A HISTORY OF WOMEN IN 101 OBJECTS

ANNABELLE HIRSCH

Translated by
Eleanor Updegraff

CANONGATE

For my mother

First published in Great Britain in 2023
by Canongate Books Ltd, 14 High Street, Edinburgh EH1 1TE

canongate.co.uk

1

British Library Cataloguing-in-Publication Data
A catalogue record for this book is available on
request from the British Library

ISBN 978 1 80530 087 8

Original interior design: Dörlemann Satz, Lemförde
English language typesetting by Biblichor Ltd, Scotland

Printed and bound in Great Britain by Bell and Bain Ltd

CONTENTS

	INTRODUCTION	7
1	HEALED FEMUR, c. 30,000 BC	11
2	CAVE PAINTINGS, c. 20,000 BC	15
3	STATUE OF HATSHEPSUT, 1479–1458 BC	19
4	SAPPHO PAPYRUS, 7th century BC	23
5	AMAZON DOLL, 5th century BC	27
6	BAUBO FIGURINE, 4th–2nd century BC	31
7	ISIS STATUETTE, 332–330 BC	35
8	LILITH AMULET, undated	39
9	HNEFATAFL GAME, 10th century BC	43
10	THE BAYEUX TAPESTRY, 11th century	47
11	*THE TALE OF GENJI*, PAPER SCROLL, 17th century	51
12	NUN'S CROWN, 12th century	55
13	IVORY MIRROR, c. 1300	59
14	MINIATURE FROM *THE BOOK OF THE CITY OF LADIES*, 1405	63
15	TITLE PAGE OF *MALLEUS MALEFICARUM* (*HAMMER OF WITCHES*), 1486	67
16	FIGURINE OF MARY MAGDALENE, 1490–92	71
17	CHOPINES (PLATFORM SHOES), 16th century	75
18	PERFUMED GLOVES, 16th century	79
19	DISH WITH THE LIKENESS OF ROXELANA, mid-16th century	83
20	CHEQUERS RING, c. 1570	87
21	MICHEL DE MONTAIGNE, *THE ESSAYS*, 1571–85	91
22	GLASS DILDO, 16th century	95
23	THUMBSCREW, 17th century	99
24	METAL CORSET, 17th century	103
25	DRESS POCKET, 17th century	107
26	MADAME DE POMPADOUR'S SEALING STAMP, mid-18th century	111
27	BIDET, mid-18th century	115
28	'LA MACHINE', 18th century	119
29	WAX BUST OF ANNA MORANDI MANZOLINI, 18th century	123
30	'THE GOOD MOTHER', GROUP OF PORCELAIN FIGURINES, c. 1760	127
31	LADIES OF LLANGOLLEN FIGURINE, undated	131
32	PHRYGIAN CAP, 1789	135

33 RECAMIER, c. 1800   139

34 BOARD GAME, 'PLEASURES OF ASTRONOMY', 1814   143

35 *BEAUTY REVEALED*, SELF-PORTRAIT, 1828   147

36 THE BRONTË SISTERS' MINIATURE BOOKS, c. 1830   151

37 ANALYTICAL ENGINE, 1834   155

38 ANTI-SLAVERY COIN, 1838   159

39 LITHOGRAPH, *L'AVENIR. PERSPECTIVE D'UN PHALANSTÈRE OU
    PALAIS SOCIÉTAIRE DE L'HUMANITÉ*, c. 1840   163

40 GEORGE SAND'S RIGHT ARM, c. 1847   167

41 WASHING PADDLE, 1850s   171

42 SINGER SEWING MACHINE, 1851   175

43 ASHLEY'S SACK, 1852/1921   179

44 PLANCHETTE, 1853   183

45 *FANOOS* LAMP, c. 1854   187

46 'AU BON MARCHÉ' RECEIPT, 1860s   191

47 THE KILLING OF AEGISTHUS, RED-FIGURE VASE, 500 BC   195

48 KNIFE BELONGING TO LA MÈRE FILLOUX, late 19th century   199

49 REMINGTON TYPEWRITER, 1874   203

50 PAGE FROM *ICONOGRAPHIE PHOTOGRAPHIQUE
    DE LA SALPÊTRIÈRE*, 1878   207

51 MARIE BASHKIRTSEFF, *IN THE STUDIO*, 1881   211

52 SAFETY BICYCLE, 1889   215

53 'ROUND THE WORLD WITH NELLIE BLY' GAME, 1890   219

54 CINEMATOGRAPH, c. 1900   223

55 THE HATPIN, 1900   227

56 POSTER, 'CLAUDINE AT SCHOOL', 1900   231

57 WONDERFUL HAIR GROWER, 1906   235

58 RADIUM CHOCOLATE, undated   239

59 HUNGER STRIKE MEDAL, 1912   243

60 ATHENA STATUETTE BELONGING TO SIGMUND FREUD,
    1st or 2nd century BC   247

61 FIRST WORLD WAR POSTCARD, 1914–18   251

62 THE FOUNTAIN, 1917   255

63 PLAN OF THE 'TEMPLE DE L'AMITIÉ',
    SALON OF THE AMAZON, post-1910   259

64 100 MPH COAT, 1920   263

65 CHANEL NO. 5, 1921   267

66 MILADY DÉCOLLETÉE GILLETTE, 1920s   271

67 'WITCH DANCE' MASK, c. 1926   275

68 TINA MODOTTI, *WORKERS PARADE*, 1926   279

69 LIPSTICK, 'LE ROUGE BAISER', 1927   283

70 GRETA GARBO'S BALLPOINT PEN, 1927   287

71 INTERNATIONAL WOMEN'S DAY BADGE, 1930   291

72 *REVISTA SUR (SUR* MAGAZINE), 1931   295

73 PLATE, 'THE FAMOUS WOMEN DINNER SERVICE', 1932   299

74 MARJORIE HILLIS, *LIVE ALONE AND LIKE IT*, 1936   303

75 EXILE DIARY OF MASCHA KALÉKO, 1941–44   307

76 STICKER, 'RED ORCHESTRA' RESISTANCE GROUP, 1942   311

77 WOMEN AIRFORCE SERVICE PILOTS INSIGNIA, 1943–44   315

78 ROBERT CAPA PHOTOGRAPH,
    THE SHAVED WOMAN OF CHARTRES, 1944   319

79 THE BIKINI, 1947   323

80 ALBERTO GIACOMETTI, *SIMONE DE BEAUVOIR* PORTRAIT, c. 1946   327

81 BASIC LAW FOR THE FEDERAL REPUBLIC OF GERMANY, 1949   331

82 FRONT PAGE OF THE *DAILY NEWS*, 1 December 1952   335

83 DANCE-CARD FAN, 1950s   339

84 MIELE 'MODEL A' VACUUM CLEANER, 1951–61   343

85 TUPPERWARE, 1950s   347

86 'ENOVID' CONTRACEPTIVE PILL, 1957   351

87 HANNAH ARENDT'S BROOCH, undated   355

88 THE MINIDRESS, 1966   359

89 ARETHA FRANKLIN, 'RESPECT', 1967   363

90 SCISSORS, 1970s   367

91 GOLDA MEIR POSTER, c. 1970   371

92 MAGAZINE COVER, *LE NOUVEL OBSERVATEUR*,
    'MANIFESTO OF THE 343', 5 April 1971   375

93 VHS TAPE, *DEEP THROAT*, 1972   379

94 DESICCATOR, 1977   383

95 THE RABBIT PEARL, 1984   387

96 DIOR 'WE SHOULD ALL BE FEMINISTS' T-SHIRT, 2016   391

97 KIM KARDASHIAN'S RING, 2016   395

98 THE MOBILE PHONE, 21st century   399

99 MENSTRUATION CUP, 2010s   403

100 THE PUSSYHAT, 2017   407

101 BUNCH OF HAIR, 2022   411

SELECT BIBLIOGRAPHY   414

ACKNOWLEDGEMENTS   416

INTRODUCTION

A couple of years ago, on a trip to the Danish coast, I visited the childhood home of the novelist Karen Blixen. To my own astonishment, I realised that I wasn't so much fascinated by the place itself – the desk where she wrote, her paintings adorning the walls – but by what seemed an insignificant detail: a number of copper pans stacked up in a corner of the kitchen. I found myself trying to imagine that small, slender woman pottering around with them, how she might have felt, what she might have been thinking about. Did she even cook? Were those her pots, or had they belonged to her staff? What, I asked myself, did her kitchen utensils say about the author of *Babette's Feast*? Did they even say anything – about her, her everyday life, her existence as a woman, as a Danish woman, a European woman of that era? Pans and other such objects are the very opposite of monuments. They don't commemorate revolutions or victories on the battlefield; don't allude to great contracts or those moments of upheaval that have an undeniably transformative effect on society. It's rarely possible to link them to one specific date, to say: 'From that day on, everything was different.' They don't belong to the so-called 'big picture' of history, but instead to a realm that is far more intimate. Quiet, and overlooked. A realm that was long considered female – and, accordingly, insignificant.

I hadn't long embarked on my research for this book when I had an interesting experience. At a dinner party one evening, I started telling the table about the new project I had in mind: to narrate the history of women through objects. What would that look like, one of the women there asked curiously – what sort of objects, for example? Before I could answer her question, before I'd even had the chance to explain that they would be objects which told the stories of women's everyday lives, of big moments and small ones . . . objects linked to topics that have a bearing on women – the body, sex, love, work, art, politics – objects that bear witness to the movements women instigated, and to all the myths to which they've been forced to conform since time immemorial. That say something about how they dealt with that, how they fought, how they freed themselves, sometimes loudly, sometimes quietly. How they always found, or at least tried to find, a way to be themselves. That some of those objects would, of course, make reference to a particular woman and the influence she had – but not all of them. Because this wasn't going to be a book about 'the hundred coolest women in history', but a cabinet of curiosities showing how rich and diverse, how complex and non-linear the history of all women is . . .

No, before I could say any of that, an elderly gent brayed loudly, 'Women and objects? But women *are* objects!' A stupid line, crude and not at all funny. But, underneath, it does hint at something: at the fact that history has so often been narrated as though this comment were true. As though, for most of it, women really did have about as little influence or significance as a vase you'd put on display in the corner and occasionally fill with something (a baby). Even today, with inspir-ational women and their stories being pulled out of the swamp of oblivion, it can sometimes sound as though active, thinking, fighting, storytelling, tightrope-walking women are something quite new. As though – with a couple of notable exceptions – all those who came before us were asleep, mere onlookers. As though their story is largely one of passive victims.

None of that is true. None of that has ever been true. At least, not in the way we usually tell it. Women have always been there, and they have always contributed. The objects for which they were so often mistaken, and with which they shared their domains – the personal, and the public, too – bear witness to this. To this side of history that has so long been overlooked, so often ignored or dismissed as insignificant, irrelevant, trivial. These objects don't reference drum-beating, big-picture history – at least, not always – but point instead to details and anecdotes, to things that only gained in importance over time and with great perseverance. They narrate the world in a different way. Some can be set within a larger context, some played a role at a very specific moment; some speak to a wider tendency, still others of one particular woman whose story I didn't want to omit. Because: this collection of objects is absolutely subjective. It wasn't curated by a historian, but by a woman who grew up between France and Germany at the end of the twentieth century, a woman who loves women, their objects and their stories. A collection chosen by a woman who has a penchant for the unimportant and anecdotal, and who enjoys taking imaginary walks through the distant past. The focus here is on the history of women in the western hemisphere – not out of any lack of interest in the rest of the world but, on the contrary, because it would have seemed to me dishonest to extend this intuitive, subjective approach to cultures with which I am unfamiliar such that I could not do them justice.

A History of Women in 101 Objects extends through the past like a long hallway, along which, here and there, I open a door or pull something down off a shelf, to shed light on certain aspects of history or tell a particular story. There are one hundred and one objects here, but there could just as well have been two hundred, three hundred, a thousand . . . it was hard to place a limit. Because the history of women and their objects is unbelievably rich, so much richer than you might think. It is manifold, and sometimes sad, often absurdly amusing. Sometimes it makes you want to shout for joy to see how strong and resourceful and wily women always have been, how close even our most distant relatives are to us, how similar our thoughts, concerns and ambitions, despite all that separates us. This history of women is neither exhaustive nor definitive, but nor does it want to be. Above all, it hopes to inspire you to dig deeper, to get things down from the shelves of history, to look for details and anecdotes and all those supposedly irrelevant matters. And to find in them material links to a world still far too unknown to us: the world that belongs to the women of history.

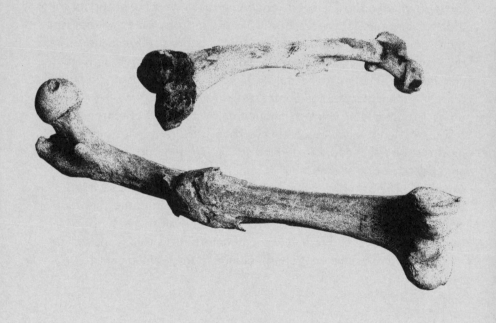

HEALED FEMUR

c. **30,000** BC

Several decades have now passed since American anthropologist Margaret Mead gave a university lecture during which she was asked to name the object that, in her opinion, could be regarded as the first sign of human civilisation. The student asking this question probably expected her to start talking about a clay pot or an arrowhead, maybe even some form of technological achievement, but after a brief pause for thought, Mead answered cryptically: 'A healed human femur.' In the natural world, she argued, if an animal breaks a bone, its chances of survival are pretty much zero. It takes several weeks for a fractured bone to knit itself together again, and during this time the animal wouldn't be able either to get to a water source or to hunt; it would die of starvation or thirst, or fall prey to another animal. Bone finds indicating that a human managed to survive a broken femur many millennia before Christianity imply that someone must have been there to look after them. Someone who brought them food and drink, who stayed with them and gave them the chance to heal in peace. The first sign of civilisation, then, isn't a weapon or some other kind of invention; it's proof of our ability to look after not just ourselves, but others too. 'We are at our best when we serve others,' said Mead, concluding with the appeal: 'Be civilised.'

When we think of the Stone Age today, we probably conjure a mental picture based on our primary-school textbooks. On one side of this image, we see a timid-looking creature in tattered clothes, crouching beside a scrum of children: the Woman. On the other side is a hairy thing, not sitting but standing upright on two legs, not trapped inside a gloomy grotto but outside in the wilderness; active, not passive. A round of applause for . . . the Man. Holding a spear triumphantly aloft as he faces down a creature the size of a house – a mammoth, let's say – he, the Man, knows no fear. He will conquer this colossus and carry it home to his grateful family. What this image suggests, of course, is that it has always been the Man who has propelled humanity forward with his conquering spirit; the Woman was 'only' there for the purpose of producing children, but otherwise pretty much useless. After all, hunting requires courage; caring for children, on the other hand . . . nothing. There is, however, one fundamental problem with this image, which continues to haunt us and still legitimises many things: there's just no evidence to suggest that life in the Stone Age really looked like this.

Just like the vast majority of images that have shaped our collective idea of history, this one was also created by men – in this particular case, in an era (the nineteenth century) when middle-class marriage and the corresponding gender roles were becoming the norm, making 'discreet housewife' the new ideal woman. Early archaeologists and anthropologists viewed their finds through the filter of their own rather misogynistic era, and they went more or less unchallenged in transferring both the prevailing gender relations and value categories of the time onto prehistory (hunting: great; childcare: not so much). These interpretations enabled them to underpin the current attitudes of the time, which they were only too happy to have confirmed by science: that women had always assumed the inferior role (it was 'natural') and, right from the very beginning, had sat around in a sweet but baffled way while men single-handedly carved the course of evolution.

The only thing is, there's no concrete evidence to suggest these narratives are accurate. For one, archaeological finds indicate that prehistoric gender roles were less fixed than some would have them; women, too, went hunting on occasion. For another, it seems unlikely that our ancestors from the Stone Age – an epoch in which 'Don't Die' was top of the agenda – could have enjoyed the luxury of giving half their society the sense that they were worthless and peripheral. After all, the fight for survival required as many motivated participants as possible. We can even assume that Stone Age men knew that hunting and conquering wouldn't get them very far in evolutionary terms, and that caring for others played a central role in the life of the community. Which is just what the so-called 'grandmother hypothesis' has been trying to prove for some time.

Much like Mead, the grandmother hypothesis argues that the fact that we take care of others is what originally gave us our strength as a species. The reasoning behind it is as follows: apart from whales, women are the only mammals to experience menopause; in other words, the only ones to survive beyond the point at which they can no longer bear children. Thanks to Darwin teaching us that not many things happen just for the sake of it, but mostly to serve an evolutionary biological purpose, scientists began asking themselves: why did the menopause prevail in humans? Possibly, they answered, because grand-mothers, or women no longer capable of reproducing, were able to support their daughters in raising their own children, thereby ensuring that they could produce offspring while still contributing to the life of the group. These grandmothers also played their part in helping a larger proportion of that progeny reach adulthood, when they in turn could reproduce.

At the time, of course, no one would have been explicitly aware of the contribution these older women were making, but it's still entirely possible to imagine that in an age before sedentism and agriculture, before the concept of possession and its attendant structures of power and oppression, our ancestors lived in a more egalitarian society that was less divided along gender lines than ours. Because they instinc-tively knew that they needed all elements of society in equal measure: young men who could wave spears around, young women who had children and were good at tracking animals. And grandmothers, who brought up those children and watched patiently over the injured until their bones had healed.

CAVE PAINTINGS

c. 20,000 BC

For centuries now, the assumption in Western cultures has been that a genius – especially an artistic one – will naturally be male. Women can be artists, yes, but even if every few decades or centuries have turned out a woman with vision and genuine talent, she's always been considered an anomaly and, despite maybe enjoying success during her lifetime, usually been erased from history after her death. Recent years have seen us rediscovering many of these forgotten artists, and exhibiting their works in group shows predicated by the word 'women' – as though their being women was, by necessity, of greater significance for their art than being men was to the work of their male colleagues. Sometimes, we even credit them with more talent than they actually had, as though trying to prove something we still don't quite believe ourselves: namely, that women are kissed by the so-called muse no less frequently than men; that art isn't normally male, and female only in exceptional circumstances; that inspiration and artistic potential actually have very little to do with testosterone.

One of the factors contributing to this unapologetically persistent notion probably lies right at the very beginning, in the origins of art history. In the image we have of the very first artists: cave painters. Most of the cave frescoes discovered in the nineteenth and twentieth centuries portray grotesque female bodies or, more commonly, large animals (bison, mammoths, horses) in hunting scenes. Of course, up until these discoveries, it was always presumed that women hadn't taken part in hunting; at the most, they would have gathered berries and nuts, but otherwise they sat around at home with the kids – which automatically led to the assumption that these early works of art had been painted by men. How could women have reproduced the experience of combat in the wilderness if they'd never gone through

15

it themselves? This thesis seems legitimate, but . . . is that how things really were?

As previously noted, early scientists clearly found it very hard to imagine that gender roles might once have been quite different to those that prevailed in their own day, and this caused them to make several errors of judgement. In recent years, for example, new technology has helped us discover that many of the skeletons once exhibited as the bones of a 'Stone Age man' – and admired for their perceived strength – are, in fact, the bones of a Stone Age woman. It seems that for a long time women were almost exactly as tall and robustly built as their men, which, on the one hand, suggests they were similarly well fed – and, accordingly, must have enjoyed a roughly equal status in society – but above all that they very likely did take part in hunting expeditions. They tracked animals, served as decoys (how nice) and maybe even carried the meat back home to the group. Hunting was – contrary to the popular claim still widely celebrated today – not a boys-only club. Women had their place on the hunt; they played a role and thus were definitely in a position to sublimate what they'd seen into artistic vision. Nonetheless, the possibility that women didn't just have practical things in mind but also felt the same urge men did – to express themselves and their view of the world – was long thought out of the question. Or, to be more precise, no hypothesis of the sort was ever even ventured.

That is, until one afternoon around ten years ago, when the American researcher Dean Snow found himself standing in front of his bookshelves at Pennsylvania State University. He pulled down an illus-trated volume on the Pech Merle cave in the south of France, and began to wonder. Only the day before, he'd stumbled across a study by a British biologist, a certain John Manning, who'd discovered that men's and women's hands differ in the proportional relationship between their fingers: women's index and ring fingers are mostly identical in length, whereas men's ring fingers are usually longer. And so, as Snow sat down and opened his book on Pech Merle, the very first page of which showed this outline of a hand sprayed on a wall, he thought to himself, *Something's not right here!* Over the preceding century, several hundred of these handprints had been found in caves and grottos in Latin America, Africa, Australasia; most, however, were in Europe, where they were between 12,000 and 40,000 years old. Our Stone Age ancestors seem to have sprayed them onto cave walls using an early air-brush technique: they'd position their hand, get out a reed tube or a hollow bone taken from a bird's skeleton, fill it with red pigment (the first colour we were capable of making) and blow into one end until the outline of their fingers was visible on the wall. Why they did this isn't entirely clear; it's thought that it was something like a signature. In the sense of: *I was here. I painted this.*

The more pictures Snow looked at, the more obvious it seemed to him that the usual designation of these hands couldn't be correct. According to the finger theory, most just didn't look like men's hands, and so he developed a special algorithm to follow up on his suspicion. His most recent studies of the Cueva del Castillo in Spain as well as France's Gargas and Pech Merle caves have revealed that 75 per cent of the handprints displayed there are women's.

Now, Snow's theory is just as famous as it is controversial. Some simply don't believe it; others are completely convinced and have even taken it beyond the art aspect. They maintain that these handprints weren't simply painted on the caves – this wasn't *l'art pour l'art*, nor a form of signature – but are traces left behind after some kind of ritual. In caves like these, according to the theory, the lack of oxygen makes it entirely possible to lose all your sensory reference points after a very short time and drift off into a kind of trance. As such, the paintings and handprints were less works of art than elements of a shamanic ritual. Which, in turn, would mean that women might have been shamans. We still don't know if this is true or not, just as the now allegedly female handprints on the walls don't automatically prove that the paintings of animals displayed next to them were also created by women. But it would be worth considering as a possibility, if only for a moment. Because, who knows; maybe the very first artistic geniuses in human history were actually women.

STATUE OF HATSHEPSUT

1479–1458 BC

Almost all biographies of famous and powerful women contain the following scene somewhere in their opening pages: the little girl's father, or grandmother, sits down with her and tells her how clever she is, how brave and smart and brilliant, before groaning in despair: 'Why weren't you born a man?' Some cases feature the addition of an idiotic brother perched next to them, which only serves to heighten the adult's distress: why has the one sharp mind among their offspring been placed in the wrong body? How could nature have made such an error?

This, too, is roughly what happened in the case of the Egyptian pharaoh Hatshepsut, whose statue you see opposite. The daughter of Thutmose I, she was born around 1500 BC and seems to have displayed remarkable intellect from a very young age – something that both delighted and grieved her father, seeing as the throne had been promised to his less keenly minded son, Hatshepsut's half-brother. In the hope of at least providing this good-for-nothing with an intelligent advisor, he determined that Hatshepsut would marry her brother. She was twelve when she became queen as the bride of Thutmose II, and not much older when she stepped into his shoes as regent. Her husband had died shortly after his coronation, and his only son – the child of a concubine – was still too young to rule. So, in the interim, our heroine ascended the throne. So far, so normal – in the Ancient World, after all, Egyptian women had a rather unusual status. While the Nile civilisation was as male-dominated as all other societies at the time, women (at least those of the upper classes) enjoyed a comparatively large number of freedoms. Unlike the women of Ancient Greece, they were able to move around at liberty, received an education and were allowed to take part in festivals, to dance and to sing. Above all, however, they were permitted to rule as regent if their son or husband was absent or otherwise not in a position to govern.

Yet Hatshepsut didn't leave it at that. When her stepson was old enough to take his rightful place, she somehow managed to have herself appointed pharaoh and put the young man off until some other point in the future. For twenty years, the reins were firmly in her hands – and, astonishingly, she never needed to have Thutmose III killed.

There have been many queens in the long history of Egypt – Sobekneferu, Nefertiti, Twosret – plenty of whom had great power and influence. But there were only ever a few female pharaohs, and Hatshepsut was the most important. Her reign was a period of peace and prosperity for Egypt; she was a patron of the arts and commissioned some of the country's most beautiful buildings, like the temple complex at Deir el-Bahari. Today, she's regarded as one of the most influential pharaohs in history, and yet, when push comes to shove, it's much more likely to be the tragic story of Cleopatra that springs to mind, as though we're in constant need of reminding that women who want too much and behave 'like men' will inevitably end up dying by suicide. We tend to honour the failed examples, not the successful ones.

But perhaps this shift of attention also has to do with the fact that Hatshepsut was regarded with a degree of suspicion until very recently, even in academia. Even in the 1950s, a curator at the Metropolitan Museum of Art in New York called her the 'vilest type of usurper'. She was accused of being unscrupulous, power-hungry and sexually depraved, and one of the reasons for these assumptions was this very statue. When it was discovered in the 1920s, it lay smashed into finger-sized pieces, broken and defiled – which, given the divine status of the pharaohs, gave rise to several questions. What had this ruler done to so anger his descendants? And, more importantly, who even was this fragmented man? As soon as the statue was identified as Hatshepsut, the answer became clear: she was a woman who had usurped a man's position. And, indeed, Thutmose III did have all traces of her reign destroyed, which historians were all too keen to read as a sign that he was out for revenge because she'd stolen his throne.

It took a few female Egyptologists to straighten out this skewed image. Contrary to the assumption that a hate-filled Thutmose III had had Hatshepsut erased from history as soon as she died, he actually turned out to have done this twenty years later, at the end of his own reign. We can assume, then, that his thoughts were less focused on revenge and more on the future: what kind of example would Hatshepsut be, a woman who had broken rank as she did? What kind of incentive might she provide to others who also wanted to assume that role? Might her likeness introduce too much confusion into the clear order of the sexes? A particularly interesting question in the context of this statue. After all, Hatshepsut hadn't just managed to rule her nation thoughtfully and successfully, she'd also blurred the boundary between the sexes – she liked being portrayed as a man, with a beard, python crown and bared, flat chest. In official records she was referred to as 'His Majesty, herself', while the word 'pharaoh' was treated as a feminine noun. She was, to all intents and purposes, employing a form of gender-neutral language, mixing up attributes willy-nilly: he, she, it, whatever . . . This statue, which is now on display in the Metropolitan Museum, shows her as both man and woman at once. Her head is that of a man (we can tell from the mostly black-and-gold-striped Nemes headdress) while her chest is that of a woman.

Nonetheless, many historians are reluctant to believe that she saw herself as a fluid third sex, a man in the body of a woman, as something outside these categories – or, as the artist Claude Cahun would later muse, 'Masculine? Feminine? It depends on the situation.' Hatshepsut clearly felt herself to be a woman, these historians say, begging the question of how they can be so certain. Because the way this pharaoh chose to communicate suggests something else entirely, namely a queer form of self- and power-portrayal that confidently blurred the lines of gender. Hatshepsut seems to have been well aware that not everyone would accept this in the future. She had the following words carved on an obelisk erected at Karnak: 'Now my heart turns this way and that, as I think of what the people will say – those who shall see my monuments in years to come, and who shall speak of what I have done.'

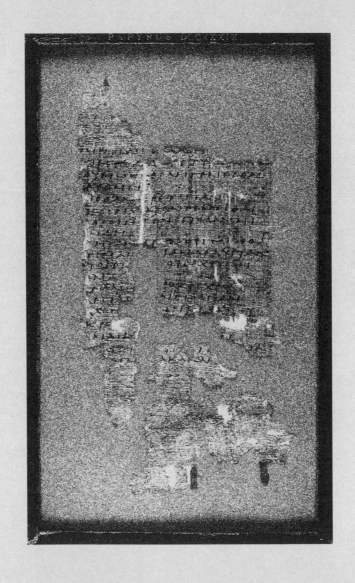

SAPPHO PAPYRUS

7ᵀᴴ CENTURY BC

For the longest time, only men were permitted to dream of making such an impact on history that people would remember them even centuries after their death. For the women of Ancient Greece, who had absolutely no influence on public life, it was a foregone conclusion that they would be forgotten. And most of them probably accepted this fate without question. Not so Sappho. In 603 BC, on the beautiful island of Lesbos, she decided – with some delusions of grandeur – that things would be different for her: 'to Sappho, you / in Kypros queen / and yet greatly / to all on whom the blazing / everywhere glory,' she wrote.[1] And again: 'someone will remember us / I say / even in another time'.[2]

As improbable as this self-prophecy may have seemed back then, Sappho was right. In all of human history, scarcely any other female name has become such an integral part of our everyday lives. 'Lesbian' women are so called because Sappho lived on Lesbos and same-sex relationships between women take their name from her: 'sapphic'. This is despite the fact that we know very little about her and only a few of her poems for the lyre have survived to the present day. The majority of her once comprehensive body of work – a whole nine volumes – is believed to have vanished when the Great Library of Alexandria went up in flames in the third century BC; a further part seems to have been destroyed in the Middle Ages, when it was considered too salacious. But wildest of all is what was later done to her poems in Egypt: the papyrus scrolls on which she had written were used to make papier-mâché coffins and stuff taxidermy crocodiles.

---

1   Sappho, Fragment 65, in: *If Not, Winter: Fragments of Sappho*, tr. Anne Carson (London: Virago Press, 2003), p. 135
2   Sappho, Fragment 147, in: *If Not, Winter*, p. 297

Art created by women was treated most peculiarly for a very long time – we know that. Some people regretted the loss of this work even then. The German philosopher and early Romantic poet Friedrich Schlegel, for example, wrote: 'If we still had all Sappho's poems, perhaps no one would speak of Homer any more.' Maybe we don't need to go quite that far. Sappho is often compared to Homer, who lived roughly a century before her, but she needn't have replaced him – why would she? She would have complemented him. Her verses form a kind of female counterpart to his heroic, and sometimes rather testosterone-heavy, epic the *Odyssey*. Erudite Sappho had little time for horsemen, foot soldiers and ships; what interested her were the circumstances that led beautiful Helen to leave her home and husband for Troy: obeying the call of 'what you love'. Her heart, then. 'I would rather see her lovely step / and the motion of light on her face / than chariots of Lydians or ranks / of footsoldiers in arms,' wrote Sappho.[1] Men write about war, women about love – it sounds like a cliché, but in this case, at least, it was true. Someone once said that Sappho was basically an early hippie; what she preached was a rather more poetic version of 'make love, not war'. And perhaps that person was right. Conquests, battles, muscular men with sharp sabres – she had no interest in any of the heroic stories that continue to shape our culture to this day. What fascinated Sappho was sensuality; the beautiful, the tender, the soft.

We know, of course, that a laughable idea established itself in Western societies in the early nineteenth century: namely that women were immune to sexual desire – or if, surprisingly, they did seem to enjoy it, they would be too prudish to talk about it. These days, naming and describing female desire can seem brand new to us at times, as though we were the first to dare to do so. Sappho is the proof that we are giving ourselves too much credit here, that there have always been women – even centuries before Christianity – who didn't just feel lust but also had no problem articulating it. It's rare to find an anthology of erotic poetry that doesn't feature at least one of Sappho's verses; she's the first known female poet who intellectually probed her body and observed what was going on inside her: 'when I look at you, even a moment, no speaking / is left in me / no: tongue breaks and thin / fire

---

1 Sappho, Fragment 16, in: *If Not, Winter*, p. 27

is racing under skin / and in eyes no sight and drumming / fills ears / and cold sweat holds me and shaking / grips me all'.[1] A shorter fragment is equally beautiful: 'Eros shook my / mind like a mountain wind falling on oak trees'.[2]

There has been much speculation about whom Sappho might have loved. Was she a lesbian? Was she bisexual? Was she neither? For a couple of centuries it was said she'd thrown herself into the sea on account of a young fisherman, but the current belief is that this story was invented to free Sappho from the 'charge' of homosexuality, so people could enjoy her poetry without a guilty conscience. We do know for sure that she had a close relationship with several of her (female) students and suffered greatly when it came time for them to leave her. We can imagine Sappho's 'circle of women' a little like the one in Alma-Tadema's slightly kitschy painting: young girls sitting on a terrace under the sun of Lesbos, listening raptly to their teacher's every word. Sappho's students came from across the entire Mediterranean region: well-heeled girls who wished to be instructed in dance, music, poetry and deportment in preparation for marriage. Their education was a 'school of femininity' – only, the self-assured femininity espoused by their free-thinking, free-loving teacher was radically different to the established ideal of the Ancient Greek world: a woman who was submissive, silent, hidden away. As such, Sappho didn't just leave us her poetry; she planted a seed which, in time, would propagate itself and make possible the emergence of female poets and thinkers, like Erinna and Hypatia, over the centuries that followed. Not for nothing did the lesbian artists of later years – especially the 1920s – so often name her as a point of reference. Sometimes, as Sappho proves, it doesn't take an epic to change things. A fragment of papyrus fished from the stomach of a stuffed crocodile will do it too.

---

1   Sappho, Fragment 31, in: *If Not, Winter*, p. 63
2   Sappho, Fragment 47, in: *If Not, Winter*, p. 99

AMAZON DOLL

5TH CENTURY BC

We generally regard it as a modern-day achievement that we raise our children in a more or less gender-neutral fashion, assuring little boys that they may play with dolls, put on make-up and wear pink clothes, and letting little girls wave swords around. Thirty years ago, however, many people thought it strange if a girl preferred toy cars to Barbies; some doubtless still do today.

Which makes this Ancient Greek doll from the fifth century BC all the more astonishing. She's an Amazon, a female warrior, who was found in the grave of a young girl. Not quite fifteen centimetres high, with movable arms and legs, her hair and Phrygian cap were originally painted in bright colours. She's one of the earliest examples of her kind, made at a time when the Ancient World had only just begun producing dolls. Later versions, such as an Amazon doll from the first century BC, display distinguishing features such as a missing left breast, characteristic patterned clothing and an even more striking headdress. But let's stick for a moment with this one, which portrays a woman in a style normally reserved for male heroes alone: 'heroic nudity'.

Perhaps it might be worth reminding ourselves of the status Athenian women held in those days, in order to understand just how unusual this toy is. According to one legend, their subjugation went right back to the founding of the city, which was going to be named for either Athena or Poseidon. The two deities vied for the affections of the townspeople, but in the end it was the goddess who won out – thanks, apparently, to enormous female support. Poseidon was so angry at the result that women were stripped of the right to vote and, consequently, of their status as citizens. They no longer had any rights at all, and became the possessions of men. Apart from a few exceptions, women were banned from religious and public life and instructed to stay in the gynaeceum, a specially designated area of the home, where they were to weave cloth and look after the children.

In the Ancient Greek imagination, Amazons were the exact opposite of this: the very definition of female freedom. They lived elsewhere, beyond the known borders of the Greek world, in a purely female society with absolutely no men. They were strong and courageous, brought up to be warriors; they knew neither pain nor fear and could measure themselves against any Greek hero. Their devotion to combat was apparently so total that they even cut off their left breasts in order to be able to shoot better with bow and arrow. Their sexuality, too, was 'not very feminine': they utilised men purely to satiate their desires or conceive children. It's said that Alexander the Great had a passionate affair with an Amazon queen – just as most heroes seem to have come into contact with them at some point. Achilles, for example, is supposed to have clashed with Penthesilea in an intense battle fought during the Trojan War, in which the Amazons took the side of the besieged city. He eventually defeated her, ramming his spear into her chest. As he did so, he looked her in the eye for the very first time and was instantly love-struck. Alas, too late.

For the Ancient Greeks, the Amazons were the embodiment of a topsy-turvy world in which all rules and the balance of power had been turned on their heads. They found them frightening yet fascinating: besides Hercules, these female warriors with their caps, tattooed arms and bared right breasts are the most common figures to appear on painted vases; in Athens, their image is everywhere – on the façades of temples, in private homes and numerous texts, and, as we see here, even in the form of toys. The question is: why? If we were to give a little girl a female warrior figurine today, we'd be doing it in an attempt to embolden her, to encourage her to feel strong and break down barriers. But what were the Ancient Greeks thinking? Why would they give a little girl a fighter like Penthesilea, only to teach her that in real life – too bad! – she was destined to be a weaver like Penelope? Perhaps they weren't thinking much at all. Their theatre, Greek tragedy, is absolutely teeming with strong women – iron-willed Antigone; murderous Medea, out for revenge after her lover abandoned her – and yet they seem never to have worried that one of these figures might function as a role model and inspire the ladies of Ancient Greece to revolt. Perhaps it was because women never went to the theatre anyway. But perhaps, too, it was because these heroines seemed so large, so magnificent, so far removed from the weak 'nature' of 'real' women that it never even occurred to the chaps that their wives and daughters might identify with them.

The question of whether the Amazons really existed has been raised repeatedly over the centuries. Some believe they did; others dismiss them as nothing more than a figment of the Ancient Greek imagination. The truth probably lies somewhere in between: artefacts found in graves belonging to the Scythians, an ancient nomadic horse people from Central Asia, show that there were most likely female warriors and riders who lived among them. In Scythian society, women could indeed attain high status and command attention thanks to their fighting prowess; most were buried alongside their weapons: hatchets, axes and sabres. Contrary to legend, however, these women didn't live in purely female groups, but alongside their menfolk. They were equal partners, in life as in war.

Yet this reality can't touch the myth of the wild Amazons who lived completely independent of men. Ever since ancient times, the Amazons have been the very definition of freedom and strength: throughout all eras, in almost every corner of the world, female thinkers and revolutionaries have made reference to them, from the first feminists of the seventeenth century, to the lesbian women's circles of the early twentieth, right up to the Femen of the new millennium. That this ideal should have been dreamed up by men and pressed into little girls' hands in the form of toy dolls – meant, perhaps, as a kind of bogeywoman or symbol of an unrealistic, never-to-be-achieved goal – seems, funnily enough, to have bothered very few of them.

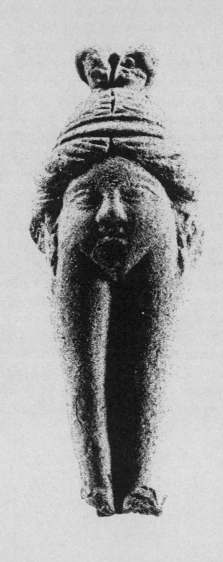

BAUBO FIGURINE

4TH–2ND CENTURY BC

Anyone who grew up in the 1990s and early 2000s, like the author of this book, will have learned from action films of the period that if you want to save the world from meteorites, monsters, rising sea levels or any other manner of catastrophe, you need three things: plenty of courage, a bit of megalomania and – crucially – a penis. The Ancient Greeks seem to have had a similar view of things. Not only were Hercules, Odysseus and such fellows always at the ready to protect their world from the threats lurking everywhere, but the Greeks also paid very visual tribute to manhood in the corporeal sense, which was thought to offer protection, happiness and prosperity. At the Dionysia, the famous festival of Dionysius, giant phalli were borne through the springtime streets of Athens; children wore small versions around their necks for protection; and, in Pompeii, a penis jutted out above the entrance to a bakery, bearing the inscription: *Here lives happiness.* Conversely, there wasn't a single house decorated with a vulva, a part of the body that was basically never seen – or, at least, only seldom. In Greek depictions, female genitalia are almost always covered up, and if we do manage to catch a quick glimpse, they look more like a Barbie's – smooth and artificial.

And yet it appears that the Ancient Greeks also ascribed a kind of world-saving power to the vulva. It was in Priene, in the year 1898, that a team of German archaeologists excavating a temple to Demeter from the sixth century BC stumbled upon a group of unusual statuettes. They were composed of oversized heads with an ostentatious hairdo set on top of two slender legs. In the place normally occupied by the stomach were two eyes, a nose, a rather cheerful-looking mouth and, directly underneath, a pudenda with a clearly visible slit. In short: a vulva. It took a few years to realise that this vulva-woman was probably connected

31

to the myth of Baubo. There are various versions of the story, which goes roughly as follows: one day, Persephone, daughter of the goddess Demeter, was out picking flowers when Hades suddenly appeared out of nowhere and carried the girl off to his realm, the Underworld. Demeter, who loved her daughter above all else, was beside herself with grief and began neglecting her divine duties. The longer she mourned, the more the harvest suffered, until the entire earth had dried up, the fields were dry and barren, and people had begun to starve, often to death. Until the day on which Demeter, wandering aimless and desolate through the human realm, ran into Baubo. The old woman tried to cheer her up, showed her sympathy, offered her food and drink – but Demeter was inconsolable and refused everything. The situation looked hopeless; the end of life on earth. But then Baubo played her last card. Without warning, she lifted her skirt and showed the goddess her bared vulva. Demeter was apparently so surprised by this move that she let out a resounding peal of laughter. Her pain thus dulled, she ate and drank and finally mustered the strength to force Zeus into finding a solution. It was agreed that Persephone would spend half the year on Mount Olympus and the other half in the Underworld. The earth was saved, and the seasons were born.

For the women of Ancient Athens, this story about a lost daughter must have been extremely relatable – after all, things were much the same in their own lives. As the uncontested head of any family, a father would simply promise his daughter to some man or other without consulting either his wife or the girl; she would then be married, handed over to her new family in a grand ceremony, and mother and daughter would henceforth see each other seldom in the best case, at worst never again. But Baubo must have played another role in women's lives as well. She's closely linked to the Thesmophoria, a festival from which men were barred. We don't know exactly what happened during those three days in October when married women slept all together in tents beyond the city walls and celebrated the goddess Demeter. Just that it drove men crazy. They imagined their spouses indulging in obscene acts, taking part in orgies and generally doing everything they were forbidden to do. In the later Roman version, the feast of Bona Dea, one gentleman couldn't keep his curiosity in check and snuck into the ceremony disguised as a matron – which, in 61 BC, caused a national scandal.

But let's return to Ancient Athens, scene of just as much male brooding on the subject of what women could possibly be up to after evading men's control. Some believed they were all making like Baubo and showing one another their vulvas – not unlike the modern-day workshops that aim to inspire women to look at their own a little more closely. Perhaps they were all sitting around in a circle with their legs spread, just like the artist Valie Export would do a few millennia later, conjuring their very own collective power.

But perhaps it isn't all that important to know what they were really doing. Let it remain their secret. What's interesting about this Baubo figurine is the kind of power with which female genitalia were imbued: a world-saving one, yes, but also one which – unlike that of a phallus – didn't wage wars or feel the need to bellow and beat its chest. It functioned much more simply, but clearly just as effectively. In this story, things took a turn for the better thanks to the simple act of laughing. What exactly makes a vulva so funny is another question altogether.

ISIS STATUETTE

332–330 BC

Look a little closer at this statuette of the Egyptian goddess Isis. Imagine her without her pearl-studded hairdo and towering crown for a minute, and focus solely on her pose. The way she sits there, a proud mother, divine child naked in her lap. The way she stretches her right breast towards her baby, the peace that envelops them both. Does it remind you of anything? Might you be able to see here a more radiant, sensual version of the Virgin Mary with the Christ child?

If so, you aren't alone. There's long been speculation that Christianity drew inspiration for its narrative and imagery from the cult of the goddess Isis, which emerged on the banks of the Nile around 2,500 years before Christ. We don't have any clear answers, but it seems as though the idea isn't that unreasonable. After all, both 'sects' coexisted in Rome and, as they shared similarities in so many respects, found themselves more or less in direct competition. They were, for one, unlike the more male-dominated cults, open to all genders and social classes; they welcomed men and women, rich and poor, young and old – even social outcasts, like prostitutes, were accepted into their circles. Then, they were all-encompassing: while most other gods concentrated on their own specialisms, both Isis and Christ were available for nearly all life situations, problems and questions. This was despite the fact that Isis didn't represent a monotheistic worldview. The Ancient Greeks, who discovered the goddess around 300 BC (thanks to Alexander the Great, apparently a big Isis fan) and went on to export her to the entire Mediterranean region, called her 'the goddess of a thousand names' on account of this universal power. Yet perhaps the biggest and most important similarity between the two lies in the promise – very new at the time, and made by Isis long before Jesus – of rebirth, or eternal life.

A quick recap of the Isis legend: Osiris and Isis were brother and sister, husband and wife, king and queen of Egypt, the most important of all the divinities in heaven. All was well until jealous Seth set a trap for Osiris, the brother he hated; he imprisoned him in a sarcophagus and sent it floating down the Nile, then hacked his body into fourteen (or forty-three) pieces, which he distributed throughout Egypt. Devastated by her loss, Isis set out with her sister Nephthys to find the scattered pieces of her husband's body, mummify them and bring him back to life. With the help of a bit of magic, the goddess somehow managed to impregnate herself using the penis she'd fashioned for her lover (the original having been swallowed by a fish), and later gave birth to her son Horus – the baby on her lap in this statuette. In this, too, she evokes the Virgin Mary; Isis also conceived quasi-immaculately, the only difference being that she didn't wait around for an angel to tell her she was carrying the son of God, but took matters into her own hands. Essentially, she assumes the active role in this myth. Does what needs to be done. Her relationship with her sister is also significant: without these two women and their sisterly collaboration, there would have been no rebirth.

The fact that we're looking at a female saviour here, and not, as in the case of Jesus, a male one, changes a lot of things. It's believed that the relatively equal status enjoyed by women in Ancient Egypt – unlike their counterparts throughout the rest of the Ancient World – which permitted them to inherit, sometimes to reign, and to move around with a degree of freedom, was at least partly to do with Isis's power and how venerated she was as a goddess. We also know that her influence spread quickest in regions where women were treated with even a hint of esteem and respect. Such as in Ancient Rome, where aristocratic women, at least, wielded a certain power and could make a name for themselves as priestesses or vestal virgins. In the first century BC, Rome was even home to a mystery cult dedicated to Isis – a secret society that staged equally secret initiation rites. We know hardly anything about it, only that its disciples carried around a sistrum (a kind of rattle) and that during the ritual they likely underwent something akin to their own death in order to liberate themselves from fear. For a time, Isis was extremely popular; temples were built in her honour – many in the vicinity of brothels – and people identified with both her goodness and power.

But then along came Cleopatra, and Isis's influence began to wane, as the queen – who styled herself as the earthly embodiment of Isis – chose to cast her divine sister in a bad light. Thanks in no small part to Elizabeth Taylor and Joseph Mankiewicz's magnificent *Cleopatra*, we know that she was loathed by the Romans and spoken of in connection with all manner of depravities, with the result that Isis, too, was henceforth associated with sexual perversion, seen as just as great a moral threat as Cleopatra herself. To circumvent this danger, her cult was banned: her statues thrown into the Tiber, her temples destroyed. Yet her banishment was not to be an enduring one: in the first century AD, during the reign of Emperor Caligula, Isis mysteries resurfaced in Rome. The goddess grew in influence, even as far away as England. Her progress was triumphant, and yet the stronger Christianity became, the more she was driven back again, this warmest and most benevolent of goddesses. In the fourth century, when Christianity became the official state religion, her cult vanished entirely from the European stage. Perhaps the Romans were afraid of the role-model function that a woman of such unusual power might be able to assume. Perhaps they were bothered by her foreignness. Perhaps Jesus simply had better answers to life's most urgent questions. Who can say for sure? But wouldn't it be nice to have an answer to the question asked by ancient history expert Sarah B. Pomeroy: what might the history of women have looked like if, all those years ago, it hadn't been the sect of Jesus, but that of Isis which had won?

LILITH AMULET

UNDATED

We will never know how the history of women might have looked if, in that 'neck-and-neck race' between Isis and Jesus, the former and not the latter had won the favour of Ancient Rome. But one thing's for certain: one figure in particular would never have existed, a figure who would inform the lives of women from then on. Eve. Eve the sinner. Eve the curious. Eve the weak, who couldn't get a grip on herself; who allowed herself to be led astray by the first snake she clapped eyes on, and so brought about the end of innocence and mankind's expulsion from paradise. While it's true that Greek mythology boasts a similar figure, Pandora – who, in opening her box, also unleashed on humanity all manner of evil, death, sickness and war – she is at least acknowledged to have liberated hope as well. Eve, on the other hand, was bad through and through, and the pretext for all female suffering. Even the pain of childbirth was attributed to her terrible misdemeanour. All women are daughters of Eve, and Eve messed things up for humanity: pain and centuries of repression are only to be expected. Naturally.

You don't need to be religious to be conversant with the story of Eve, the serpent, the apple and the end of innocent nudity – the so-called Fall of Man. In its various guises, it haunts all our museums, all manner of stories, proverbs and TV shows; some would even prefer to believe it over Charles Darwin's theory of evolution. But one detail that's often withheld from this cornerstone of Western culture is that Eve wasn't actually Adam's first wife. She was his second. The first was called Lilith, and she was a rebel. At least, that's what it says in Hebrew mythology, which offers a rather different version of the creation story. With slight variations depending on the text, it goes roughly as follows: once God had created the first man, Adam, he decided it wouldn't be good for him to be all alone in the world, and so he made a woman for him. Not from one of his ribs, no, but from the same material as man: earth.

Unlike Adam and Eve, Adam and Lilith were born equals. Only, that seemed to be a problem: whenever they had sex, they couldn't agree on who got to go on top. Lilith said, 'But I don't always want to be lying underneath you', and he said much the same, adding that it was her job to submit to him – he was the man, after all, the boss of everything. But Lilith insisted they had equal rights. Hadn't God made her from the same earth as him? Unable to find a solution, they argued constantly, until Lilith called the 'magic name' of God and rose into the air. She just flew on out of there. This, of course, made Adam sad, and so he complained. 'The woman has fled from me,' he said. What was the deal with that? So God dispatched three angels in pursuit of the runaway, tasking them with making her see reason. But Lilith, who by this time had reached the Red Sea, remained steadfast. She had no wish to return, certainly not to that petty-minded Adam. The four of them came to an agreement: from then on, Lilith would be a child murderer, snatching away newborn boys under eight days old, and newborn girls under twenty, with one exception – and this is where this nineteenth-century amulet comes into play – 'should I ever see your three names or images on an amulet worn by a newborn, I promise the child shall be spared'.

And because Lilith wouldn't be returning after all, Adam got a second wife. Not one made from the same earth this time, but one who was carved from his rib and thus promised greater obedience: the famous Eve. The idea that Adam created humanity with a woman formed from his own body because he didn't get on with his first wife, a woman who was his equal, is disconcerting and doesn't exactly say much for him, but that's irrelevant here. Of greater import is that as soon as Eve came on the scene, we forgot all about Lilith. Or, to be more precise, the Bible, and thus the whole of Christianity, forgot about her. In Judaism, on the other hand, she continued to crop up in texts and mythology, and was clearly so well known that people used amulets like this one to protect themselves from her. Made from metal, embroidered fabric or paper, women wore them during pregnancy or placed them in newborns' cradles so that Lilith would turn away and spare their children. People were afraid of this creature, who had transformed into a child-eating, blood-drinking monster after her separation from Adam. What else would a woman who refused to subjugate herself be? She was portrayed as a demon, a dark power, sometimes also a prostitute. A few people even believed she'd disguised herself as a serpent and smuggled her way into the Garden of Eden in order to tempt Eve. In pop culture she's become a vampire queen, Satan's wife, a hideous witch. Whichever form she's taken, she's always been something from which we need protection: a wicked, renegade woman.

But, as is so often the way, one person's horror is another's salvation. In the 1960s, Lilith experienced an unexpectedly brilliant comeback. Suddenly, she was no longer a terrifying figure to be staved off with an amulet round the neck, but a role model for feminists, Jewish ones especially. It was enthusiastically established that the very first woman hadn't in fact been an easily influenced little idiot, but a strong-willed and sensual lady. She hadn't just been Adam's de facto equal, she'd insisted on this equality and preferred to be cast in the role of demon for ever than to subject herself to the patriarchal rule of her husband. She was, as French rabbi Delphine Horvilleur once said: 'The free woman who eludes our control.'[1] In this role, she made many people afraid, but she also allowed others to rethink completely the place of women in religion – in Judaism, at least.

---

1 Sweeny, Nadia, 'Delphine Horvilleur: Le livre est sacré à condition que vous le laissiez parler à l'infini', *Le Courrier de l'Atlas*. Available at: <https://www.lecourrierdelatlas.com/dossier-du-courrier-delphine-horvilleur-le-livre-est-sacre-a-condition-que-vous-le-laissiez-parler-a-l-infini-20537/>

HNEFATAFL GAME

10TH CENTURY BC

In popular perception – which is to say, to those of us who aren't specialist historians or fans of excessive masculinity – Vikings have rather a bad reputation. We imagine them as men built like wardrobes, with red beards and horned metal helmets, travelling around in dragon boats and spreading terror wherever they landed (their usual mode of greeting being to plant an axe in their opposite number's skull). It's hard to say why some images have stuck and others haven't, why we imagine the past to be the way we imagine it, but what is certain is that we're doing the Vikings a great disservice. Even the matter of the horned helmet, for example, which to our minds has become every Viking's favourite accessory, is most likely absolute rubbish. No archaeological evidence has ever been found for its existence, while we can say exactly when the association of Vikings and horned helmets first appeared: in 1876, at the premiere of Wagner's *Der Ring des Nibelungen*.

Generally speaking, the German nationalists' passion for Vikings – or, to be more precise, for what they wanted to see in the Vikings, namely maximum masculinity – didn't do this Norse people any good. But that's not what we're here to discuss. Our subject is the role of women in the Viking world and a spectacular discovery made in 2017. That year, a group of researchers from the University of Stockholm published an article in the *American Journal of Physical Anthropology* revealing how DNA testing had shown that the human remains found in 'Bj. 581', a famous Viking grave in Birka, weren't those of a man, as previously thought, but were in fact the bones of a woman. The article was titled 'A female Viking warrior confirmed by genomics', and it landed like a bombshell. Ever since the discovery of the Birka burial site in the nineteenth century, grave Bj. 581 had been assumed to be that of an outstanding Viking warrior, thanks to its size and the many

43

weapons it contained. This only served to confirm what everyone thought already: Viking men were fantastic fighters, strong and brutal, while their women were . . . something else. But now, in a blend of excitement and confusion, global headlines were making announcements such as: 'Viking "Warrior" Presumed to Be a Man Is Actually a Woman'.[1] It's true that, back in the 1970s, a (female) researcher had cast doubt on the skeleton's gender – its forearms were unusually slender, she noted; something wasn't quite right here – but she'd been kindly advised not to worry her pretty little head about it. A grave containing so many weapons could only have belonged to a high-ranking warrior, and only men could be high-ranking warriors – hence it was a man's skeleton. Simple.

Essentially, it's always the same story: if society can't or doesn't want to imagine something, archaeology will probably struggle to find evidence of it as well. Finds are interpreted in line with what seems plausible, until modern technology or methods potentially bring something different to light. This has happened often in recent years: male warriors have become female warriors, what seemed certain has become shaky. But back to Birka, which was discovered in the 1890s on the island of Björkö, just off Stockholm, by Swedish archaeologist Hjalmar Stolpe. At the time, his find was sensational: Birka is still regarded as Sweden's very first town, with a harbour that was an important centre of international trade from the eighth to the eleventh century. When Stolpe began exploring the site, the aforementioned Bj. 581, a grave located near the trading post's barracks, immediately stood out as unusual. Out of more than a thousand graves, only seventy-five contained weapons, and only two of these a full set: axes, shields, spears, swords, bows and arrows. Two horses, a mare and a stallion, had also been buried alongside them – one of them wearing a saddle. But aside from all those symbols of strength and power, what made this grave truly unique were these little balls made of elk horn. Lying in the corpse's lap, they were part of a board game known as hnefatafl. The exact rules of the game – of which further examples have been found in shipwrecks – haven't survived, but it clearly involved two opposing

---

1 'Viking "Warrior" Presumed to Be a Man Is Actually a Woman', Tia Ghose, Live Science, 14 September 2017, available at: <https://www.livescience.com/60418-viking-warrior-was -a-woman.html>

armies and required its players to use skill and concentration to get their pieces safely across to the other side of the board.

Now, this game can point to two things: either this woman was so rich that she was able to engage in such unproductive activities as playing games, or hnefatafl was a game of military strategy, and the dead woman wasn't just a warrior but a military strategist. Yes, we already knew that Viking women – unlike their sisters from the south – were allowed to inherit, and even to divorce their husbands, and perhaps we might have been able to imagine them reaching for a weapon now and then, if the need arose. But a military strategist? That really was taking things a bit far.

Some people still think this way. When the skeleton's gender could no longer be refuted, some scientists suddenly expressed doubts they'd never appeared to nurse when the skeleton was still understood to be male. Who ever said, they wondered, that the things with which a person was buried actually indicated their role in life? What's to say that weapons and military-strategy games pointed to a military position? Maybe the stuff just happened to be lying there! Now, we could allow ourselves to be amazed that some people are so desperate to believe female warriors never existed that they're willing to rethink the entire interpretation of graves. Or we could honestly say: *True, maybe.* Maybe those weapons were just lying there for no reason. It's unlikely, but not impossible. But it could just as well be that Vikings had a different concept of 'gender' to the one we do. Maybe, to them, 'woman' and 'man' weren't categories associated with certain roles; perhaps they fluctuated, sometimes one and then the other; perhaps it depended on how tall and broad you were, not what you had between your legs. Who knows? But no matter what role the woman from grave Bj. 581 in Birka actually played in the tenth century, she has succeeded – ten centuries after her death, with her hnefatafl pieces still in her lap – in breathing fresh life into discussions about her people, and in calling our perception of women's roles into question once again.

THE BAYEUX TAPESTRY

11ᵀᴴ CENTURY

Fighting and playing games were the order of the day in Sweden, but what was going on in the rest of Europe? What were women doing? Contrary to what you might imagine was happening in the Middle Ages, they weren't sitting around in towers guarded by dragons, but were out being active and visible. Unlike in the Ancient World, when they'd spent most of their time in the gynaeceum, and unlike in later epochs, when they'd be increasingly forced out of the cityscape, urban areas in the Middle Ages were buzzing with working, toiling women. You'd find them at markets, behind the counters of bakeries, in taverns, butcher's shops and pubs, in hat, glove, spice and shoe shops, in goldsmiths' and in breweries. They worked alongside men on building sites, raised the foundations of the cathedrals slowly shooting up all over Europe; they were book illustrators and barber-surgeons (a profession that included not just beard-trimming, but also tending to broken bones). Many women worked with their husbands; others, widows, ran a business or boutique as a *femme sole* (single woman) and single-handedly fed their family. It's telling that French – a rather masculine language which still hesitates to speak of an *écrivaine*, a female writer, and instead prefers to use the all-encompassing *écrivain*, male writer – had the female forms of many professions to hand at this time: women could be *médecines* (doctors), *porteresses de lettres* (postwomen), *trobairitz* (troubadours).

And then, of course, many women of the Middle Ages did what they'd done in antiquity and all the centuries that followed: they worked in the textile industry. They weaved, knitted, sewed and embroidered. Viking women, for example – to return to them for just a minute – must have been champion sail-makers. While Viking culture is often admired for its magnificent ships, we usually only think about the bottom part, the wooden structure. Yet a ship without a sail is nothing but an aimlessly floating nutshell. Viking women's sails were fantastic; it took longer to make one than it did to build an entire ship, and they were essential for voyages of expansion. As American textile historian Virginia Postrel wrote, we tend to ignore the history of textiles and its importance. This is partly to do with the fact that it's a female domain, and until recently female domains were mentioned only in whispers. But it's also linked to the fact that feminist retrospection often prefers to mention how our female ancestors did carry weapons and could be just as strong and brutal as men, while the fabric-based activities generally perceived as more 'feminine' are discreetly swept under the carpet. Which, in turn, may have to do with the fact that sewing and weaving didn't just furnish a woman's family with clothing, but also served to tie her to the home and keep her busy – anything to prevent her thinking too much. This was why the seventeenth-century British feminist Mary Wollstonecraft advised women against embroidery. It was a form of intellectual repression, she thought; gardening or writing was much better.

While this is surely true, there are exceptions, such as this one here: the Bayeux tapestry. Ever since its creation in the eleventh century, power-hungry men in particular have been scrambling to get at it. Napoleon was so fascinated that he had it brought to the Louvre; Himmler found it so brilliant that he desperately wanted it in Berlin; France and England squabble over it from time to time. What's so special about it? Plenty. First, there's its size: almost seventy metres long and roughly fifty centimetres wide, it was embroidered on linen using woollen threads in ten different colours, and depicts 623 people, 202 horses and 560 other animals, some of which look as though they're moving. Above all, however, it offers unique insights into the daily life, architecture, clothing, even military strategies and language of the time. Some have gone as far as to call it the world's first comic strip. And the story it tells is that of the Battle of Hastings – the Norman victory over the Anglo-Saxons.

The story, which unspools in the tapestry over fifty-eight episodes, begins in 1064, when the English king Edward the Confessor tasked his brother-in-law, Harold Godwinson, with informing the Norman duke William the Conqueror (still known as William the Bastard back then) that he would inherit the king's throne following his demise. Harold did as instructed, but when Edward duly died, he himself ascended the throne. Naturally, William was fuming. He promptly sallied forth with his troops, and in October 1066 the two sides met in battle at Hastings. Armed with spears, swords, bows and arrows, the men set upon each other. Many of them died – so many that the lower portion of the tapestry, which had been set aside for the dead, was soon overflowing with corpses, hacked-off body parts and horses, too. The scenes show a fierce battle; looking at them, you can almost hear the screams and pounding hooves. Finally, an arrow pierced Harold's eye, bringing an end to the conflict. Having conquered England, a victorious William was finally crowned king.

The legendary Bayeux tapestry is a monumental work and, as is sometimes the case with legendary works, shrouded in myths and questions. As an example, no one knows exactly who made it. One popular legend has it that Matilda, William's wife, set herself up as a Norman version of Penelope and sat there embroidering while her husband was off in battle, hoping to bolster his image through her work. This, however, isn't really plausible. Even with the help of her ladies-in-waiting, she would never have managed to create such a work with this degree of precision and craftsmanship. A more likely story is that Odo of Bayeux, bishop of Bayeux and half-brother of William the Conqueror, commissioned the tapestry. The question then is: from whom? For a long time it was assumed it had been made by a male-run embroidery workshop in the south of England, but for several years now, many scholars have been pointing to a more obvious option: nuns. In England at that time, many women, many nuns, were attracting attention for their exceptional needlework. Their technique of stitching gold thread onto satin – or, as in this case, linen – was known as *opus anglicanum* (English work); they mostly created pieces for ecclesiastical use, but not exclusively. To complete a work like the Bayeux tapestry, a large group of extremely skilled and experienced embroiderers must have come together and worked side by side for several weeks, if not months. We'll probably never be able to say with any certainty, but it is at least possible that this tapestry isn't just propaganda for manly conquest, but also a rare example of the outstanding craftsmanship and creativity of sisterhoods. Not a masterpiece, then   a mistresspiece.

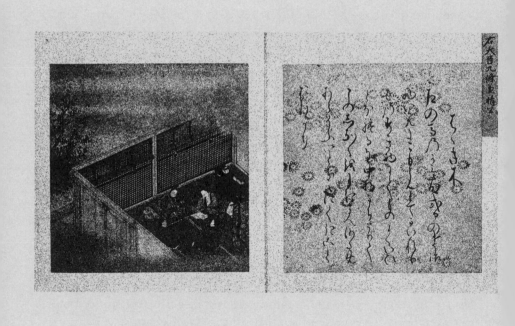

THE TALE OF GENJI, PAPER SCROLL

17ᵀᴴ CENTURY

Asked which writer she admired most in the history of the world, the French author Marguerite Yourcenar answered: 'Murasaki Shikibu [. . .] She was truly the great writer, the great novelist, of eleventh-century Japan, which is to say, of the period when Japanese civilization was at its height. In a word, she was the Marcel Proust of medieval Japan, a woman of genius with a feeling for social gradations, love, the human drama, and the way in which people will hurl themselves against the wall of impossibility. Nothing better has ever been written in any language.'[1] Murasaki Shikibu's *The Tale of Genji*, represented here by a page from an illustrated version published in the seventeenth century, is said to be the first psychological novel ever written. Some even call it the world's very first novel. In Japan, and especially in Kyoto, where she lived and wrote as a lady-in-waiting during the Heian period, it's almost impossible to visit a museum gift shop without encountering her and her thirteen-hundred-page magnum opus. You'll usually find them right next to contemporary Japan's hit export, Haruki Murakami.

A succinct summary of the story of Genji would go something like this: we find ourselves in the distant past, in an era not entirely clearly defined but sometime before 1008 (the year in which Shikibu seems to have begun work on her novel). A son, named Genji, is born to the Japanese emperor and his favourite concubine, but the boy's mother dies when he is just three years old. This event – and here Shikibu displays a good deal of psychological sensitivity for her day – will have a major influence on his future relationships with women: the 'brilliant'

---

1   Yourcenar, Marguerite, *With Eyes Open: Conversations with Matthieu Galey*, translated by Arthur Goldhammer (Boston: Beacon Press, 1984), p.87

Genji becomes a Don Juan, a rakish figure more charming than cynical. He shuttles between women, finds them fascinating, writes poetry and falls in love perpetually, even with the women he really shouldn't be falling in love with. His own father's wife, for example. The lady in question evidently reciprocates his feelings, and soon gives birth to a son whom they pass off as the emperor's own – until their illicit relationship comes to light after all. Genji is banished from court until several years later, when he returns to find his son the newly crowned emperor, a development that does ultimately lead to prestige and a high political rank for our protagonist. *The Tale of Genji* is a story of power, seduction and poetry, but first and foremost a coming-of-age novel, one that recounts the life of a man from childhood to old age. It tells of childhood loss and a thirst for love that can never be sated. Murasaki Shikibu also used her novel to describe the Japanese nobility, the intrigues and affairs of the Heian period – the world in which she spent her everyday life as a lady of the court and teacher to the empress. It's a world that seems alien to us, yet she describes it with such sensitivity and precision that we can still recognise ourselves in it, despite the temporal, geographical and cultural distances that separate us. Or, as Argentinian author Jorge Luis Borges once put it: her characters unfold and develop with 'impressive naturalism'; what we find is an accurate analysis of 'human passions'.

Opinions were apparently much the same even during Murasaki's lifetime: her work was received at court with great enthusiasm; readers were entranced by her keen observations and portraits. Later, in the nineteenth century, when Japan opened up to the world, it was decided that the book should be exported to the West as a classic of Japanese culture, which explains why it's still one of the country's best-known and most-admired works. Little is known about Murasaki herself – not even whether she was really called Murasaki or simply given that name after one of her main characters, Genji's great love. What we do know is that she was of noble birth and lived at court, though she never felt particularly at home there. In her diary, she wrote that the other women insulted her as stupid, unlikeable, good for nothing. They clearly had no idea who they were dealing with: none other than a pioneer of Japan's future literary culture. Quite apart from its nuanced psychology, *The Tale of Genji* is such an interesting book because it speaks to the role of women in the development of Japanese script. At that time, during the

Heian period, Japan was only just taking its first small steps out from under the yoke of Chinese culture. The search was on for its own aesthetic, own language, own style – and, in the course of this, a new Japanese writing system was developed at court.

Up until this point, anyone who was important or had important things to say would always and exclusively have written in Chinese, the language of the literate and learned. Expressing yourself in katakana or hiragana, the systems that used Japanese characters, had long been considered an inferior art, for which reason it was gladly left to women. Unlike Murasaki Shikibu, who had taught herself Chinese, most of her contemporaries weren't familiar with the language – simply because it had never been taught to them. This was a means of keeping them in their places, but it also meant that from the eighth century onwards, woman composed their letters – and, above all, short poems, *waka* and impressions – in hiragana. And so it was that the country's first authors (or, at least, the first to write in the national language and leave their mark on Japanese script) were female. Murasaki Shikibu was the very first among them to move away from those small-scale forms, which typically described private matters or affairs of the heart, and instead use this new script for an entirely new mode of expression: the novel.

NUN'S CROWN

12ᵀᴴ CENTURY

In its early years, Christianity had recognised women as kindred spirits – in Rome, apparently, it was the aristocratic women in particular who converted en masse and persuaded their husbands to do likewise – but in the Middle Ages, the Church and its representatives began moving in a very different direction. The original female martyrs, such as Perpetua and Felicitas, who'd been executed for their loyalty to Christianity, were now forgotten, and the once so multifaceted and powerful goddesses of Mount Olympus had long been heresy and bygones. From now on, women could and must measure themselves against three possible options: Eve, the sinner; Mary, the virgin; and Mary Magdalene, the atoner. Much as groups of friends in the 2000s would ask each other, 'Are you Carrie, Charlotte, Miranda or Samantha?' the question back then was probably, 'Who do you think you're most like: Mary? Mary Magdalene? Don't tell me you're an Eve!'

This had downright fatal consequences, such as entrenching the assumption that women inherently maintained an intimate relationship with the devil, and thus had to be monitored extremely closely or else incited to inflict self-punishment. But in the early twelfth century, the High Middle Ages, Christianisation did also have its good sides: the positive revaluation of virginity, the ideal of the Virgin Mary, opened up a new prospect for women. Until that point, they'd had the choice between being wife and mother, or wife and mother; a woman without a husband simply didn't exist, or only on the very fringes of society. Now, for well-heeled women at least, there was another variation: a life devoted to God – in other words, in a convent. These days, of course, that sounds more like punishment than progress. Letting yourself be locked up behind cold walls in the very bloom of youth, abstaining from all sexual activity (at least theoretically) and worshipping a cross day after day is something that appeals to very few people as an attractive template for life. But, back then, at a time in which geographical mobility barely played a role anyway, the convent was a place of freedom for many women. Instead of having to deal with the risks of many (not infrequently fatal) childbirths, the wishes of a husband they quite possibly didn't love, and an often less-than-fulfilling sex life; instead of being treated with mistrust, as a potential Eve, these women lived among themselves and were able to indulge in a spiritually and intellectually sophisticated life instead of slaving away for their family. They could sing, dance, read, garden and, above all – and this was an enormous luxury in those years – they could think. It's no surprise then that so many nuns were appalled when Luther and his disciples came along and broke down the convent doors in order to 'liberate' them. They didn't want that. They were happy right where they were.

At least, this was true for many of them. Of course, there would still have been instances of brutality, perversion and rivalry, even in a convent. Life among (ostensibly) abstinent women wouldn't always have been easy, not least because many mistook self-mutilation and punishment for love and devotion to God. But around that time, there were also a few women who achieved respect and power without any need for self-chastisement, but simply through their thinking and writing. The abbess Hildegard of Bingen, who was born roughly thirty years after the Bayeux tapestry was stitched, isn't exactly an unknown example; during her own lifetime she was a superstar among nuns, and she remains one even now. Nonetheless, she's still worth remembering in the context of this object, because her example shows that all eras and all corners of society have indeed seen women who spoke their minds and – sometimes – found themselves listened to. At least, after a while. Because even for such a brilliant intellectual as Hildegard, things can't have been easy. People didn't take her visions seriously, she complained to Pope Eugene III, writing in the 1140s. And all because they came from a 'poor woman' who was 'formed from a rib'. Even back then, Hildegard was appealing for the words of women not to be written off as inferior or half-witted: 'Do not reject these mysteries of God,' she urged the Pope. It seems she found in him a willing listener, as she did in so many other ruling powers: the Pope became one of her most loyal advocates, encouraging her to publicise her visions and thereby contributing to her international star status.

Today, it's popular to look at Hildegard as an early feminist, though it's questionable as to what extent this is useful. What is certain, though, is that she was interested in the female perspective and rejected the brutality with which her religion sometimes treated her fellow women. So it was that in her convents – in Disibodenberg and later in Rupertsberg – there was a prohibition on self-punishment, even if it was enacted out of love for God. Instead, the nuns celebrated this love together, eating and drinking well and plentifully, singing about the beauty and goodness of the Virgin Mary and other female saints, and seemingly not shying away from luxury and a hint of eccentricity. And this is where our object finally comes into play: contrary to the custom observed in other convents, the Rupertsberg nuns didn't shave their heads; on feast days, apparently, they even wore their hair loose beneath a long white veil topped by a towering, gold-embroidered nun's crown, like this one. As the Abbess of Rupertsberg, it clearly didn't make one jot of sense to Hildegard that the clergy should be allowed to celebrate their status through their clothing – tippet, pallium, mitre and so on – whereas nuns were denied this opportunity. She'd written about nun's crowns in her famous *Scivias*, but for a long time people didn't believe that she'd really dared to make such items. We still don't know whether this cap – which until recently was classified as a monk's crown – was one of a kind or just one among many. Scandalised reports by nuns from other convents suggest that the women of Hildegard of Bingen's empire, with their magnificent headdresses and jewellery, went against all the rules of modesty. Many found this completely shocking but, at the height of her reputation, Hildegard seems not to have cared. She was willing to put up with a bit of criticism in order to crown her sisters equal Christians.

IVORY MIRROR

c. 1300

Associations with objects relating to both 'Middle Ages' and 'women' often mean that the first thing that springs to mind is 'chastity belt'. For some reason, people seem to enjoy imagining how the aristocratic ladies of that era sat around at home with metal teeth protecting their modesty as they waited for their husbands, who were clearly insanely jealous, to return home from their barbaric crusades against Islam. In truth, however, this fabled belt seems to have been more myth than reality. A couple of specimens did exist, of course; it was invented in Padua, Italy, in the fourteenth century and sometimes also used there. But such an archaic practice of policing female virtue wasn't really very widespread. On the contrary: beginning in the twelfth century, there was a brief moment in which female sexuality downright blossomed.

The starting gun was fired by France and the court of its already thrilling queen, Eleanor of Aquitaine. As a young woman, quick-tempered Eleanor – who dreamed of a tumultuous romance in the same vein as that of her famous contemporaries Abelard and Héloïse – was married off to the rather chilly and extremely pious French king Louis VII, with whom she had little joy. To escape a life entirely devoid of passion, she had the marriage annulled after a few years and instead married like-minded King Henry II of England. She was the mother of Richard the Lionheart, joined in spreading the legend of Lancelot, was exceptionally strong-willed and – of interest to us here – a great supporter of all things beautiful and joy-inducing: art, music, song and, above all, love. As the granddaughter of supposedly the very first troubadour in history, she – and, later, her daughter – staked a lot on disseminating a new idea that would completely change the life of women at court. This was the idea of fin'amor, or amour courtois: courtly love. In De Amore, André le Chapelain wrote on the subject: 'Men cannot amount to anything or taste of the fountain of goodness unless they do this under the persuasion of ladies [. . .] For whatever good things living men may say or do, they generally credit them all to the praise of women.'[1] Suddenly, a woman – a noble one, at least – was queen of all. Men dedicated their every action to her, sang to her, admired her, even made themselves ridiculous by pre-Romantically threatening: 'It's her or death!'

Depending on your view, this will sound either wearisome or wonderful, but thanks to the new concept and its heightened appreciation of passionate love, women did at least obtain a new role and respect outside of religion. For perhaps the very first time in history, a particular thought was gaining currency among men: that affection should be based on mutual feeling, and that they'd need to come up with something good if they hoped to get anything from a woman – her favour, a kiss, perhaps even more. For the first time, it dawned on them that it wasn't possible to obtain a woman as a 'present' from her father, or simply to pounce on her if they felt like it; they'd need first to seduce her and kindle her love (or desire), because 'a woman must admire her lover as a friend, not a master', as the female troubadour Marie de Ventadour once wrote. From now on, in this culture of love, things no longer involved an active man and a passive woman, but a game between two like-minded opponents.

This ivory hand-mirror from the thirteenth century expresses this exact thought in a particularly beautiful and memorable way. At first glance, it appears to show an ordinary game of chess: two opponents, a man and a woman, are brooding over the board, each carefully considering their next move. In reality, however, this is an allegory of *amour courtois*. In the Middle Ages, chess was often used to symbolise love of this sort, as can be seen in the story of Tristan and Iseult. This scene suggests peace, an encounter on an equal footing, less a battle between the sexes and more a game they've entered into mutually. Both are sitting on the same level, both playing on the same board. In other versions of this mirror, a couple of curious onlookers are also depicted, keen to know what will happen. The man could be victorious, but he might not – in this story, the end wasn't determined before it

---

1   Capellanus, Andreas, *The Art of Courtly Love*, tr. John Jay Parry (New York: W. W. Norton, 1969), p. 108

even began; the woman could get up and leave, could say no, or even, if she wanted to, yes. One advantage of this new, playful communication – quite aside from the element of fun – was that people now saw great value in women having a little bit of education. In order to play with one another, it was important not just to know the rules of the game, but also to stay mentally agile – otherwise the whole thing would be no fun at all. This meant that women at court were taught literature and philosophy and encouraged to formulate sharp, original thoughts, to have an opinion and express it, too. It was a revolution.

Now, it would of course be both naïve and wrong to claim that courtly love changed the balance of power between men and women. It didn't, and there are reasons for this. First, because it was only 'noblewomen' who met with respect and a degree of deference, while among the general population women continued to receive rough treatment. And then there was the fact that these two opponents – no matter what the image might suggest – were never really on an equal footing. At least, not in social terms: a man could only play against a woman of a higher social class than himself; true equality, a concept that remains difficult to this day, simply wasn't wanted. What's more, the woman had to have been claimed by another man already. Married, engaged – preferably to a much-admired ruler. Seen from this angle, it was less about the woman herself than about the idea of her, about making a conquest and pitting oneself against another man. The fact that these women were actually unavailable was to the men's advantage; ultimately, they didn't want to win so much as simply to play the game. And yet, this new definition of love and the interaction between the sexes made the lives of many ladies at court far more interesting, amusing and lively, and threw open the door to knowledge in an otherwise mundane existence. It taught them that they didn't need to stand passively by while others made decisions for them; they could sit at the board themselves and challenge an opponent to a game.

Cy commence le liure de
la cité des dames Du 3c
er ma celle auidonnce &
ro Lucena Colunna de 3.

MINIATURE FROM
THE BOOK OF
THE CITY OF LADIES

1405

In her 1920s essay entitled 'Medieval Ideas About Women', the economic historian, feminist and medievalist Eileen Power, a neighbour and friend of Virginia Woolf, wrote: 'it might with truth be said that the accepted theory about the nature and sphere of women was the work of the classes least familiar with the great mass of womankind'.[1] She was referring to the clergy. And indeed it was mainly men of the cloth – in other words, those who didn't have the faintest idea about or contact with women – who explained to the masses what womankind was, who she was, and what place she should be afforded in society. As they had been in most other centuries, the women of the Middle Ages were mostly studied and described by men, only seldom offering their own view on their state of being.

Seldom, but not never. Even then there were exceptions to this rule. One of the most visionary accounts from this time was the hand-book of a certain Dhuoda, who believed even back in the ninth century that the lives of women would only be good if and when men were brought up to demonstrate more generosity, love and respect. In her *Liber Manualis*, she assumed the role more commonly reserved for fathers, listing for her son all the qualities she believed would make him an honourable man and husband. Only, it seems that no one actu-ally read this book – perhaps not even her son. Because even after a few women had gained some influence, respect and doubtless also

---

1   Power, Eileen, *Medieval Women*, M.M. Postan (ed.) (Cambridge: Cambridge University Press, 1995), p. 1

self-confidence – a development seen chiefly from the twelfth century onwards – and even after the troubadours had sung women's praises as the most beautiful and precious creatures in the world, misogynist tendencies increased enormously, particularly among the aforementioned late medieval clergy, and were enforced with considerable vigour.

Many of them weren't at all happy with the idea that women could now be educated, perhaps even more educated than men. Sermons suddenly erupted in fulminating hatred of all that was feminine; the literature that had once been so romantic now incited the reading public against women. Like *The Romance of the Rose*, a poem that was extremely popular at the time, and not just in France. At first glance it was a love story, but its subtext presented a downright catastrophic image of women: that they were permanently horny, stupid and weak, and it was necessary to take protective measures against their perversity. This opinion, expressed in almost so many words, seems to have fallen on fertile ground in Europe. In the decades following the poem's publication, the whole continent saw heated discussions about the essence of womankind. What even was she? Was she human like 'us' (men)? Was she even capable of thinking, what with that uterus and all her other problems? Didn't everything about her prove that she was intellectually challenged? People puzzled over the issue – no, *men* puzzled over it; women were never invited to take part in this discussion. Until one of them had suddenly had enough. Her name was Christine de Pizan and, according to Simone de Beauvoir, this would be 'the first time a woman takes up her pen to defend her sex'.

What de Pizan said was something de Beauvoir would echo, even more incisively, five centuries later: namely that women weren't naturally 'more stupid', but were simply never given the chance to develop their talents. In her book *Le livre de la cité des dames* (*The Book of the City of Ladies*) – represented here by one of its most famous illustrations – she created a kind of utopia: a 'city of women' a little like Fellini's, only less chaotic. A place, then, that was built by women, for women; stone by stone, just as we see here. This city was to be an intellectual space, a peaceful one, far removed from the world's misogynists. It would be founded on the example of all the brave and impressive women who had gone before, the ones who continue to be left out of the history books even to this day.

Essentially, what de Pizan wrote was an early history of women, but she was equally passionate about the time in which she lived. She was, for example, the very first person to write about Joan of Arc, of whom she was a contemporary. De Pizan seems to have been an ardent fan of this heroic woman, an innocent yet incredibly strong phenomenon at just sixteen years old. Finally, the real world had brought forth a woman just like the ones de Pizan had dreamed up for her city of women: a girl who achieved what an entire army of men had failed to do. 'Oh, what an honour for the female sex!' she wrote in July 1429, the month in which Charles VII was crowned in Rheims thanks to Joan of Arc. She compared her to Hector and Achilles, to both male and female heroes of antiquity: 'I have heard of Esther, Judith and Deborah, who were women of great worth, through whom God delivered His people from oppression, and I have heard of many other worthy women as well, champions every one, through them He performed many miracles, but He has accomplished more through this Maid.'[1]

Her ode is positively bubbling over with enthusiasm, and probably also with hope – after all, this was the first time a fully armed, triumphant woman had stood up and been taken seriously, even by men. Perhaps de Pizan saw it as a good omen for the future, but perhaps she was also clear-sighted enough to write her homage as a foil for the oblivion to which history tended to consign women. Fortunately, she didn't live long enough to see the Maid of Orleans meet her end. De Pizan died shortly after penning her joyful ode, while Joan was arrested two years later and accused of witchcraft. The crazy thing about her story – which, of course, was later written by men and is nowadays eagerly seized on by right-wing extremist parties like Rassemblement National – is that none of the charges brought against her stood up in court, and she was eventually convicted on the most inane grounds possible. On 30 May 1431, Joan of Arc was burned at the stake – because she had been wearing trousers when she'd rescued France.

---

1   de Pizan, Christine, *Le Ditié de Jehanne d'Arc*, ed. A. J. Kennedy and K. Varty (Oxford: Society for the Study of Medieval Languages and Literature, 1977), available at: <https://www.jeanne-darc.info/contemporary-chronicles-other-testimonies/christine-de-pizan-le-ditie-de-jehanne-darc/>

MALLEVS
MALEFICARVM,
MALEFICAS ET EARVM
hæresim framea conterens,

EX VARIIS AVCTORIBVS COMPILATVS,
& in quatuor Tomos iustè distributus,

QVORVM DVO PRIORES VANAS DÆMONVM
versutias, præstigiosas eorum delusiones, superstitiosas Strigimagarum
cæremonias, horrendos etiam cum illis congressus; exactam denique
tam pestiferæ sectæ disquisitionem, & punitionem complectuntur.
Tertius praxim Exorcistarum ad Dæmonum, & Strigimagarum male-
ficia de Christi fidelibus pellenda; Quartus verò Artem Doctrinalem,
Benedictionalem, & Exorcismalem continet.

TOMVS PRIMVS.
Indices Auctorum, capitum, rerumque non desunt.

Editio nouissima, infinitis penè mendis expurgata ; cuique accessit Fuga
Dæmonum & Complementum artis exorcisticæ.

Vir siue mulier, in quibus Pythonicus, vel diuinationis fuerit spiritus, morte moriatur,
Leuitici cap. 10.

LVGDVNI,
Sumptibus CLAVDII BOVRGEAT, sub signo Mercurij Galli.
_____
M. DC. LXIX.
CVM PRIVILEGIO REGIS.

TITLE PAGE OF MALLEUS MALEFICARUM (HAMMER OF WITCHES)

1486

The increasingly virulent hatred of women, which manifested both in Joan of Arc's execution and in subsequent debates about the essence of womenkind, reached its climax with the witch-hunts of the early modern period. In general, the whole witch-burning business is regarded as a phenomenon of the Middle Ages, a peculiar characteristic of an era apparently deeply dark and misogynistic. In reality, this madness – which had people right across Europe accusing their neighbours, children and friends of associating with the devil – ushered in the so-called Renaissance. In the 1970s, the American historian Joan Kelly asked a provocative question in an essay of the same title: 'Did Women Have a Renaissance?' She went on to answer it herself in the very first paragraph – with a resounding 'no'. The Renaissance didn't just see women lose the playful access to love and freedom that women of the court had enjoyed in the Middle Ages; now, they were also being hunted. Women were the 'scapegoats of modernity', as historian Michelle Perrot once put it, and back then things were probably much the same as they are with modern-day conspiracy theories: overwhelmed by the new times in which they were living, an era marked by epidemics, bad harvests, a prolonged cold snap and new sets of values, people went in search of an explanation for all that was going wrong in life. And they soon found it in one imaginary figure. The witch.

The book pictured here, the so-called *Malleus Maleficarum*, or *Hammer of Witches*, was instrumental in the wholesale spread of a panic that soon had all levels of society in its grip. Its author, the German Dominican friar and inquisitor Heinrich Kramer, laid out in its pages a simplified, twisted version of the theories of Thomas Aquinas, Augustine and others, finishing it off with a sprinkling of misogynistic 'truths' (Eve as 'proof' of all women's susceptibility to sin). It says, for example: 'For truly, without the wickedness of women, to say nothing of witchcraft, the world would still remain proof against innumerable dangers.'[1] Or: 'It is better called the heresy of witches than of wizards, since the name is taken from the more powerful party.'[2] Just as many lies are spread today with the help of the internet, so too did a brand-new technology contribute to the popularity of this work, as well as the theories expounded within: letterpress printing. This was the first time it had been possible to disseminate ideas to a huge number of people in a very short space of time. Until that point, it had been necessary to copy books by hand, which took forever (and pretty much no one had been able to read them anyway). Over the years following its publication in 1486, the three volumes of *Hammer of Witches* were reprinted countless times, and 30,000 copies sold throughout Europe. The consequences are well known: thousands of women, plus a few men, were subjected to Kafkaesque trials and executed with absolutely no evidence against them.

The general public learned about the contents of *Hammer of Witches* from preachers and expanded upon them with the help of their own imaginations. It must have been a terrifying time in which to live. After all, absolutely anyone could turn out to be a witch: your mother, your best friend, your sister . . . perhaps even yourself. In the mid-sixteenth century, a young woman from the small town of Pau in the south of France is said to have accused not just her entire family but also herself of witchcraft. During her trial, she explained that yes, they did indeed ride on broomsticks, also regularly had sex with Satan, and of course ate small children. In the end, her family were burned at the stake, but she was spared in light of her 'honest atonement'. Most alleged witches, however, tended to be 'betrayed' by third parties. For the majority, it was because they were deemed to be different: old, alone, possibly foreign, or, in the worst case, Jewish (it was no coincidence that witches supposedly flew their broomsticks on Shabbat, of all days). But often, it was the women who possessed some kind of non-academic knowledge of whom people were most afraid. This applied

---

1   Kramer, Heinrich, *Malleus Maleficarum*, tr. Rev. Montague Summers (London: The Pushkin Press, 1948), Part I, Question 6, available at: <https://archive.org/details/b31349717 /page/n7/mode/2up>
2   ibid.

particularly if they were able to heal gynaecological afflictions. Even in the nineteenth century, the novelist George Sand had the protagonist of *Little Fadette* say: 'Well, instead of being thanked kindly by all the children of my own age whose wounds and illnesses I had healed, and to whom I had taught my remedies without asking for any reward, I was accused of being a witch'.[1] The clergy put it somewhat more harshly: 'If any woman dare to practise healing without having studied, she is then a witch and must be condemned to death.'[2]

The general public seems to have gone blindly along with this proclamation. Contrary to what you might think, most trials weren't conducted by the Inquisition but by 'ordinary' people. A people's court would be established, the job of which was to determine whether this child or that really had fallen ill because of a midwife's curse, or whether the malignant glances of an elderly neighbour had indeed killed that poor cow. Women had their heads shaved and were tortured; they were inspected for 'marks of the devil' and, if none were found that only meant Satan was protecting them particularly well. After a while, nearly every victim would plead guilty to even the most insane allegations.

Although somewhere between 30,000 and 60,000 people – three-quarters of them women – were executed for alleged witchcraft in the period from 1560 to 1630, almost no one who lived in that supposedly so enlightened age actually spoke out against this barbaric practice. Michel de Montaigne is reputed to have murmured that it was a little bit crazy to burn a human being on the grounds of an unsubstantiated suspicion, but he found himself entirely alone in this observation. Women had absolutely no support in the face of the outlandish accusations being made against them, and it's hard to escape the thought that many people – while not necessarily pro, but also not actively against witch-hunting – took the stance they did because women (or those accused of witchcraft, at least) represented access to a world that worked more on intuition than on pure rationality. It's probably for this reason, too, that the figure of the witch has continued to experience a revival every three decades or so, especially in modern times: she embodies alternative forms of existence, a primordial female power.

1   Sand, George, *Little Fadette*, tr. J.M. Lancaster (Portland: Hawthorne Classics, 2020), p. 106
2   Duby, George and Michelle Perrot, *Histoire des Femmes en Occident 2. Le Moyen Âge* (Paris: Éditions Perrin, 2002)

FIGURINE OF
MARY MAGDALENE

1490-92

If, in Christianity, Eve represented female weakness and legitimised the hatred and mistrust of women, while the Virgin Mary embodied the ideal of modesty, what then was the significance of Mary Magdalene? Unlike these other two models of womanhood – the one that was more or less fundamentally tainted, a slave to 'the flesh'; the other so pure she was able to conceive a child without even having sex – Mary Magdalene, seen here in a particularly wild portrayal made in the fifteenth century, is hard to place within this good–evil schematic. She's a grey zone. A woman neither entirely good nor entirely bad, but a bit of both at the same time.

At least, that is, if we go along with the most common story about her. In this tale, Mary Magdalene was a prostitute who 'redeemed herself' during an encounter with Jesus. One day, when Jesus was paying a visit to Simon the Pharisee, she threw herself at his feet, washed them with the tears now streaming wildly down her face, then dried them with her long hair before applying oil to them. *If only he knew what a terrible woman she is*, thought Simon, but Jesus countered with something along the lines of: *She washed my feet with her tears and dried them with her hair, covered them with kisses and rubbed them with oil. You didn't. So, don't be so sure of yourself.* Or: 'her sins, which *are* many, are forgiven, for she loved much'.[1] This sounded like a conciliatory message to all the female sinners out there, a chance to set themselves on the right path after all, if they only wanted to. It was supposed to be a sign of divine benevolence and forgiveness, yet this scene, which has been

---

1   Luke 7:47, *New King James Bible*

taken as the subject of various paintings, comes across as really quite troubling. It shows a group of men sitting around a table, eating, drinking and making conversation, while a woman lies on the floor, sweeping her hair across one of the men's feet. The sight alone is a bit nauseating, nowadays, at least.

In the twelfth, thirteenth, fourteenth and fifteenth centuries – the period in which Mary Magdalene was especially popular – people probably thought she'd done everything right. After all, this act of subservience spelled the end of her life of sin, after which a new one was able to begin: she became one of Jesus's closest confidantes and is said to have been the first person to see him after the resurrection, standing dressed in white at the entrance to an empty tomb. Naturally, the apostles didn't believe her at first. Peter was particularly indignant: *Why should the Lord reveal himself to a woman first? And, of all of them, to this sinner!* The fact that he had apparently done just that was explained away by saying that she'd shown herself to be so meek and repentant, clearly so acutely ashamed of her previous life and everything she'd been in it, that she was forgiven. Today, this is what we'd call a toxic relationship, but at the time the message to women was clear: if you don't want to be treated with contempt, accept the place we're offering you, keep your head down and don't make a fuss. While Mary Magdalene did bring a certain 'softness' to the otherwise awkward and overwhelmingly masculine world of saints, as French historian Michelle Perrot once said, her veneration did also go hand in hand with an extreme boom in female atonement. Women abused themselves in the worst possible ways, subjecting themselves to various means of suffering in order to prove their boundless love for Jesus: binding belts of nails around their waists, pouring hot wax into their vaginas so they wouldn't feel any stirrings of desire when engaged in obligatory marital sex, sometimes weeping frenetically or renouncing personal hygiene. They were debasing themselves, just as Mary Magdalene had once done. Surely one of the most spectacular methods of proving your devotion to God was one that was especially popular in France during the Late Middle Ages: immurement. Women who couldn't afford to join a convent – or who simply wanted slightly harsher treatment – would have themselves locked up in tiny cells (just under nine square metres was considered ideal) and spent the rest of their lives there. They survived on alms handed out by passers-by and were roundly admired and revered for their devotion and self-sacrifice, sometimes even canonised. The fact that some women still think that love and self-neglect, or love and suffering, belong together is quite possibly down to traditions like these.

This spectacular figure made of lime wood, which was carved in the fifteenth century by renowned Bavarian sculptor Tilman Riemensch-neider, is related to this ritual of immurement. There are, of course, plenty of stories about Mary Magdalene: the author Dan Brown, for example, promoted the idea that she was Jesus's lover and gave birth to his child; still others claim she was his wife; while, more generally, love or even just sex between Jesus and Mary Magdalene is a recurring and popular theme. Riemenschneider, however, makes reference to a different story in his sculpture. One in which Mary Magdalene is amalga-mated with the figure of Mary of Egypt. According to legend, this Mary of Egypt was a prostitute; when she found religion, she retired to the desert for the rest of her life. She lived there alone, like those medieval women in their cells, and was afflicted by an excessive growth of hair that soon covered her 'sinful charms'. Why exactly Riemenschneider chose this lesser-known variation on the Mary Magdalene story is unclear – perhaps it was its visual appeal. But over and above that, his decision is proof of the difficulty we had in the past in finding one consensual story for this woman who wouldn't let herself be pigeon-holed in any of the normal ways.

A little while ago, historians discovered that Mary Magdalene, as we know her, was probably an invention of the sixth century, when Pope Gregory is thought to have combined three female figures from the gospels – including a harlot – into one. Mary Magdalene, however, according to this theory, was never a prostitute, never threw herself at Jesus's feet and never had to beg for forgiveness. She was a disciple who enjoyed equal rights with the others, the only female apostle. It's just that such a proud figure of a woman clearly didn't fit the patriarchal interpretation of Christianity, and so she was made into a woman who had to subject herself to lifelong debasement.

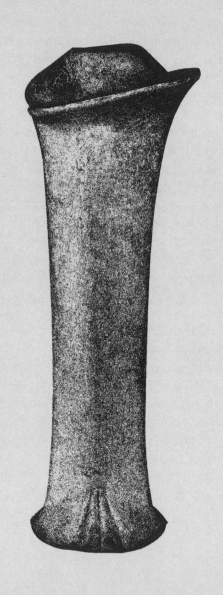

CHOPINES
(PLATFORM SHOES)

16TH CENTURY

A sixteenth-century visitor to Venice, taking their first stroll around the Piazza San Marco, may well have found themselves wondering what on earth was up with the women of the Venetian Republic. Enormous, and rather unsteady on their feet, they lurched across the piazza like drunken giraffes, generally on the arm of a husband or servant. As they shuffled inelegantly over the cobblestones – often with a deafening noise – it was clear that they considered themselves extremely beautiful. 'The noblemen stalking with their ladies on *choppines*,' the writer John Evelyn observed in his diary in 1645.[1] He surmised that these extraordinarily high shoes had a similar effect to that of the 'golden lotus' feet fashionable in China: to restrict women severely in their movement and keep them tied to the house. They were, he joked, 'half flesh, half wood'.

In fact, Alexander McQueen's versions of these shoes (you remember: 1990s Givenchy, then Lady Gaga) seem like comfy slippers compared to the fifty-centimetre stilts of the sixteenth century. A brief attempt was made to pass a decree reducing heel height, but the women of Venice seem to have roundly ignored it. Unlike the 'golden lotus' feet, the idea wouldn't have been to keep women locked up at home; quite the opposite. The chopine, one of the first versions of the high heel – or, to be more precise, the platform heel – wasn't designed to hide, but to reveal. Being taller than everyone else on the piazza was a very effective way of drawing attention to yourself, a symbolic demonstration of how you floated above the lowly rank and file. The

---

1 Evelyn, John, *The Diary of John Evelyn*, Vol. I, ed. William Bray (Washington, London: M. Walter Dunne, 1901), p. 202, available at: <https://www.gutenberg.org/files/41218/41218 -h/41218-h.htm>

higher the better. It was also a good way of illustrating wealth. After all, a higher heel required a longer dress – meaning more fabric, meaning more money. For a time, chopines were the accessories of noble-women, who, beginning in the sixteenth century, were increasingly encouraged not to work and instead to serve merely as a surface on which to display their husband's wealth. But then, all too soon, court-esans also adopted their style of footwear.

It is well established that prostitution experienced an upturn in Italy at exactly the same time as efforts were being made to curtail it in most other European countries, where it was no longer seen as a means of preventing male violence and sexual assault. It's said that Rome invented the courtesan, but Venice raised her to an art form. At least, it seems as though in sixteenth-century Venice it was impossible to tell the difference between a *cortigiana onesta* – an honest courtesan – and a noblewoman. While courtesans may have been exhorted (like other minorities) to distinguish themselves from the rest of the popula-tion – for example, the law forbade them from wearing silk – the small group of elite good-time girls was so famous and so admired that they were almost a tourist attraction, and the occasional extravagance on their part was willingly overlooked. On a visit to the floating city, where he called on Tintoretto, Titian and other important men of the time, the French king Henri III was presented with a rather unusual book: the *Catalogue of All the Principal and Most Honoured Courtesans in Venice*, a kind of sexual guidebook. Almost 210 women were listed within its pages, each with a miniature portrait and basic information. Henri's choice fell on the courtesan who is still the most famous of them all: Veronica Franco. Theirs, it seems, was a successful interaction; after-wards, the king assured her that he would help to publish her poems, and he did indeed go on to do so, as a result of which she dedicated her first book to him.

Franco's is an example of an extremely successful career in this field. Where many women had to sell themselves to any and all passers-by beneath the Ponte delle Tette (the Bridge of Tits) and lived under very difficult conditions, a small number – those 210 in the guide-book – managed to carve out a good, highly privileged, and above all unusually liberated way of life. Franco was akin to a queen among them. As was common for the daughter of a courtesan, she had been inducted at a young age into the profession that was supposed to help her maintain her independence and earn a living for herself. She had learned to read and write, to think, to sing, to hold a witty conversation – all the things that were denied to normal girls because it was believed they had no use for them. Courtesans, on the other hand, turned this into their art: they weren't just supposed to entertain men physically, after all, but also intellectually. Veronica seems to have been so good at this that she became the most-admired woman in Venice, moving in illustrious circles, attending parties and intellectual discussion groups, and, for a time, hosting such events herself, in the manner of early salons. She wrote and published, was painted by Tintoretto, moved freely through the rich and exciting creative scene of her island city. Of course, she had to pay a price for it. Of course, she sold herself and her body for that apparent freedom, and of course we mustn't romanticise her situation. But, if we look at the particulars, her life wasn't all that different from those of other women. After all, as Mary Wollstonecraft would write a hundred years later, marriage was often nothing but a form of 'legal prostitution', the necessity of giving yourself to someone you quite possibly neither desired nor loved, merely in order to survive.

Women like Veronica Franco, who walked through life proud and tall, both feet planted firmly on the ground in their extravagantly high chopines, as though on a podium, were at least recognised for talents that extended far beyond the bedroom, did at least have their unique voices heard. And perhaps they even taught a couple of truths about women to the men on whom – as was inevitable from such a height – they looked down by several centimetres. Or, as Tullia d'Aragona, another famous courtesan, once admonished a client: 'If Socrates was so wise and clever, why do you not do the same as him? You know that he discussed everything with his friend Diotima and learned all manner of wonderful things from her.'

PERFUMED GLOVES

16TH CENTURY

Let's stay on the subject of fashion for a moment and devote our attention to a chic scandal and consequence-laden transfer of culture. As we know, the sixteenth century was a society of outward appearance; suits, dresses, shoes, hats and gloves were a kind of calling card, the ID papers of your social standing. These days we see people slung about with bags stamped with large Ds or serpentine Cs, and at that time, too, your choice of wardrobe said something about who and what you were – or wanted to be – in society. It revealed how many pieces of gold you had lying around in boxes at home and how much power you wielded. Fostered by increasingly close trade relations with the Far East, sumptuous and expensive fabrics flooded the European markets. People were prepared to pay horrendous sums for a length of silk, velour or taffeta, merely to prove to others that they could.

This applied particularly in Italy and France. If a lady were to spend some time away from court, she would be well advised to inform herself about the latest fashions before her return and select her wardrobe accordingly. If she didn't, she was in danger of making herself a laughing stock and losing her place at court; after all, it was a duty of aristocratic ladies to dress in elegant attire. As the concept of naturalism had recently been rediscovered, giving preference to delicate silhouettes, fair complexions and a generally sylph-like appearance, this required the following: a velour mask to protect that pale skin, a corset and – to emphasise your own natural sweetness – perfumed gloves known as *frangipane*. The gloves pictured here are one such pair, and they belonged to the fantastic Catherine de' Medici.

Catherine de' Medici is known to history first and foremost as a woman of great political influence, admired by some and regarded by others as the mastermind behind the bloody St Bartholomew's Day

Massacre. A two-time regent of France, she ruled in her sons' stead for almost thirty years, which earned her as much hatred as it did celebrity. Alongside this, she left her mark on French fashion and, consequently, further aspects of French culture – a fact that has largely been forgotten. She was, apparently, the first woman at the French court to wear underpants. The side-saddle posture she introduced for horse riding required practical underclothing – it wouldn't do to have people see absolutely everything – so she simply wore men's underpants. And because she was so famous and admired, other women copied her. Suddenly, they all wanted underwear; a few pairs were made in various colours from lace and other fabrics, and a small fashion scandal erupted. In France, after all, long undergarments were predominantly accessories for prostitutes. That women of noble birth should now also be wearing them scandalised the clergy above all others – though, admittedly, they did have a rather rough time when it came to *la mode*: the very deep décolletage that was a trend in those years shocked some men of the cloth so thoroughly that they simply refused to give communion to women whose bosoms were too abundantly on display.

But let's return to Catherine de' Medici and her gloves. Without them, Grasse, the ultimate French perfume town, might never have become the place it has been ever since the sixteenth century. In 1533, when Catherine married the man who would later become Henry II of France, the trunks she brought with her contained an accessory as yet unknown in her new home: a pair of *guanti* perfumed with essences manufactured by the famed Florentine convent of Santa Maria di Novella. Perhaps we should quickly remind ourselves at this juncture that washing was not a favourite pastime in the Renaissance. Or, to be more precise: people were afraid of water. Ever since plague and cholera had descended upon Europe, the public baths had been closed or were barely used, and people avoided water because they were convinced it would open their pores and let in disease. Best not to imagine what a nose-numbing experience a day at court must have been. This was partly the reason why the fashion for perfume had been introduced in Florence: anyone of any significance, or who at least thought quite a lot of themselves, possessed a bespoke scent from Santa Maria di Novella. Catherine's gloves were a particularly refined execution of this new trend; instead of having to decide on one perfume, it was possible to switch gloves, and thus scent, several times a day, to suit the mood or occasion. The ladies of the French and other European courts were impressed. They all wanted such a luxurious pair of gloves for themselves – or, no, make that two, even three! And so a local manufacturer needed to be sourced, and quickly. At that time, Grasse was a leather-making town; it produced bags, pouches and, yes, gloves. But thus far no one had hit upon the idea of scenting them to rid the leather of its appalling animal stench. Only in the course of the new glove trend launched by Catherine did the master crafts-men of Grasse develop new techniques for perfuming their products and, in doing so, completely incidentally discovered how rich in fragrant flowers and aromatic plants, in lavender, mimosas, roses and other essences, their region actually was. Over the years that followed, leather was jettisoned *peu à peu* and ever more focus placed on the art of fragrance.

Despite this small cultural revolution, the Medici gloves did not come off well in history. In 1572, with Catherine's daughter due to marry the son of Jeanne d'Albret, Queen of Navarre, this soon-to-be mother-in-law succumbed to an unknown malady. Rumours abounded about Catherine and the perfumer she had brought with her from Italy: Renato Bianco, also known as René le Florentin. It was claimed that on the day of Jeanne's death, Catherine had sent her a pair of perfumed gloves to poison her, Medea-style. The rumours even reached the pages of Alexandre Dumas' novel *La reine Margot*. Naturally, no evidence was ever found.

DISH WITH THE LIKENESS OF ROXELANA

MID-16ᵀᴴ CENTURY

Around the same time as Catherine de' Medici was turning fashion at the French court on its head, a certain Roxelana, a Russian slave, was shaking up the balance of power in Constantinople and laying the foundations of what would later be known as the Sultanate of Women: an exertion of female influence on state affairs in the Ottoman Empire that would last for nearly a hundred years. If you haven't heard of it, don't be surprised: the Turkish government sets great store by sweeping this unusual episode of history quite literally under the harem carpet. A few years ago, when Turkish TV series *The Magnificent Century* made reference to this era of influential women, President Recep Erdoğan had the extremely successful soap unceremoniously banned, simply because this historical truth didn't fit into his patriarchal version of national history.

All the same, it doesn't quite seem to fit with the image we have in Europe of women's lives in the harems of the sixteenth-century Ottoman Empire. Ever since European artists set out in the eighteenth century to describe and paint the so-called Orient – and, as they did so, plainly relied a good deal more on imagination than observation – the cliché of an oriental woman has been one of overwhelming sensuality, and that of a harem one of a plush, luxurious brothel. The wishful thinking of a few Europeans made these places out to be ones in which every element – every velvet cushion, every wall tile, every tea glass – was aimed at two things alone: sex and seduction. Yet they weren't nearly as dissolute as some people clearly wanted them to be. The harem was less a place of endless (male) pleasure and more one designed to ensure the line of succession. What went on there was serious and important: it was about conceiving a pool of potential heirs with the roughly three hundred concubines who lived within its walls, in order to decide later on which of them might be most suited to the throne. The sultan didn't simply march in, nor did he pounce on the very first concubine who happened to catch his eye; instead, he followed a strict protocol and order. The idea was to impregnate as many women as possible, which meant not spending too much time with any one of them, but swiftly moving on to the next as soon as she was pregnant. Most sultans adhered firmly to this principle, until Suleiman the Magnificent was gifted the aforementioned Roxelana, a woman so beautiful and clever and brilliant that he quickly threw all the rules overboard and devoted his attention entirely to her.

When his mother, who governed the harem, finally died, he completely cast off all conventions and constraints, freed Roxelana from her status as a slave and made her his wife. At that time, this must have been a sensation. Right across Europe, from Paris to London to Florence, people gossiped and tittle-tattled about little else: the sultan had married a woman from his harem! What was going on there? This Venetian dish, which was made in the mid-sixteenth century using an extremely expensive, very recently developed technique of reverse painting on hollow glass, is indicative of the fascination this woman elicited at the time, even beyond the empire's borders. She was painted again and again, sometimes alone and sometimes with Suleiman; a portrait of her even emerged from Titian's atelier, according to reports made by the Italian ambassador to the Ottoman court. Above all, though, these pictures testify to one thing: namely that the clichéd idea of the harem favourite, kept far away from the prying eyes of the rest of the world, reclining on plump cushions and stuffing sweet treats into her mouth as she considers how best to give the sultan sexual satisfaction, was pretty far removed from reality. Roxelana didn't live hidden away but was very much visible to important visitors; her main occupation wasn't sex but state business. When foreign ambassadors came to court, they sometimes met with Suleiman and sometimes Roxelana; when the sultan was away on a campaign of conquest, it was she who informed and advised him about events at home. And she seems to have done that very well indeed; the Ottoman Empire was seldom more powerful than under their joint rule.

Naturally, not everyone appreciated the power she wielded. People said all kinds of awful things about her, for example that she had set fire to the original harem (which wasn't in Topkapi Palace back then) in order to move into the palace and so bring the harem closer to the centre of power. Accusations of witchcraft were also very popular (how else could she have held one man's attention for so long?); others saw her as a schemer and murderer. The British Museum in London houses a seventeenth-century playing card depicting Roxelana as 'the cruel one'. The game brought together the most important queens in history; Hurrem Sultan, as she was known back then, plays the role of the wicked queen who has the son of her rival killed in order to secure the throne for her own offspring. It's not clear whether this really happened or not; at any rate, it didn't do her sons any good, as neither of them became sultan.

The power of the harem, which was ushered in by Roxelana and later discredited by small-minded people as a 'gynocracy' – if not ignored altogether – nonetheless persisted for several decades after her death. It was a kind of state within a state, a command centre from which women could see everything, hear everything and exert their influence discreetly but effectively. Perhaps even with the support of Europe's female rulers, such as Catherine de' Medici and Elizabeth I. At the very least, Hurrem Sultan's successors, Safiye Sultan and Nurbanu Sultan, kept up a lively correspondence with both of them.

CHEQUERS RING

c. 1570

When Elizabeth I, one of the most powerful women of the Renaissance, died on 24 March 1603, something very unusual took place at her deathbed. The story goes that her cousin Robert Carey sneaked into her chamber in Richmond Palace that day, furtively slipped a ring from her cold fingers and rode off like a shot. For three days he galloped north, never once stopping. When he finally crossed the border and stood breathlessly before James VI of Scotland, he told the king that he was now James I of England.

The extent to which this legend corresponds to reality is just as unknown as the ring around which it was built. But many of the people who choose to believe it suspect that ring is the one pictured here. A magnificent specimen made of rubies, pearls, diamonds and gold, it is nowadays housed in the collection at Chequers, the official country home of the British prime minister. The upper part features a large diamond E, underneath which is a cobalt-blue R: Elizabeth Rex, Elizabeth Regina. Elizabeth the King, Elizabeth the Queen. But the truly interesting feature of this ring is not the part it plays in a tenacious legend or the fact that it's almost never on public view, but rather the secret it contains. This ring is a 'locket ring': the E can be opened like a small casket to reveal two portraits nestled within. There are two women in here, one on either side, facing one another across the locket. One is clearly Elizabeth in her younger years, the identity of the other the subject of keen guesswork. Generally, she's assumed to be Anne Boleyn, Elizabeth's mother, who was accused of treason and executed on the order of her husband, King Henry VIII, in 1536. Elizabeth was a mere two years old when her mother's head rolled, and afterwards she had a tough time at the English court. Often branded a bastard, aspersions were cast on her legitimate place within the royal family, just as they had been on her mother's position as queen. When her half-sister, Mary Tudor, became queen, Elizabeth was even locked up in the Tower of London for several years, until Mary's death finally forced her to concede the throne. It's said that Elizabeth rarely spoke of Anne. But if this picture really does show 'the Boleyn girl' who would meet such a tragic end, then the ring is proof of quite a different story. Namely that the queen may not have hawked her mother's name around – surely a clever move, given that Anne's reputation was abysmal (she was described as power-hungry, a seductress, perverse, a witch with six fingers) – but she always carried her close. In this tiny, well-hidden space.

Anne Boleyn, a figure who recently resurfaced in Pablo Larraín's Diana film, *Spencer*, must have appeared as both a role model and a nightmarish spectre to her daughter, Elizabeth. The king had initially made Mary Boleyn his mistress, but had later fallen madly in love with her clever, quick-witted sister, Anne. She, however, rejected his advances so stubbornly that Henry did everything in his power to make her his new queen. The good man, who at that time was still married to Catherine of Aragon, doubtless thought the prospect of a posting as queen was something no one could refuse, not even Anne. And perhaps he was right. When the Pope failed to answer his request to annul his marriage to Catherine, Henry went ahead and married Anne without the blessing of the Church, thereby causing England's break with Rome, the Reformation and ultimately a civil war. For a long time, Anne was held responsible for this religious fracturing of the country. She was despised by the people and, even decades after her death, shunned as a seductive schemer. Not least because the king's interest, too, soon waned: after a mere three years of marriage, he accused her of adultery, treason and incest with her brother, and, despite her credible protestations of innocence, had her executed. Some historians have since begun to question this image of the manipulative queen. They doubt, for example, that she deliberately balked at becoming the king's mistress so as to make him lose his senses and force him into marrying her. Instead, they believe something many people clearly considered impossible: namely that she just didn't really want him.

Nonetheless, one can't help but think that Anne's ill-fated relationship with the man who began by worshipping her and ended by condemning her to death must have been a factor in Elizabeth's decision never to marry. While it's rather unlikely that the so-called Virgin

Queen was actually a virgin – she's rumoured to have had various affairs with younger men – she did refuse all the offers of marriage she received in her lifetime, which was something highly unusual for that period. She was married to England, she often said, and that was enough for her. In Renaissance eyes, this made her a 'man-woman', a kind of Amazon, simultaneously unsettling and fascinating. She was seen as a rather masculine virgin, not unlike Joan of Arc; she herself preferred to be described as a ruler 'with the body of a woman and the heart of a king'. If it's true that her mother made use of her femininity to obtain a position of power, then Elizabeth did exactly the opposite: like Hatshepsut, she created for herself the image of an androgynous ruler, king and queen in one. Shakespeare, who seemed to greatly admire Elizabeth I, may have drawn inspiration from this fluid transition between man and woman. He was adept at incorporating the prohibition on female actors into his work: his plays often feature women playing men (the actors themselves actually being men); the dividing lines of gender are often removed and become the subject of the play. It's doubtful what effect – if any – this dissolution of boundaries had on the lives of 'ordinary' women; but the Venetian ambassadors, at least, reported that Elizabeth had 'improved the situation of women' with her intelligence and skill. She never, unfortunately, rehabilitated her mother.

MICHEL DE MONTAIGNE, *THE ESSAYS*

1571–85

It was Michel de Montaigne who notably taught us about the close affiliation between humanism and friendship, and that this new philosophy favoured enriching relationships over the dry obligation of brotherly love. With the most beautiful simplicity, he wrote of his friendship with the poet Étienne de la Boétie: 'Because it was he, because it was I.' It's a clear statement that sounds markedly different to: *Thou shalt love thy neighbour (no matter how stupid and unlikeable he is)*. It encourages us really to engage with the person opposite, and to allow a new, important thought-space to form within the framework of each encounter. In the sixteenth century, what was known as platonic love – passionate friendship without sex – was the notion on everyone's lips, the only question being: to whom did this newly appreciated form of friendly togetherness apply? Did it apply to just men and just women – in other words, only to same-sex relationships? Or could men and women also be friends? Even in the twentieth century, the wonderful 1989 film *When Harry Met Sally . . .* (written by the equally wonderful Nora Ephron) was asking this very question: is friendship between a man and a woman even possible? Isn't there always just the smallest, teeniest bit of sexual tension in the room?

While this book, *The Essays* by Michel de Montaigne – or, rather, the lesser-known story behind it – doesn't at all prove that people involved in such relationships didn't occasionally notice that their opposite had really very lovely lips, nice hands or a sexy bum, it clearly wasn't at the forefront of their thinking. It shows that humanism (which history has generally looked on as a purely male party) quite possibly wouldn't have got as far as it did if a couple of women hadn't added their thoughts and suggestions to the mix. One of them was named Marie de Gournay, and she was in charge of administering the aforesaid Montaigne's estate.

Heard for the first time, Marie and Michel's initial encounter doesn't sound at all sixteenth century, but far more like a literature-groupie story from the era of social media. Marie – who, at the tender age of eleven, had demonstrated a very independent spirit by spending her time studying Latin and philosophy instead of sewing and spinning – experienced a kind of philosophical shock when she was eighteen. She had just read the first version of Montaigne's *Essays* and was so impressed that she immediately picked up her quill and wrote to the author. Montaigne, who was clearly equally impressed by her clever remarks, wrote back at once, and there developed between them a rather unusual friendship which some parties regarded with scorn. On several occasions, de Gournay spent a few weeks at the house where Montaigne lived with his wife; he dictated new chapters of his *Essays* to her, and supported her decision not to marry but instead to try to live off her writing. In him, she found – or so it seems – someone who took her ideas and thoughts seriously, who discussed them with her and in turn tried out his own thinking on her young mind. When he eventually died, Madame de Montaigne wrote to Michel's good friend Marie that her husband had wanted her to act as his trustee and publish the final version of his life's work. Which, of course, de Gournay duly did.

At the time, this kind of friendship between a man and a woman, one that had less to do with love or seduction and more with mutual intellectual passion and understanding, was very new, and indicative of a shift in women's position in society. Even if a few critics continue to maintain that there must have been something more than just philosophy between Michel and Marie – there must have been *something* going on; such an intelligent older man would never have been interested in a much younger woman's ideas 'just because' – all they're proving with claims like these is their own narrow-mindedness. In the sixteenth century there were numerous examples of friendships like this: a couple of decades after Montaigne, the philosopher René Descartes embarked on a correspondence with Elisabeth of Bohemia, a woman twenty years his junior, which would endure till his death. It was Elisabeth to whom he dedicated *The Passions of the Soul*: the insights she had given him into her thoughts, along with their intimate conversations about the body and soul, were what had inspired him to write the book. Of course, in her own treatise, *The Equality of Men and Women*, Marie de Gournay was right to take issue with the fact that women had contributed less than men to cultural achievements only because of their poor or even non-existent education. And yet this had already begun to change during her lifetime – at least in higher circles. Women were no longer regarded merely as silent objects of affection or – as in the tradition of courtly love – erotic playmates, but instead were recognised (at least occasionally) as conversational partners who were to be taken seriously.

They demonstrated this in part by patronising the development of the philosophical movement. While men were out busting each other's heads on the battlefield, the ladies of the French and Italian courts in particular were scratching *their* heads over Plato's theories, questions of love and friendship, and all the other concepts whizzing around and churning up minds all over Europe. It was women who invited great thinkers to their courts, who encouraged debate and took on the role of patrons. They commissioned works, exchanged ideas with their friends throughout Europe and had texts translated from one language to another. And some simply wrote themselves. The author Marguerite de Navarre, for example, clearly felt so inspired by Boccaccio's *Decameron* that she wanted to pen her own version. Interestingly, her *Heptameron*, a collection of sometimes cheeky, sometimes thoughtful, sometimes moralising short stories, is one of the texts that Michel de Montaigne quotes most frequently in his *Essays*. He evidently engaged far more with Madame de Navarre's writing than with that of many of his male contemporaries. Partly to criticise it, true, but less with a 'women are stupid' attitude than to argue with her on a level playing field. Which is precisely what you do with your friends and equals.

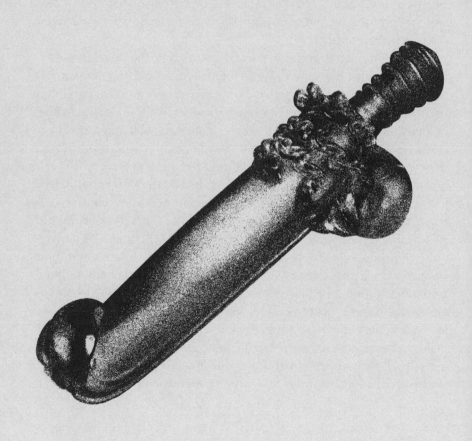

GLASS DILDO

16ᵀᴴ CENTURY

Set out in search of women's relationship with sex and you will – with a bit of luck – find a very amusing engraving from the seventeenth century lurking in the shallows of the internet. It shows three young women standing at a sales counter. You could be forgiven for thinking they're at a regular weekly market, except that in the places where cheese, salami, fruit and vegetables would normally go, there hang instead a selection of penises. Big and small, thick and thin, any shape you could ever imagine or wish for. Behind this display stands a woman who appears to be explaining each one in detail. The two women at the front are pointing at a couple of examples with interest, no doubt asking, 'Oh, and what can that one do?' while the third woman hovers in the background, tearing her hair in excitement and – one can only hope – anticipation.

This picture comes from the English translation of one of the first French handbooks of its kind: the *École des Filles ou la Philosophie des Dames*, in English *The School of Venus, or The Ladies Delight*. What exactly constituted a lady's 'delight' at that time, we cannot say for certain. Throughout history, female sexuality and female desire have been tricky terrain, heaped with shame, fear and many a myth. In the late eighteenth century, for example, the medical profession began the rumour – which stubbornly persists to this day – that women fundamentally don't enjoy sex, are only out for relationships, and will commonly feign a migraine in order to evade their duty. Yet in all the preceding centuries, people had believed quite the opposite: namely that women were wild, hyper-sexualised creatures – animals, almost – who were at the mercy of their own urges and would fall on anything and everything if not restrained from doing so and monitored for their own safety. It was for this reason that cucumbers, courgettes and similarly phallic vegetables were strictly off the menu in many convents.

Even Ovid, writing in antiquity, claims that women feel around nine times as much desire as men. Nowadays we'd probably agree without hesitation, but what did the women of early modern times think about their appetites? Did they believe what men told them and feel afraid of their alleged sexual unpredictability? Or did they laugh among themselves about the husbands for whom their female potency was clearly too much? Did they complain, like so many women today, that men – despite all claims to the contrary – just didn't want it as often as they did? We don't know. At any rate, they seemed not to want to wait around for a man to 'do them the honour' in his brusque and no doubt less-than-satisfying manner, as suggested by the object pictured here: a sixteenth-century dildo.

As already mentioned, Venice was in those days what you might call the capital of refined sex. Accordingly, the glass-blowing island of Murano wasn't just in demand for its famous chandeliers, candlesticks, glasses and other pretty objects – but also as a dildo factory. In a well-to-do household, masturbation (if indulged in) was to be aided by the very finest glassware, if you please, despite the fact that onanism was second only to *coitus interruptus* – which, incidentally, is linked in the Bible to the story of Onan – as the Church's worst nightmare. Masturbation was a sin to be punished. Even sex itself was extremely problematic at the time. In principle, it was a sin, but if you did do it, it needed to serve a purpose – namely reproduction – which meant that any practices which wouldn't result in a child were ruled out by default. So: no fellatio, no cunnilingus, no sodomy, no *coitus interruptus* and, of course, no masturbation. From the Church's perspective, sex should be exclusively aimed at having children; it was a box to be ticked rather than a way to have fun. At least when it took place within a marriage. Outside this union, and depending on which century you were in, it could be regarded with a slightly more relaxed attitude. In the Middle Ages, for example – and this was very much in accordance with the idea of courtly love – the general opinion was that passion and marriage should have nothing to do with one another, that sex could most certainly be pleasurable, just not at home. Coveting your own wife was a sin, as it were, with one particularly blinkered priest writing that there was nothing more despicable than a man who loved his wife as he would a mistress. The likelihood of women finding sex with their husbands boring, or being frustrated by the rarity of the act, was therefore pretty high, all the more so as they were only allowed to do it in one position: missionary. Lilith, Adam's first wife, had tried to take measures against this, as we all know, and actually preferred to quit paradise altogether rather than submit to the position of 'board' for all eternity.

The women of the early modern era found less radical methods. During the brief wave of libertinism, some high-society ladies did have lovers. But those who found the risk of compromising their reputation and livelihood too great (while men have always been able to cheat to great acclaim, women have not) survived attacks of acute boredom by reaching for objects like this one. The sex-toy business seems to have experienced a small boom in the seventeenth century: they were produced in greater numbers and various materials; some could be filled with liquid to simulate ejaculation.

And maybe these phalli weren't used exclusively for self-pleasuring but, over time, came to occupy a place in marital sex. For one thing, after the Reformation there was generally a renewed appreciation of marriage; partners were encouraged to show one another love and affection in fulfilling sexual relationships that weren't aimed solely at making babies. And for another, right the way from antiquity to the late eighteenth century many social circles were of the pleasing persuasion that a woman could only get pregnant if she had an orgasm. Why else would God have given her orgasms? To the minds of many, female desire was an essential component of conception. In 1740, for example, the Austrian empress Maria Theresa received some friendly advice from her doctor: she shouldn't fret too much about producing an heir, he said, but should simply let her clitoris (a discovery of the previous century) be 'tickled' a bit in bed. With success, it seems: she didn't just become an outstanding ruler, but also a mother sixteen times over. Looked at this way, we can assume that even the most pious husbands at least occasionally made a bit of an effort – especially as it was said that the prettiest children were conceived through mutual climax. Those who were denied this might have reached for one of these glass contrivances. Or repurposed their glass penis as a 'drying rack' – for the condoms made from animal intestines that gradually went on sale in the eighteenth century.

THUMBSCREW

17ᵗʰ CENTURY

In the foundational myths of Western culture, the subject of rape is assigned a large and sometimes shockingly benign role. If you look closely, ancient mythology is positively teeming with gods who just thrust themselves upon women without asking. They impregnate them by means of golden rain and other such tricks, or else force them into having sex, then somehow ensure that punishment is meted out not to them but to their victims.

One of the best examples of this is the story of Medusa. We remember her as a monstrous woman with piercing eyes and snakes for hair, a mythological figure slain by a heroic Perseus for the good of everyone. But we've forgotten that Medusa didn't always look like this, that she once had gleaming hair instead of hissing creatures on her head, that her gaze was once entrancing instead of paralysing. According to the legend, Medusa was so beautiful and enticing that the sea god Poseidon just couldn't help himself and raped her in the Temple of Athena. Athena was understandably outraged by this desecration of her sacred site – only her anger wasn't directed at her colleague but at the young woman. To ensure she wouldn't lead anyone else into temptation in future (she just looked too good!), the goddess transformed her into a monster. And this certainly isn't the only story of its kind. Even the Roman Republic was supposedly founded on the consequences of a rape: that of a virtuous wife, Lucretia. After being raped by one of King Tarquinius Superbus's sons, she chose to end her own life: 'I may be able to acquit myself of sin, but I wish not to evade punishment; and, in future, no woman who has lost her honour shall live on by invoking the name of Lucretia,' she said.[1]

---

1   Girod, Virginie, *Les femmes et le sexe dans la Rome antique* (Paris: Éditions Tallandier, 2013)

Her suicide apparently appalled the general public so thoroughly that they overthrew the monarchy – which, unfortunately, rather consolidated the example she'd set: the ideal of the self-punishing victim.

This disconcerting object, a so-called thumbscrew, is also indicative of the sad tradition by which victims are punished when accused of lying. It was employed mostly during trials, in many cases as an instrument of torture that was used to 'verify' whether women were telling the truth in their statements: their thumbs would be placed between the plates and the screws turned. Ever more, ever tighter. If the lady stuck to her testimony even under this torture, it would eventually be considered true. Yet most of them probably succumbed to the pain and 'admitted' to having lied. Lots of witch trials were decided by thumbscrew, with well-known consequences. But this instrument also played a role in one of the most famous and important rape trials of the Renaissance: the painter Artemisia Gentileschi versus Agostino Tassi. The trial was held in Rome in 1612 and caused quite a stir at the time. In the court transcript, the young woman describes the crime as follows: 'With a blow to the chest, he threw me onto the bed, then forced his knee between my thighs and stuffed a handkerchief into my mouth so I could not cry out. Now he pushed up my skirts, brought his second knee between my legs and plunged his member into my private parts. Then he let go my hand and began to thrust. As he forced himself into me, I felt a powerful burning and sensation of pain. I resisted but was unable to call for help as he continued to stop my mouth. I scratched his face, ripped out his hair and, before he thrust it in, dealt his member such a powerful blow that a piece of flesh came away. But he would not be deterred, and persisted with the deed. Only when he had finished his business did he dismount from me. When I was once again at liberty, I ran to the desk drawer, took out a knife, threw myself upon Agostino and cried, "With this knife shall I kill you, for you have defiled me!"'[1]

Tassi, a friend of Artemisia's father, who had invited him into their home, took to the stand and denied it all. He hadn't raped her, nor had he ever even slept with her, and he also had never promised to marry her, which Artemisia and her father steadfastly maintained he had. Instead, however, he claimed that the young woman was prostituting herself – a

1 Gentileschi, Artemisia, *Actes d'un procès pour viol en 1612* (Paris: Des Femmes, 1984)

clever move on his part, you could say, as society automatically looked with suspicion on a woman who painted, and was inclined to believe in her wickedness. The brutal climax of this sensational trial came when Artemisia was tortured: as the thumbscrews crushed her fingers – her painting tools, the very things she needed to live – she cried out, 'This is the ring you have given me, and these are your promises!' It is, of course, entirely typical that we once again find the plaintiff and not the defendant being tortured. And yet, after a hearing that lasted many weeks, it all ended with something that even today occurs sadly rarely: the court found in favour of Artemisia. Tassi was convicted of rape and taken to prison. But the public scandal had hit the young painter hard, so she left Rome shortly afterwards and went to live in Florence.

In the pictures Artemisia painted later, as a highly regarded artist, she repeatedly referenced myths and stories about rape or sexual assault. She painted the aforesaid Lucretia fatally stabbing herself, and Susanna in the baths being ogled by two lecherous old men. Her most famous painting, though, is *Judith Beheading Holofernes*. What stands out in her depiction of this scene is that – contrary to nearly every other version of it – the serving girl isn't merely standing by, but instead, in a sisterly gesture, helping her mistress to decapitate the man. In Artemisia's trial, exactly the opposite had happened: her nanny had given her no support whatsoever, instead delivering a cagey witness statement that rather reinforced doubts about the plaintiff's innocence. It's often said that her rape and the experience of the trial that followed made Artemisia Gentileschi the first painter of female anger and revolt against the patriarchal order and its violence. The writer Anna Banti – whose husband, art historian Roberto Longhi, rediscovered Artemisia in 1916 after she'd spent long decades languishing in oblivion – wrote in the introduction to her novel *Artemisia*: '[Artemisia Gentileschi was] one of the first women to uphold, in her speech and in her work, the right to do congenial work and the equality of spirit between the sexes.'[1] Her courage in insisting on truth and justice, despite the pain and the risk of never being able to paint again, stands alongside her pictures in proving this to be true.

---

1   Banti, Anna, *Artemisia*, tr. Shirley D'Ardia Caracciolo (London: Small Axes (HopeRoad), 2020)

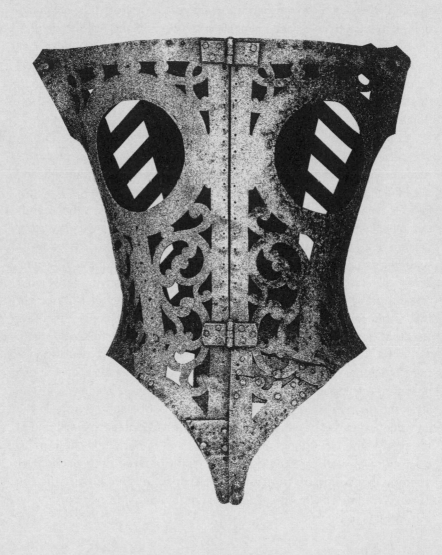

METAL CORSET

17TH CENTURY

If there's one piece of clothing that determined the female silhouette all the way from the Renaissance into the twentieth century, it was without doubt the corset. Devised in Spain in the mid-sixteenth century, it was loved, celebrated and perfected in Italy, whence it would go on to conquer the fashionable heart of Europe's aristocracy. It came in different guises depending on the era – sometimes in hourglass or funnel form, sometimes with a deep décolletage, sometimes without. Some held their shape through a wooden structure, others through whalebone, and some, like this scary specimen here, were made of steel or metal. It's often said that men invented this particular contraption to torment women. They wanted to keep them immobile and thus obedient, a little like the way women in China had their feet bound so they couldn't run but only tiptoe along. The corset was intended to suffocate women, leaving them capable only of sitting quietly and lethargically in the corner. But is the image we've had of them for at least a century at all accurate?

In many respects, it is. With a corset around your torso there are many things you simply can't do, or only very painfully: you can't run, you can't swing yourself up on a horse and ride off, nor can you just quickly undress for your lover. You'll talk more quietly because you can barely breathe – best avoid laughter altogether – and, squeezed in like that between panels of brocade, even dancing isn't much fun. All these factors are clear arguments against the corset. And yet, in assuming the corset to be just one more example of misogyny-disguised-as-caring, we might actually have been hoodwinked. At least, that's the theory put forward by American fashion expert Valerie Steele (who, incidentally, believes that corsets were never laced as tightly as we think). After all, the objection that corsets aren't good for women doesn't just go back to Chanel or the liberty bodice, but right to the garment's very beginnings. And it was men who raised it.

As far back as 1588, a French military doctor, Ambroise Paré, was declaring that while metal corsets – which were probably used for medical purposes originally – might be good at correcting bad posture, under no circumstances should they be worn for reasons of fashion. They could deform the body and even lead to death. 'To get a slim body, Spanish style, what torture do women not endure,' wrote Michel de Montaigne, seeing this suffering for beauty as a very unfeminine act of heroism. He compared women to Roman gladiators, which was ridiculous but somehow also fitting: after all, metal corsets were modelled on male suits of armour. Tellingly, Eleonora of Toledo, who seems to have been one of the first people to have such a garment made didn't commission her dressmaker to construct it, but instead went to an armourer.

Seen in this light, the Spanish corset was probably intended less to mortify the flesh of women than to lend aristocratic ladies a proud bearing that would underline their superiority. It wasn't to make them smaller, but bigger and more majestic. Catherine de' Medici is said to have threatened her female entourage with banishment from court if they refused to wear a corset. Maybe that's why the structure so quickly became a must-have, one that radically altered women's silhouettes: the laces that were affixed first at the breast and later the back (in the non-metallic versions) meant that the waist could be cinched even tighter, thereby making bust and bottom appear more expansive. The entire body could be well and truly sculpted, which led to complaints with increasing regularity. Especially from the eighteenth century onwards, many voices maintained that both corsets and the pain associated with them (which, by the way, was reported more often by men than by women) were a sign of female weakness. The women who wore them were 'fashion victims': so silly, vain and easily influenced that they were prepared not just to subject themselves to terrible suffering but even to risk death in order to follow a crazy trend.

What those poor, disconcerted men found even worse, though, was that in re-sculpting their bodies this way, women were 'criticising' nature. In the same way some purists still look askance today when a woman is prepared to spend good money in order to go around wrinkle-free or with a straighter nose, many men of that period found it immoral to mess with God's work. Shaping your silhouette to suit your own taste instead of gratefully accepting what nature had given you was, in their opinion, a sin. But what unsettled the gents most of all was the possibility of deception: now how were they meant to know how a woman 'really' looked if she was able to 'transform' herself with a corset, some expensive fabric, a pair of heels and a bit of make-up? Didn't all this fakery give women incredible power over men, who would be left entirely at the mercy of those artificial charms? And, as Jean-Jacques Rousseau asked, wasn't this also a way for women to step away from their 'natural' role as gentle, loving mothers and instead stand as sexualised subjects in their own right? Amusing details from the seventeenth and eighteenth centuries also suggest other uses in that era. It was common to insert flat whalebones into the bodice between the breasts so the wearer would hold herself even straighter, and particularly inventive lovers began to use this to their advantage. They had little love notes engraved on whalebones so their darlings could wear them close to their heart and in secret. One of the Duchess of Montpensier's lovers, for example, is said to have given her a metal corset bone on which was written, 'How I envy you the happiness that is yours, resting softly on her ivory breast. Let us divide between us, if you please, this glory. You will be here the day and I shall be there the night.'[1]

All of which did very little to change the fact that a garment like this was certainly not comfortable. Not for nothing did the mid-nineteenth century swell with increasing numbers of female voices, particularly in the USA, loudly demanding more practical clothing for active women. But the fact that there were also very different opinions out there – namely the women who thought doctors should finally leave them the hell alone; they felt stronger and more attractive in a corset – suggests that the relationship between women and corsets is actually more complex than we might think. Which would also explain why this garment has made repeated comebacks in softer, fabric forms, and has been worn – at least since Jean Paul Gaultier and Vivienne Westwood – in a style similar to that once favoured by the ladies of Spain: as a fortifying item of clothing. In the end, every woman should be allowed to decide for herself what makes her feel beautiful, strong, brilliant, sexy, brave, heroic . . . or just plain good.

---

1 Quoted in Valerie Steele, *Corset: A Cultural History* (New Haven: Yale University Press, 2003)

DRESS POCKET

17TH CENTURY

Often, it's the smallest things that make the biggest difference. In the lives of many women, one such thing was a bag. Not a handbag, no, but an altogether smaller kind of bag – or, to be more precise, a pouch – that was long withheld from them but finally sewn into garments like dresses and trousers. The pocket.

Until late into the seventeenth century, European fashion didn't differentiate between men and women when it came to bags. Every-one carried their worldly possessions around with them in little pouches; until a fashionable rift opened up between the sexes, and suddenly we had men with their trouser pockets – and, accordingly, the option of keeping everything (keys, pieces of gold, whatever else they wanted to lug about) in pouches handily integrated into their clothing. Women, on the other hand, continued to be denied such a practical opportunity.

Nowadays, we rarely think about them – they're one of those things we just tend to possess – but having pockets in your skirt, dress, trou-sers or jacket amounts to a certain kind of freedom. A certain nonchalance, too. Even at the beginning of the twentieth century, the sight of a woman sticking her hands casually into her jacket pockets was regarded as incredibly disturbing and unfeminine. When Coco Chanel added pockets to her shirts and jackets, she caused a furore. And back in the seventeenth century, this would have been simply unimaginable. While men paraded about with pockets in their trousers and jackets, women went around with flat pockets, like this specimen from 1740s England – pouches in the shape of a squashed pear that measured around thirty to forty centimetres end to end. They were worn tied around the waist, with items pushed in through a slit at the top. Depending on your social status, you'd tie your pouch over or under your petticoat. Elegant ladies hid them between the many layers of their dresses or directly on top of the structure known as a hoop skirt – so they had to more or less undress to get to their pocket. Working women usually wore them on top of their aprons, for easy access to their money or tools at the market or in the workshop. It was in pockets like these – mostly made of linen and sometimes, like this one here, decorated with pretty embroidery – that women carried just about everything they needed: boxes of chocolates, thimbles, snuffboxes, nutmeg graters, tiny books, the obligatory sewing kit (just in case you spontaneously wanted to mend something), coins and all sorts of other stuff. They were essentially a cross between today's tote bags and the recently revived bum bag: just as many of us schlep around half the kitchen sink with us these days, women back then also went about their business with the most absurd items in tow. Treats and secrets, love letters, mementos, money – of course – but also maybe a small knife or, later, revolver for self-defence. At night, many of them slept with their pockets under their pillows. They were their treasure chests, a kind of safe.

As such, these pockets – though decidedly less practical than the integrated male version – most definitely did have emancipatory value. They were secret little spaces that weren't terribly easy to peer into – which soon gave them something of a disreputable image. By the early nineteenth century, they had to some extent become a yardstick for female virtue: if her pocket was full, a woman was anything but pure, whereas a modest, empty little pocket was a symbol of virginity. We can see this especially well in George Eliot's first novel, *Adam Bede*, in which we find Captain Donnithorne standing in front of four-year-old Totty, whose cousin Hetty he will soon be seducing. 'Has she got a pocket on?' he asks of the child, upon which the girl lifts up her skirt, shows him the little thing and says, 'It dot notin' in it.' Donnithorne replies that he, as it happens, has something for her: five silver sixpences, which are soon making 'a pretty jingle' in Totty's little pink pocket.[1] It would hardly be possible to make a clearer allusion to female sexuality.

And perhaps it was this association that increased the symbolic power of the pocket until, by the mid-nineteenth century, in England and the USA particularly, there was an outright battle being waged

---

1 Eliot, George, *Adam Bede* (London: J. M. Dent & Sons Ltd, 1911), p 86

for trouser and breast pockets. In the eyes of women, especially the suffragettes, pockets were more than just little pouches stuck to the leg or chest in which you could keep coins or hankies. They were political. A battlefield of gender order. The women's magazine *Vogue*, for example, noted around 1900 that the slogan 'Pockets for Women' appeared at suffragette demonstrations almost as often as 'Votes for Women'. And, as the American novelist Charlotte Perkins Gilman explained, writing in the *New York Times* in 1905: 'One supremacy there is in man's clothing [. . .] its adaptation to pockets. Women have from time to time carried bags, sometimes sewn in, sometimes tied on, sometimes brandished in the hand; but a bag is *not a pocket*.'[1] For women, as is so often the case when it comes to fashion, the point was mobility. It was about no longer having to rummage around in layers of fabric if you needed anything, and also not having to spend your whole life tying and untying three pockets. The idea of lugging around all your possessions probably wasn't very attractive either; after all, the aim was to move about freely and easily.

And indeed, beginning in the nineteenth century, women opted less often for tied-on pockets and instead began to go around with little handbags – only these turned out to be even less practical. You no longer had your hands free, stood about with your little bag in a stiff and strained manner, and probably never had any fun because you were always afraid you were just about to lose or forget something. Anyone who's ever carried a clutch bag will be familiar with this feeling. It was exactly this – the historic pocketlessness of women and its freedom-robbing consequences – that the famous 'suffragette suit' hoped to address. Legend has it that it didn't just feature two or four, but rather six or even eight integrated pockets. Or, as the *New York Times* noted with concern in 1910: 'Plenty of Pockets in Suffragette Suit'. You could say, then, that one's scope of freedom is directly proportional to the number of one's pockets.

---

1 'Male Attire', Charlotte P. Gilman, *New York Times*, 5 March 1905, available at <https://www.nytimes.com/1905/03/05/archives/male-attire-charlotte-p-gilman-inveighs-against-it-but-finds.html>

MADAME DE POMPADOUR'S SEALING STAMP

MID-18ᵀᴴ CENTURY

In 1772, the French philosopher and writer Voltaire wrote rather irritably to a friend: 'Have you heard that two volumes containing the correspondence of Madame de Pompadour have been published? These are written in a relaxed, light tone, which seems to wish to imitate the Marquise de Sévigné. Some things therein are true, others false. Anyone who didn't know the woman will doubtless think the letters written by herself.'[1] Abroad, people were falling over themselves to get their hands on a copy, he wrote – the man who had once inducted Madame de Pompadour into the customs at the court of Louis XV and helped divest her of the occasional linguistic faux pas. Because this collection of letters was obviously a fake. While it was usually women who wrote under male pseudonyms, on this occasion a man had clearly decided to entertain himself by taking up his quill as 'the Pompadour' (who, at this point, had already been dead for eight years).

Audacious, yes, but also amusing. Not least because it said quite a lot about that particular era. For example, that this was probably the first time in European history that a woman was able to attain power and prestige even if she hadn't been born in direct proximity to the Crown. Madame de Pompadour, whose name no doubt everyone knows, was no aristocrat but a young woman from Paris's financial bourgeoisie. According to the perennially sharp-tongued Goncourt brothers, Jeanne-Antoinette Poisson (as she was formerly known) made the acquaintance of the king by planting herself directly in the path of the royal hunt on the edge of a forest, either 'dressed in pink, sitting in

---

1   Berly, Cécile, *Lettres de Madame de Pompadour: Portrait d'une favorite royale* (Paris: Éditions Perrin, 2014)

a blue calèche' or 'dressed in blue, sitting in a pink calèche'. Like most young women in the country, she was in love with the allegedly very attractive young king, and keen to catch his eye – something she seems to have succeeded in doing. It's said they first got to know each other better at one of the many masked balls held to celebrate the dauphin's engagement: Louis approached her in the guise of a tree, she seems to have recognised him under all that greenery, he took her home at the end of the night, and that was pretty much a wrap. The fact that she was married didn't really matter much – her furious husband was easily appeased – but her background was a far greater issue. It was common knowledge that the French kings (particularly Louis XV) enjoyed extra-marital entertainments and kept favourites – no one had any objection to that. But it was considered tasteless for a parvenu, a lady of the nouveau riche, to get into bed with the sovereign. She was the first royal mistress who wasn't of noble birth; her arrival at Versailles and purchase of the title 'Marquise de Pompadour', and especially her years-long influence on state affairs, were a never-ending scandal.

She was known among the people as 'the king's whore' until the bitter end; at Versailles, noses were wrinkled as courtiers whispered that you never knew what kind of ignoble games she was playing to maintain her top-level status. Even today, we more or less automat-ically assume that a mistress must have 'slept her way to the top' and only retains her position by being particularly entertaining, or else particularly compliant in the bedroom. This is no doubt true in some cases, but it wasn't entirely so for Madame de Pompadour. Her sexual relationship with Louis didn't even last four years. It's said he found her cold and devoid of passion; in bed, she was a *macreuse* (a sea duck with a reputation for coldness). Yet this never did anything to change her position. The marquise was never more powerful than in the fifteen years after her brief sexual relationship with Louis ended. She was the only mistress never to be banished from court, dying there at the age of forty-three.

This sealing stamp, which she had made for her correspondence with the king, speaks of the intimate bond between the two of them, one that went far beyond pillow talk. It must have been sometime in the mid-eighteenth century that she commissioned it from gemstone-engraver Jacques Guay; around three centimetres tall and made of gold, it is inlaid with precious stones and a cameo. The stamp underneath shows a miniature Cupid carrying a bunch of roses; the lettering around it reads 'love unites them'. It is unclear whether Madame de Pompadour used the stamp herself or gave it as a present to Louis XV, but their correspondence was certainly lively. She was one of his closest advisors; as a rather unwilling king, he trusted her intuition. Letters were an important means of communication, even if they did live in close proximity.

The marquise is said to have written a lot in general, which would also explain the fake correspondence mentioned earlier. But those volumes – and the success they enjoyed, much to Voltaire's disapproval – are indicative of something else, too: namely the role that letter-writing played in the lives of women back then, and the growing appreciation of this particular pursuit. It still seemed to be out of the question that women should write novels or books, whereas it was quite acceptable for them to sit in their rooms composing missives in which they shared their thoughts and experiences, or perhaps even invented the odd detail to make their lives sound more exciting. Eventually such letters no longer had to be kept private, but might even be published in the form of a collected correspondence, like the famous letters written by Madame de Sévigné to her daughter. This collection would later go on to inspire Marcel Proust, but even in the eighteenth century it enthralled men and women alike with its mixture of gossip from the court of Louis XV and a mother's smart advice to her daughter. Some women also penned epistolary novels, like the German writer Sophie von La Roche, whose *History of Lady Sophia Sternheim* became an unexpected hit in 1771.

Looked at from this angle, it isn't surprising that a man should publish letters under a female pseudonym; correspondence and its very intimate tone was female territory. Territory that paved the way for the wave of female authors who followed in the nineteenth century. As Virginia Woolf once wrote of British letter-writer Dorothy Osborne: 'Had she been born in 1827, Dorothy Osborne would have written novels; had she been born in 1527, she would never have written at all. But she was born in 1627, and at that date though writing books was ridiculous for a woman there was nothing unseemly in writing a letter. And so by degrees the silence is broken; we begin to hear rustlings in the undergrowth.'[1]

---

1   Woolf, Virginia, 'Dorothy Osborne's Letters', *The Common Reader*, 1935, available at <https://www.berfrois.com/2017/11/virginia-woolf-dorothy-osborne/>

BIDET

Anyone who hoped to survive longer than a curtsey at Versailles needed to be able to do three things above all else: entertain, fascinate and even slightly overwhelm their partner in conversation. Some, like the Marquise de Prie, a famous and powerful figure at the court of Louis XV, chose to employ rather eccentric methods of doing this. For example, if you were to enter her rooms (after first being announced, of course), you'd occasionally find her in the following position: skirts hoicked up, legs spread, sitting on her bidet as though astride a small horse. Madame would greet her visitors with a friendly smile, invite them to sit down and ask for the latest gossip, all while calmly continuing her pursuit: washing her bottom and, most likely, everything else as well.

Anyone who doesn't live in Italy, Spain or France and is under the age of seventy quite possibly won't know who or what a bidet is. Until a few years ago, you'd have found such an object in any older French house, while in Italy it's still a feature of every bathroom: a pear-shaped ceramic basin, usually standing right next to the toilet, which is used for washing one's private parts (not feet!) Back then, in the Marquise de Prie's time, it was a brand-new piece of furniture. Just as they had been in Catherine de' Medici's era, people were still afraid of water and the illnesses it might cause to invade the body. People never washed – Louis XIV is said to have had two baths in his entire life. Versailles was visually very beautiful, in olfactory terms less so. But it wouldn't have done for love to suffer because of this, for which reason the royal carpenter invented a new object: this one right here, the very first version of the bidet. A little basin set in a kind of chair, which could be used to direct water in a comfortable and targeted fashion straight onto one's nether regions. There was sometimes a small box built into the backrest for storing soap and sponges. The object was christened a bidet because its users (women) were supposed to sit on it as they would on a small, robust horse – the so-called *bidet*. We can safely assume that with her extroverted way of using the bidet, Madame de Prie was rather an exception to the rule. Most ladies used their new piece of furniture in more intimate situations, either before or after sex. Or, as the French libertine Restif de la Bretonne had it in his erotic novel *L'Anti-Justine*, 'I need [. . .] at least thirty minutes on the bidet; my poor fur is in tatters.'[1]

It was, evidently, the first time questions had been asked about hygiene and, more specifically, the first time worries were raised about women's more intimate smells. Later, in the nineteenth and twentieth centuries, advertisements would peddle them the line that their husbands would probably cheat on them if they didn't smell good down there. Back in the eighteenth century, the aim was also to some extent to please, and to encourage certain sexual practices – though not necessarily with one's own husband. After all, especially at court and in the more fashionable circles, a happy realisation was slowly gaining currency: sex could – no, *should* – be a pleasure rather than a joyless marital obligation, and it could be enjoyed with many different partners. Women, too – at least those who belonged to the upper classes – were allowed to amuse themselves outside the bonds of marriage, just as long as it didn't result in any 'bastards'. And here, again, we find our bidet coming into play: women used it to wash themselves out, just as they would later use vaginal douches and spraying. It was even believed this could keep sexually transmitted diseases at bay. Thanks to its association with libertinism, the bidet was often called a woman's 'confessional', or the 'lady's confidant'. She would tell it everything, and use it to cleanse herself of all her 'sins'. It became so popular that in 1790 an editor of the *Almanach des honnêtes femmes* (*Almanac of Honest Women*) even suggested introducing a national 'feast of the bidet' to honour women's new best friend in a manner befitting it.

And yet, it seems this association didn't exist everywhere – not everyone knew how or why bidets were used. One funny story involves a French ambassador giving just such a basin-chair to a lady in Rome – a

---

1   Rétif, Nicolas-Edme, *L'Anti Justine: The Delights of Love*, tr. Charles Carrington (Lincoln: Locus Elm Press, 2014)

typically disreputable French party gift, that – only for her to serve the fish course in it at her next dinner party. Its real function clearly hadn't been obvious to her. Or perhaps she was simply afraid of other people's judgement – after all, the bidet and women's sexual liberation went more or less hand in hand at this point. Unfortunately, the advent of the nineteenth century would close this brief window of increased sexual freedom for women. From now on, female desire would again be viewed with fear and scorn, while fun and levity were *passé* once more. This caused the bidet, an object so closely associated with the culture of permissiveness, to be banished to other circles. Instead of Versailles, it now stood around in brothels, thereby becoming an item of furniture associated more with profligacy than fulfilment. The fact that some manufacturers chose to market it as a 'protector' – in other words, explicitly as a method of contraception – didn't improve its image. In the puritanical USA, the bidet was the object of a veritable witch-hunt; the Ritz in New York City, for example, had its bathrooms entirely stripped of them in 1900. Altogether, the bidet was so successfully banished from the scene that around this time, the beginning of the twentieth century, an American stood squealing excitedly at a ceramic bidet in a Parisian hotel, asking: 'Oh, how lovely! Is it to wash the babies in?' The chambermaid's reply was sobering. In cool tones, she answered: 'No, Madam, it is to wash the babies out.'

'LA MACHINE'

18TH CENTURY

Life and death have always been women's remit. Even back in antiquity, a time in which women were excluded from almost all areas of life, men – who were clearly creeped out by these things – called on their wives for help when faced with either the end or the beginning: when it came down to pulling out a baby or anointing a dying person for the final time. In the eighteenth century, the two sadly overlapped with increasing regularity. Infant and maternal mortality were extremely high in almost all European countries; one in four mothers died in childbirth, and few infants survived their first weeks or months.

One of the reasons for this was poor hygiene. Another, yet more significant factor was the poor – or non-existent – education of midwives: bringing children into the world was women's business, yes, but most went about it with more intuition than planning. They copied the manoeuvres they'd learned from their mothers or aunts, not necessarily knowing what was where or what needed to be done in certain situations. To bring all this dramatic dying of young women and babies to an end, it was decided that the half-knowledge being passed from generation to generation should be professionalised and 'midwife' deemed an official job. This despite the fact that women had been very successfully forced out of medicine by that time: in the Middle Ages, there had been female doctors and even surgeons – the female physician Trota of Salerno wrote the first ever text on gynaecology – but during the Renaissance it had been decreed that women who wanted to make themselves useful in a medical capacity were dangerous. Any woman not in possession of a diploma who still worked as a healer was a witch and ought to be burned at the stake – or so a few clergymen had announced in the sixteenth century. And because women were excluded from universities and therefore couldn't earn diplomas, that was the question of a career in medicine settled – at least for those who didn't wish to be burned to death.

Childbirth, however, was an area men were all too willing to leave to women's care, and women were at least partially let in on the latest scientific discoveries relating to this field. This resulted in midwifery schools opening up right across Europe from the 1750s onwards, for example at Berlin's Charité teaching hospital. All this was good, wonderful even – only it excluded ordinary women, the kind who lived in the countryside and didn't have time to undertake a long course of education. And so Louis XV plumped for a different method. Instead of merely waiting for women to attend these schools, he decided it would be necessary to teach the ones who worked in their villages as self-appointed midwives. To this end, he summoned to court a woman, one Madame du Coudray, and asked her to start touring the country. With this doll right here.

Du Coudray was already a pro. She'd spent nearly sixteen years as head midwife at Hôtel Dieu in Paris and had been an early advocate of professionalising her chosen career. She got up a petition, for example, against the growing influence of surgeons: they had no idea what they were doing, just tugged around wildly on babies' heads with those newfangled forceps, but still they sought to contest women's place. This was absurd, said du Coudray. Childbirth required women's expertise – after all, it involved women's bodies. Who could know better what they needed than another woman? To bolster this intuitive female knowledge with anatomical explanations, and vividly demonstrate what happened during childbirth, she designed this object, 'the machine', which was accepted in 1758 by the Académie de Chirurgie as an official life-sized demonstration model. Of course, similar objects already existed. In Italy, for example, the midwives of Bologna practised on a model uterus, though it more closely resembled a glass crouched between two cushions (the ovaries).

At first glance, *la machine* (a modern replica of which is shown here) looks a little like something created by the artist Louise Bourgeois, but, in fact, no other model was as precise and detailed as this one. Du Coudray had sewn together fabric, leather and stuffing to show, as she herself wrote, 'the lower abdomen of a woman, her uterus, her ligaments, the vagina, the bladder and the rectum. To the model I also added a life-sized child.' The infant's head was modelled precisely. It had a nose, ears, drawn-on hair and an open mouth for practising what needed to be done in case of a breech birth. The umbilical cord came in two variations: one for a living and one for a dead child. You never knew, after all. The courses du Coudray gave across France on the king's instruction, beginning in 1759, consisted of a theoretical part, in which she read aloud from a handbook she had written, and a practical one, during which women could practise using the model. Over the next twenty-five years, she taught almost 2,000 women (and a few men) not only a better understanding of the female body, childbirth and what they needed to do, but also to think beyond the actual moment of birth and know what a woman needed before and after. Something many doctors now appear to have forgotten. Perhaps this is partly to do with the fact that training women to become good, professional midwives became a background matter in the wake of the French Revolution and all the subsequent social upheavals. Women like du Coudray couldn't do anything about it. Her objection that revolutionary leaders like General La Fayette – whom she herself had delivered – had only survived birth thanks to hands as skilled as hers was simply ignored. And from the nineteenth century onwards, childbirth was transferred to the remit of men, with the aforementioned consequences. The ladies who had attended courses and wanted to learn about the nature of their own bodies were now mocked. One in particular was laughed at the most: the 'fat old woman' who had once toured France with a doll tucked under her arm to explain to women what really happened in childbirth – an event of which we still speak in whispers, and which only women experience.

WAX BUST OF ANNA MORANDI MANZOLINI

18TH CENTURY

In the eighteenth century, when young aristocrats set off on the Grand Tours that were so popular at the time, there was one box that absolutely had to be ticked, alongside the Palladian villas of the Veneto, the ruins of Pompeii, the Colosseum and all the other sights of Italy that are still beloved today. This was Clemente Susini's 'Anatomical Venus' at La Specola in Florence. There, in the exhibition hall at the world's first official school of wax modelling, visitors would see a naked woman lying on a satin blanket inside a glass display case. She was young and beautiful, her head tipped back slightly, her mouth open in gentle ecstasy, a string of pearls at her throat. At first glance, she appeared to have been caught sleeping, or else in the throes of orgasm. Her face looked peaceful, even happy, but from the neck down something quite different was going on. Her stomach was wide open, giving a view of coiled intestines and organs – and, in some versions, even a foetus. Sometimes her insides were laid out at her feet, like a present. The young woman was made of wax; her eyelashes, long tresses and pubic hair were real.

After centuries of medicine being based on the theories of Hippocrates, and practical anatomy barely coming into play because it was forbidden, the fifteenth century finally saw the Church decree that human bodies could now be taken apart to see what was in there. The result was veritable anatomy-mania. People were fascinated to see what their bodies looked like beneath their skin; they met up at 'anatomical theatres' – like us going to the cinema these days – and watched avidly as men in white coats cut open bodies and pulled out intestines. Maybe it was this public enthusiasm, or maybe just the fact that we didn't yet know how to preserve bodies (and it didn't quite seem justifiable to slit open two hundred corpses merely in order to understand one particular detail of an organ better) – at any rate, the eighteenth century saw the rise of anatomical wax modelling and, with it, the trend for anatomical Venuses. In other words, for these ecstatically dying young women who were chiefly to be seen here in La Specola. The fact that the Marquis de Sade – the French author whose sexual fantasies were notoriously not what you'd call friendly towards women – saw in these wax models the realisation of his wildest dreams is cause for concern. We might also venture that their popularity was suggestive of a culture of necrophilia that would only grow during the nineteenth century – or, as Edgar Allan Poe once put it, 'The death of a beautiful woman is, unquestionably, the most poetical topic in the world.'[1]

Interestingly, this period also saw the development of an idea that was partly prompted by the findings of anatomical study: that, contrary to what had previously been assumed, men and women weren't two variations of the same sex, but two completely different ones. Ever since Aristotle, women had been regarded not as a fundamentally different sex, but simply as men that had gone a bit wrong. Their genitalia were an inverted penis, their ovaries were testicles turned inwards. Now, faced with all these beautiful corpses, people had the revolutionary idea that, actually, things might not be that way at all: women weren't just genitally challenged men, but a completely different model of human. A second sex.

You may think this realisation would have led to a greater appreciation of women, but sadly quite the opposite happened. Instead of saying they were different but equal, this 'being different' was turned into a supposedly scientifically proven state of being 'less'. In some ways, the anatomical Venus trend is indicative of the desire to use medical discoveries as an argument for the oppression of women, and so we might wonder: was this even about science at all, or more about erotic delectation? Perhaps that's a question Anna Morandi Manzolini, whose self-portrait in wax is pictured here, occasionally asked herself, too. She was the only woman who dared to venture into the very

---

1   Poe, Edgar Allan, 'The Philosophy of Composition', first published in *Graham's American Monthly Magazine of Literature and Art*, Philadelphia, April 1846, available at <https://www.poetryfoundation.org/articles/69390/the-philosophy-of-composition>

masculine territory of anatomy and wax modelling, and who distanced herself emphatically from the 'death becomes her' aesthetic adopted by her colleagues. What she was interested in wasn't erotic fantasy, but details and anatomical realities. Or, as the German scholar Johann Jacob Volkmann wrote in his diary in 1757: 'Using her wax, she creates all the parts of the body with extraordinary artistry and is capable of depicting each one in its actual colour. For more precision, she reproduces some parts of the body, such as the eye or the ear, two or three times larger than in real life . . . She teaches courses in anatomy and explains the body to young people.'

Bologna, where Manzolini worked, was experiencing a new economic upturn around this time. Educated ladies, like philosophy professor Laura Bassi, mathematician Maria Gaetana Agnesi and the aforementioned Signora Morandi Manzolini, were the poster girls for this university town's rediscovered lustre. And, thanks to her uncommon branch of science, Anna had a special place among these *madre degli studi*. It was widely accepted that, despite their 'weak bodies', women were indeed capable of thought – but for one of them to dissect bodies and study organs down to the tiniest detail, all without fainting, was unusual indeed. Anna Morandi was clearly well aware of this: this self-portrait was doubtless a provocation. She may be wearing a pearl necklace, as a Venus normally did, but aside from that this bust is the polar opposite of her male colleagues' beautiful corpses. It doesn't show us a dying girl but an adult woman, a sturdy lady with curled hair and a pink taffeta dress. She looks as though she could be on her way to a party, only she's clearly busy with more important things: grasping a scalpel and tweezers, she has just sliced away the top of a head and is engaged in studying the brain within. It's telling that she should be examining this particular area – the centre of knowledge and therefore power. Perhaps that's why Catherine the Great of Russia, who was a staunch advocate of education for girls, had a miniature version of this Manzolini bust on her desk: 'I keep the bust on my desk in St Peter's Court,' she wrote to a friend, and if ever anyone asked her who this strange woman was, she would simply claim: 'That is my grandmother.'

'THE GOOD MOTHER', GROUP OF PORCELAIN FIGURINES

c. 1760

In Mary McCarthy's novel *The Group*, there's a particular scene that has stayed with me ever since I first read it. The story follows a group of eight young women – eight friends – as they throw themselves into life after university and try to make their way in 1930s America. Reality causes some of them to fall apart, while others simply change direction; a few do manage to realise their dreams eventually. The scene in question goes something like this: Priss Hartshorn, a political activist and one of the eight friends, has just had a baby, and her husband, a doctor, has got it into his head that he could use her and the child to prove the benefits of breastfeeding. He doesn't care that people swear by baby formula or that his young wife has immense difficulties breastfeeding. He asserts his opinion, because he thinks it's best that way: for his child, for his wife, for his own notion of motherhood.

The question of breastfeeding, then – to do or not to do, and if so, for how long – is a recurrent one. The trends and attitudes around it change every couple of decades, but the fact that absolutely everyone has an opinion on it – and that includes people who have neither breasts nor milk ducts, maybe not even children – has stayed pretty much unchanged for centuries. If a woman doesn't breastfeed, because she doesn't want to or can't, outsiders will commonly allow themselves to make judgements that are rarely kind, often even harsh or hostile. One central argument is usually nature. There have always been advocates of the milk-dripping breast – even in the Ancient World, many spoke out in its favour – but when it comes to the notion of what makes a good mother, the intrusive, self-confident manifestations of the sort that we see today only really began to surface in the eighteenth century. Until that point, mother–child relationships were likely to have just as little

127

emotional charge as husband–wife relationships. A family was something you had, but not necessarily something that had an impact on your emotional life. As such, it was completely unimaginable that a well-to-do woman would feed her baby herself. After a few days it would be sent to the countryside, to a wet nurse; while anyone who had a lot of money could hire one to live in – though only, mind you, after first inspecting her like a horse (a bit like in *The Handmaid's Tale*). All this was done for good reason. Firstly, because most women simply didn't have time to spend half the day feeding a baby – the concept of 'housewife' didn't yet exist. Secondly, because you didn't necessarily want to get attached to an infant; the child mortality rate was extremely high in those days, and it was a form of self-protection only really to engage with your child after it had survived those critical first months or even years. And, especially, because most men didn't set much store by their wives breastfeeding, for the simple reason that it left them sexually out of bounds (for a long time, sleeping with a breastfeeding woman was considered taboo).

Just as some women these days will sell or loan out their bellies, at that time it was a well-paid and socially well-regarded career move to hire out your breasts and milk. For young women, wet nurse was one of the most lucrative occupations of all – until a group of men decided to invent a new myth in order to put women under a new sort of pressure: motherly love. Now, it was claimed with great gusto, a child's bond with its mother – and thus in some way with the world – began with the naked, outstretched breast.

Not for nothing is this group of Nuremberg porcelain figurines (made by Gottlieb Lück) called 'The Good Mother'. Here sits a woman surrounded by children, either sleeping or playing a musical instrument, hanging off her breasts, shoulders and hands as though from a nurturing climbing-frame. It seems not to bother her, really; she's all patience and self-sacrifice. This group of figurines, of which there are many variations and which could have been found in many well-off households at the time, depicts an ideal of the 1770s and functions both as a decorative object and something like a warning. From its place on a side table it would shout at women: *Look! This is what a 'good mother' looks like! Her body is a permanent 'open house'!* We start learning when we start living; our first teacher is the woman who nourishes us from her breast – so wrote Jean-Jacques Rousseau, who himself grew up motherless. Just like his friend and colleague Denis Diderot, Rousseau (who was, mark you, one of the most-read and highly esteemed child-development theorists of his time) thought it impossible that a woman should go against her 'nature' and farm out her children 'just like that'. In his famous treatise *Emile, or On Education* he complained: 'These gentle mothers, having got rid of their babies, devote themselves gaily to the pleasures of the town. Do they know how their children are being treated in the villages?'

As mentioned: the eighteenth century saw the discovery of women's 'biological nature', which could thenceforth be called upon to explain even the most outlandish theories. By permanently referring to the ostensibly maternal 'nature' of women, these otherwise clever and not-at-all-misogynistic gents succeeded in developing the image of 'good' versus 'bad' mothers that still persists in many places. On the one hand we had the woman in her supposedly 'natural' role as a nourishing, caring, child-rearing entity. And on the other there were all those who continued to think 'only' of themselves, or even just sometimes of things other than their babies. What was especially pernicious about this notion of 'natural motherly love' was that, while it pinned women down and imposed yet another new myth on them, it also had them believe that this development was to their benefit: it reflected a deeper appreciation of their role within the family. They were no longer just the 'vessel' – as Aristotle put it – in which a child came into being, not merely breeding machines. Now, thanks to their 'naturally' close relationship with their children, they also had something like influence. After all, nurture begins with the first drops of milk – that's what Rousseau said, anyway, thus turning the breastfeeding mother into a child-rearing entity. On the other hand, he did also say, 'Woman was made for man's delight.' The British feminist Mary Wollstonecraft, who otherwise admired Rousseau, dismissed this statement as nonsense. She, of course, died of complications from childbirth and so never breastfed her daughter Mary – which in absolutely no way prevented said daughter from going on to write the internationally renowned horror classic *Frankenstein*.

LADIES OF
LLANGOLLEN FIGURINE

UNDATED

Anyone who happened to be walking through Woodstock, Kilkenny, on the night of 30 March 1778 may have found themselves witness to an unusual scene: that night, a woman who went by the name of Sarah Ponsonby, twenty-three years young, climbed out of her bedroom window disguised as a man and ran off with her dog, Frisk, on the end of a lead, plus a pistol in her bag. Her destination: the house of one Eleanor Butler, a woman sixteen years her senior. One hundred and fifty years later, the French novelist Colette would describe Ponsonby and Butler's escape in *The Pure and the Impure*: 'Infatuated with romance, they had leaped from a window rather than leave by way of the open door. They corresponded with each other by secret means, bribed the servants, and, at the moment of leaving, had seized firearms they did not know how to use and fled on horseback, although they had never in their lives sat a horse . . . There were complications, legal processes, tragedies, childish tears . . . but from all this a unique sentiment sprang, straight and firm and flowering like the iris nestling against its green stem.'[1]

The sentiment to which Colette was referring – and for which the two escapees, the so-called Ladies of Llangollen, became famous over the years that followed – was friendship. Or, to be more precise, romantic friendship between two women. Love and emotion were fundamentally rediscovered during the eighteenth century and, against this background, the subject of relationships between women also gained in importance. The two ladies became representatives of this

---

1   Colette, *The Pure and the Impure*, tr. Herma Briffault (New York: New York Review of Books, 2000), p. 123

new development. Neither intended ever to marry, nor did they wish to join a convent, but when they met at a tea party at an elite Irish salon, they instantly recognised one another as kindred spirits and secretly plotted their escape. On their first attempt, on 30 March, their families caught them before they'd even boarded the ferry to England. Frisk, the dog, had given them away by barking. But a couple of months later, they somehow managed to persuade everyone of their novel plan for life – and so, on a beautiful morning in May 1778, they emigrated to the British mainland and settled in Llangollen in Wales. That plan was as follows: to live an independent, secluded life, spend their time reading and gardening, drink hot chocolate in the afternoons and fill their evenings with illuminating discussions. To sit at the fireside when it rained, reading the memoirs of Madame de Maintenon by candlelight. To think. To be free.

And that was exactly what they did. At this point, it would be worth mentioning again exactly when this story took place. Compared to what preceded it, the eighteenth century was more open in many respects; as noted, female friendships were en vogue, and single women or widows often lived together. Nonetheless, it must have been unusual, not to say downright scandalous, for two relatively young women – and members of good Irish society, to boot – to decide, just like that, to move to a pretty little manor in the middle of nowhere and live purely with each other and their thoughts. Like nuns, essentially, though independent of any religious doctrine. A little, too, like the artist Claude Cahun and her partner Marcel Moore, only two hundred years earlier. Their entire appearance – including their habit of wearing matching outfits and a rather masculine style of clothing – was so original that, before long, everyone in Britain was talking about them. Even the queen made curious enquiries and persuaded the king to allot the ladies a pension. Lord Byron apparently visited several times to converse with these clever, educated women, and perhaps to gawk a little, too – after all, the whole thing was pretty peculiar.

Over time, Sarah, Eleanor and their new dog – which went by the name of Sappho – became a veritable tourist attraction on account of their unusual lifestyle. Some visitors, like Byron, Sir Walter Scott, Percy Bysshe Shelley and the lesbian poet Anne Lister, came to them as kindred spirits. Others travelled to Llangollen with the sole aim of catching a glimpse of the unusual couple and their home. If they were unlucky, they might instead have pocketed one of these figurines to take back with them, as proof that they had at least been in the vicinity. The poor ladies can't have liked this at all. They had come in search of peace and seclusion and ended up accidentally attaining cult status.

The buzz elicited by their way of living also indicated the growing popularity of the idea that women could best develop intellectually and emotionally when they lived together. Of course, we had long had convents for this, but they were all about devotion and faith in God, which put rather narrow limitations on their occupants' scope of interests. By contrast, the era in which the ladies lived saw a growing desire among women to decide for themselves what their interests were, with whom they discussed them, and whose company they found enriching. As early as 1694, for example, the famous Mary Astell wrote in *A Serious Proposal to the Ladies* (signed 'By a Lover of her Sex') that women could best improve their minds with each other's help, because only in these circumstances were they free of the 'deceitful flatteries' of men, who thought merely about themselves and their own entertainment. Among their own sex, wrote Astell, it was possible for women finally to develop all the skills these men were always promising, but which they actually wanted to distract them from attaining. The Ladies of Llangollen were no doubt of a similar opinion and, in choosing so decisively to live in accordance with their convictions, they became role models for many women. For lesbian women, yes, but also for those who were slowly realising that they could probably only live the life of which they dreamed alongside another woman, or women. And, so as not to forget this at the first empty promise made by a man, they put the Ladies of Llangollen up on the mantelpiece as a reminder.

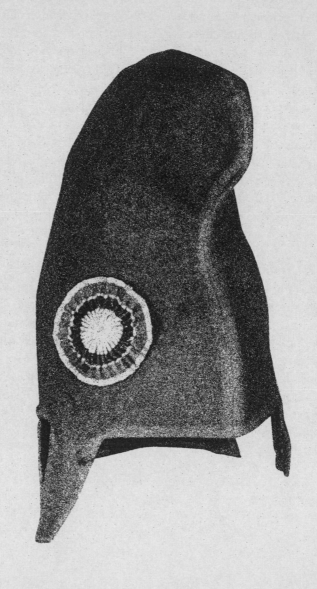

PHRYGIAN CAP

1789

Élisabeth Vigée Le Brun, one of Marie Antoinette's favourite portrait painters, said of the eighteenth century: 'Women ruled back then; the French Revolution knocked them from their throne.'[1] On one hand, she was right; on the other, entirely wrong. While it's true that many women of that era had more power, more influence, more knowledge and, consequently, more self-confidence than ever before – for some it had indeed been an exciting and enlightening century – this applied only to a very privileged section of society. The women of the people, all those who appear in the Estates-General's *Cahiers de doléances* (record of complaints) rueing the fact that they were 'the object[s] of men's admiration or hate' but never perceived as independently thinking subjects, did not experience the eighteenth century as Vigée Le Brun did – a period of freedom – but instead had high hopes of the Revolution.

It's often forgotten that it was the women of the *halles*, the market women of Paris, who marched on Versailles in the company of the National Guard on 5 October 1789 to protest against hunger and demand that the king return to Paris. Marie Antoinette's famous exclamation, 'Let them eat cake' – which is, incidentally, said to be a (male) invention, a trick to stir up anti-monarchist sentiment – galvanised the marchers. More than a thousand women set off that day with banderoles on which were written things like 'Versailles feasts while Paris starves' and 'We're coming for the baker, the baker's wife and their son'. After besieging it for a night, they succeeded in forcing their way into the palace and obliging the royal couple to follow them back to Paris. At the time, a briefly circulated rumour said it had been men

---

1 Vigée Le Brun, Élisabeth, *Souvenirs 1755–1842: 'Les femmes régnaient alors, la Révolution les a détrônées'* (Paris: Éditions Tallandier, 2015)

dressed in women's clothing who had brought the monarchs to Paris. *Mais non*, it was indeed women. Later, they would be fleetingly honoured as 'heroes of the Revolution', and a woman was chosen as a symbol of the young and supposedly equitable Republic: Marianne, recognisable by her distinctive headwear, a Phrygian cap.

In Ancient Rome, slaves who had been granted their freedom wore a cap known as a *pileus*, which looked quite similar to the one shown here. It seems that the French got the two confused and interpreted the Phrygian cap as a symbol of freedom. In actual fact, the latter is attributed chiefly to the Amazons – both the real-life warriors of antiquity, the Scythians, and their imaginary counterparts, the Amazons depicted on Ancient Greek vases, wore these caps. Looking at Marianne in the famous painting by Delacroix, the way she leads her people with the French flag in one hand and a weapon in the other, her left breast bared, it doesn't take long for a certain question to suggest itself: is this Marianne some kind of Amazon? Had someone actually listened to the Revolutionary Théroigne de Méricourt, dressed in her Amazon warrior garb, as she cried to her friends, '*Aux armes, Mesdames!*' before winding up in the Salpêtrière asylum? Not likely. We can't really see Marianne the Amazon as a metaphor for the place of women in post-Revolution society. Because even though they did actively participate in the uprising and continued to be involved afterwards, the First Republic saw women increasingly being shut out of public life. A similar thing happened after subsequent wars and revolutions: women were all too gladly mobilised at the height of the crisis but then sent back to the hob and the sewing machine. Their red caps – which they'd never been allowed to wear in public anyway – were hung up in the hallway. The Revolution was over for the time being, and it hadn't really changed things for women. In the *Encyclopédie* (said to be the ideological basis of the Revolution), for example, a *citoyen* (male citizen) was a 'member of a free society', while a *citoyenne* (female citizen) only existed in relation to a man, as 'the wife of a *citoyen*'. What was new was that a French woman was now allowed to inherit, and for a brief time she was even permitted to divorce her husband (with his agreement), though Napoleon revoked this right again in 1816. The *liberté, egalité, fraternité* proclaimed in the *Déclaration des Droits de l'Homme et du Citoyen* was no *sororité*; the new order did elevate a section of society, but sadly not the female one. Furious about this rather unexpected turn of events, Olympe de Gouges wrote the *Déclaration des Droits de la Femme et de la Citoyenne* in 1791. In her foreword, she asks accusingly: 'Man, are you capable of being just? It is a woman who poses the question; you will not deprive her of that right at least. Tell me, what gives you sovereign empire to oppress my sex? Your strength? Your talents?'[1] And in a postscript, she addresses women: 'Woman, wake up! The tocsin of reason is being heard throughout the whole universe; discover your rights.'[2]

Olympe de Gouges was in favour of the Revolution, but also in favour of retaining the monarchy. Her *Déclaration* was dedicated to Marie Antoinette, a move that would ultimately seal her fate. Along with a few other politically active women, she became one of the first victims of the so-called *Terreur*, the reign of terror. After Marie Antoinette was taken to the guillotine on 16 October 1793, Olympe de Gouges went to the scaffold on 3 November, followed five days later by another well-known Revolutionary, the former *salonnière* and *girondiste* Madame Roland. More than a hundred years later, Clara Zetkin would write about both women in her articles for *Die Neue Zeit*, reminding us that the great democratic sea-change brought about by the French Revolution was nothing but an empty promise as far as women were concerned. France might have put on its Amazonian cap and strutted around behind combative Marianne in its new role as a nation of freedom and equality, but in reality it preferred to let women fade into the background – or, if they became restive, simply guillotine them. 'Woman has the right to mount the scaffold; she must equally have the right to mount the rostrum,' wrote a clear-sighted Olympe de Gouges. And perhaps, after the disappointment of a revolution they had instigated alongside men, women realised they would only ever achieve things if they stuck together. As Amazons.

1   de Gouges, Marie-Olympe, *Déclaration des Droits de la Femme et de la Citoyenne* (*Declaration of the Rights of Woman and the Female Citizen*), 1791, available at <https://pages.uoregon.edu/dluebke/301ModernEurope/GougesRightsofWomen.pdf>
2   ibid.

RECAMIER

c. 1800

Contrary to all hopes, then, the French Revolution changed little for women. It had brought more frustration than freedom and, according to the famous writer Madame de Staël, even disrupted a very female tradition: that of the salon. Since the Revolution, she said, the art of conversation, intellectual entertainment and cheerful get-togethers had gone down the drain in France, much to her regret. Germaine de Staël had herself grown up in one of the most famous Parisian salons of the eighteenth century – that of her mother, Madame Necker – and loved what she saw as an extremely French and female custom. To her mind, other cultures struggled with light conversation; the Germans, for example, whom at heart she liked very much, were simply lacking in lightness of spirit. She found them too goal-orientated, too practical, for which reason they always slipped into serious conversations that, while interesting, just weren't any fun. Unfortunately, ever since the Revolution, the situation in Paris had been similar to that on the other side of the Rhine: people seemed to talk about nothing but specifics these days, and they didn't do it in a terribly uplifting manner.

One exception to the rule was, in her exacting eyes, the salon hosted by one of her dearest friends, the so-called *belle des belles* (beauty of beauties), a woman who was turning half of Europe's heads at the dawn of this new century – on purpose, of course. Her name was Juliette Récamier, one of the last great *salonnières*, in whose honour this piece of furniture was named: the recamier. Why exactly, we don't know. Presumably, the name for this one-person sofa stems from a painting by Jacques-Louis David, famous portraitist of Napoleon, capturing Juliette at the age of twenty-three. It shows her lying on one of these very sofas, her back to the viewer, wearing a white dress in antique style. She has bare arms, bare feet and quasi-undressed curls, and she looks back at us over her shoulder with a gentle yet self-possessed gaze. David began the painting in 1800 but never finished it, saying: 'Artists too have their idiosyncrasies, not just women.' Despite this, his portrait still became immediately famous. Just like his model and the piece of furniture on which she sat for him. If we wanted to be critical, we could say that this sofa and her suggestive pose trapped Madame firmly within the image of the Romantic period's ideal woman: young and ethereally beautiful, as popularised by ballets such as *Giselle* and *La Sylphide*. We could also say that it helped to underpin the two-sphere theory spreading like wildfire through the USA and England in particular: namely, that the exterior world – the dynamic, active one – was the sphere of men, while the interior one – the thoughtful, intimate, lying-down one – belonged to women. We might also recognise in it something else entirely: a piece of furniture as metaphor for the concept of female salon culture.

Madame de Rambouillet, for example – the inventor of the salon tradition, the very first of her kind – had only initiated these intellectual get-togethers in her own home because, back in the seventeenth century, her health didn't allow her to receive people anywhere except in her bedroom. Because she couldn't go out much and quickly grew tired at balls and receptions, she didn't just bring the natural world into her home in the form of bouquets, but also invited along the brightest minds of the period. She too will have spent most of her time in this half-sitting, half-lying position, in the fabled 'Blue Room' of her Parisian townhouse. A suggestive pose, perhaps – in Madame Récamier's case, certainly – but it was also a demonstration of power, at least when adopted by a woman, a way of saying: *I'm going to take a moment for myself, let my hair down, but please, do take a seat somewhere, while I indulge in my own interesting thoughts.* And quite apart from that: just think of all the wonderful things you do lying down. You don't knit, you don't sew, you don't darn socks; you don't do any cleaning or cooking. Nor do you trouble yourself about the children, still less about the staff. No, no. You read, you write (at least, one and a half centuries later, writers like Françoise Sagan did), you think, you dream, you talk and you love. You let your mind wander and, at least for those few moments, you're entirely free, entirely present in yourself – just as you would have been later on Freud's sofa. You also give the impression of being busy, just not with any of those boring chores. And that was exactly the point. After all, salon conversation – to paraphrase Madame de Staël – was supposed to be conducted in an entirely 'un-German manner', as a kind of aimless art form that left daily life and so-called reality at the door, and elevated itself to other spheres. The salons of Madame de Rambouillet and her successors left their mark on literature and language with these principles, but they also allowed the development of the ideas that would eventually lead to the Revolution.

Maybe Madame Récamier was just as disappointed as many other women by the empty promises of that great social upheaval. At any rate, it was forbidden to discuss politics at her salon. Conversation was to be light and cheerful; she kept discussion of life's more serious issues to letters, Madame de Pompadour-style. Preferably letters addressed to Germaine de Staël. Like twenty-first-century friends using text messages, they talked about the latest events on their turbulent continent, about gossip from Paris, about love. De Staël clearly knew that Madame Récamier was irresistible, reclining like that on her recamier – when one of her lovers set off to spend a few days in Paris, she wrote to her friend that she trusted she would do her utmost to conceal her charm and beauty from him. A couple of days later, she added the moving plea: 'Make it so that he loves me, not you.' What happened, we don't know. But one thing's for sure: Juliette didn't hide her charm and beauty from the famous political scientist Alexis de Tocqueville and his friends. When the gentlemen arrived, she was lying on her sofa, beautiful and proud, occasionally dropping a *bon mot* into the conversation and generally bewitching her entourage. 'We were all in love with her, we were all her slaves,' wrote Tocqueville. At the time, this was remarkable – in most cases it was exactly the other way around.

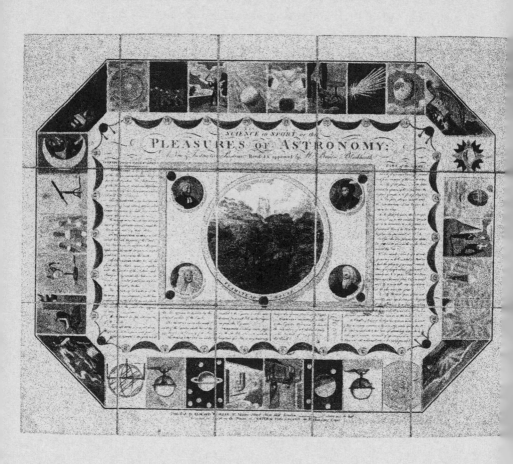

BOARD GAME, 'PLEASURES OF ASTRONOMY'

1814

If, in seventeenth- and eighteenth-century France, you wanted to describe someone as mad, or at least pretty strange, you'd say: 'He's got a quarter-moon in his head.' Or, more likely: '*She's* got a quarter-moon in her head.' After all, it was mostly women who were considered strange. In a lithograph from the period, tellingly titled 'The Influence of the Moon on the Heads of Women', we can see five women dancing in a village square in the middle of the night, with the moon above them raining beams down onto their heads as though they were its marionettes. At the opposite side of the picture, their husbands are fruitlessly searching for them. The women can neither see nor hear them (or they simply don't want to); their thoughts are somewhere else entirely, far away, in the stars. Oh, all right, then – in the moon.

The belief in women's special relationship with the moon didn't just emerge when large numbers of women developed an interest in astrology and started looking to the constellations for clues to their personal development. Even our Stone Age ancestors believed there was a correlation between the lunar and female cycles, and the moon was regarded as a potent influence on fertility. In the Ancient World, 'women's sicknesses' were referred to as 'moon sicknesses'; later, witches were thought to dance in the moonlight, their perceived relationship with this celestial body making them unpredictable. For a long time, women's allegedly unstable character, which shifted with each new phase of the moon, was used as an excuse to deny the vast majority of them any access to education. It would only confuse them; their fragile minds, so easily influenced by distant planets, would just become more muddled. But in the seventeenth and eighteenth centuries, women had caught up dramatically. There was now a new type: the educated woman. Some called them bluestockings, some laughed at them – like Molière in his play *The Learned Ladies* – but their progress couldn't really be stopped. Education wasn't just for the upper classes, either. With a bit of luck, ordinary girls would attend their village school for a couple of years, learning at least the basics of reading and writing – a development that was partly linked to the higher regard in which mothers were now held. If nothing else, this had encouraged the idea that it might not be a bad thing if the primary authority in a child's upbringing wasn't completely uneducated, for which reason the bourgeoisie in particular were increasingly sending their daughters to boarding schools for girls.

At such schools, as Jane Austen puts it in *Emma*, 'a reasonable quantity of accomplishments were sold at a reasonable price'.[1] There was very little danger that these girls would return home geniuses; in reality, the education they received only reinforced the schooling they were given in submissiveness, said this author (who never attended boarding school herself). But the creator of the board game pictured here, the astronomer and teacher Margaret Bryan, would no doubt have vehemently disagreed with her, and may even have been a little offended. After all, she invested a lot of effort in making new, rather 'unfeminine' fields of knowledge accessible to girls in as simple a way as possible. Towards the end of the eighteenth century, she was teaching astronomy in no fewer than three girls' boarding schools in England, and she wrote books familiarising her pupils with the universe and various modern technologies available for studying it. On the frontispiece to one of her first works, *A Compendious System of Astronomy in a Course of Familiar Lectures*, we see her sitting at a table with her two young daughters. They're surrounded by various instruments used in astronomy – a telescope, an armillary sphere, a compass – while Bryan herself is holding a quill and noting down some observations. An unusual picture, this. At that time, the only really well-known female astronomer was the German scientist Caroline Herschel – funnily enough, the Herschel Museum in Bath is now home to the frontispiece from Bryan's book. Herschel helped her brother William to make reflecting telescopes and was at his side for his chance discovery of Uranus, which earned him the position of court astronomer to the British Crown

---

1   Austen, Jane, *Emma* (Harmondsworth: Penguin Books, 1973), p. 52

and her the position of first professional female astronomer in history. Later, she herself discovered several comets and stars, but she still tended to play down her knowledge. She'd assisted her brother like 'a well-trained little dog', she once said, thus maintaining the illusion that women didn't have very much of their own to contribute to astronomy, or to science in general.

Bryan evidently saw things quite differently. She hadn't conducted any major research, hadn't discovered anything of note and she probably wasn't even a rebel. The prevailing idea that a girl should be delicate, sensitive and virtuous seems to have sat well with her. But she didn't understand why this should stop her reaching for the stars. This game, which was published in London in 1814 and which she reviewed for scientific accuracy (in the upper corner we see the words 'approved by Mrs Bryan') is, to some extent, proof of her conviction that studying the cosmos was something that should be open to everyone, especially young women. Her teaching methods were aimed at imparting the science of astronomy in as playful a way as possible, and making it comprehensible to everyone instead of merely addressing the handful of girls who were particularly well versed in maths. If you wanted to win at this board game, which was designed as a race across thirty-five spaces, you needed to be able to explain how a telescope is constructed and exactly how it works, be familiar with the phases of the moon, display a bit of patience – the name of the game in research, after all – remember the names of the planets and a few astronomers, and know what Newton, Copernicus and Ptolemy thought. But you would also need to be able to discuss the signs of the zodiac and their meaning. At that time, astronomy and astrology still went hand in hand; only at the end of the nineteenth century were they divided into two disciplines, one to be taken seriously and the other slightly laughable. Who knows – maybe women, with their quarter-moons in their heads, had started developing an interest in it.

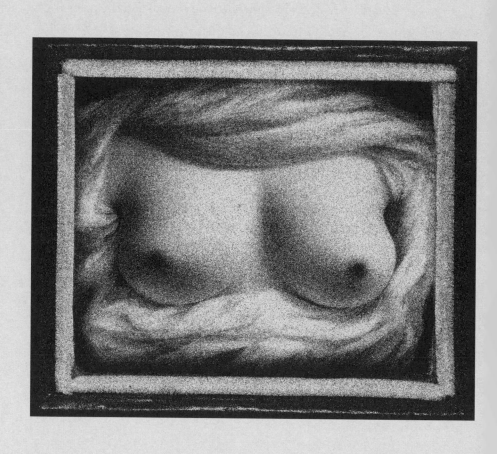

BEAUTY REVEALED, SELF-PORTRAIT

1828

Nowadays, if someone hits upon the generally well-meant but pretty wearisome idea of setting you up with someone you don't know, you don't need to stumble blindly into your first date but can arm yourself with advance information. You can comb through social media to see what the person looks like, what they think – or, at least, claim to think – and how they present themselves in public. In the early nineteenth century, matchmaking was a different kettle of fish: as a young woman, you'd have been brought to market, usually by your parents, sometimes by a so-called matchmaker, and had few opportunities to form a picture of your future intended. Men, too, didn't always get to see candidates 'in real life' but had to trust other people's descriptions. Since it wasn't just one evening at stake, but the rest of their lives, men – with whom the decision lay – wanted to get a rough idea of the face they'd be looking at every day in future. So they liked to have their potential spouse's portrait painted.

The lovely film *Portrait of a Lady on Fire*, by French director Céline Sciamma, is a good examination of this tradition. A young woman is to have her portrait painted – from her best side, of course – so that her fiancé, who is somewhere abroad, can have the pleasure of seeing her. Only, the stubborn lady refuses to sit for any of the painters. She doesn't want to show her face, doesn't want to marry at all, doesn't feel understood by these men with their paintbrushes and easels, and bristles at having a stereotypical sales portrait made of her. She remains steadfast until a woman comes along and paints her just the way she sees her: not as a sweet little woman with a gentle gaze who dreams of nothing but marriage, children and a household, but as a complex being. A real person.

The breasts portrayed in this painting under the title *Beauty Revealed* tell a similar story: they too speak of the wish to be seen as the person you feel yourself to be, instead of being forced to fit into a ready-made picture. Sarah Goodridge, who painted this 'self-portrait' in 1828, clearly felt comfortable in her own skin. Unlike Sciamma's protagonist, she didn't wait for another woman to paint her from a female perspective, but instead took matters into her own hands. Instead of painting her face, her shoulders, perhaps even the top of her décolletage, she shows herself only in the form of her naked bosom. It shines almost three-dimensionally out of the painting, beautiful and full, with rosy nipples. (On Instagram, it would have been taken down within seconds.)

This six-by-eight-centimetre watercolour wasn't just a selfie of a woman who thought herself beautiful and wanted to show off, but was very much part of a tradition in which women painted portraits for their future husbands. Yet the man in this case, a certain Daniel Webster, had no idea how lucky he was. In the early nineteenth century, Sarah Goodridge was working as a successful miniaturist in Boston, the city that would later become so feminist (if two women lived together, it was referred to as a 'Boston marriage'). She wanted to marry Webster, and this was the way she chose to tell him. She and Senator Webster had been corresponding for many years; when his first wife died, Goodridge scented an opportunity and offered herself as his next wife by sending him this self-portrait. Miniatures were very fashionable back then; they were a way of carrying your nearest and dearest with you at all times, just as people would later slide passport photos of their families into their wallets. Only, then as now, it was mostly faces rather than body parts on display – and certainly not breasts. Sarah Goodridge didn't care. Everything about this move was exceptionally brave, and brazen: the fact that she didn't wait for Webster to ask her, but made her own quasi-proposal of marriage to him. That she showed him a part of her he clearly hadn't seen before, thus telling him she wasn't just a good girlfriend and excellent miniaturist, but something else, too: a sexual being.

But what's also interesting is the way Sarah idealised her breasts, much in the way she herself might have been idealised in a regular portrait. She was forty when she painted this self-portrait and it's rather unlikely that the breasts flashing back at her in the mirror really looked this plump, fresh and rosy. Yet, she was clearly clever enough to know that self-portraits, just like seduction, aren't about reality, but about how a person wishes to be seen and what they want someone else to believe. In a time in which the male gaze – the objectivising eyes of a man on a woman and her body – was steadily becoming a significant feature of the urban landscape, with idealised images of women increasingly being used to promote goods in Europe and America, she simply allowed herself to see her own body. To wit, to see it in a way that pleased her. This was unbelievably progressive; at that time, female self-expression was regarded as shameless. Whether Mr Webster appreciated this modernity is something we will sadly never know. He chose another woman. But he never returned Sarah Goodridge's wonderful bosom to her. Her breasts remained in the family until the 1980s, when they were auctioned off at Christie's. She herself painted two further self-portraits – this time, with her clothes on.

THE BRONTË SISTERS' MINIATURE BOOKS

c. 1830

In Greta Gerwig's film adaptation of Louisa May Alcott's famous novel *Little Women*, there's a scene in Paris in which Amy dejectedly explains that she's going to give up painting and get married. She might have talent, but she's no genius – so, as a woman, she has no hope of survival. Which women have ever been let into the genius club, young Laurie asks her, to which she replies, without hesitation: 'The Brontë sisters.'

In 1869, when Alcott's *Little Women* was first published, Charlotte, Emily and Anne Brontë were indeed among the very few women to be considered geniuses – or, no, better yet: legends. For one thing, because they'd died just ten years earlier, all at a very young age: first Emily at thirty, then Anne at twenty-eight and, a couple of years later, Charlotte at thirty-eight. For another thing, because of their novels: *Jane Eyre*, *Wuthering Heights* and *Agnes Grey*, which they published in 1847 under the pseudonyms Currer, Ellis and Acton Bell. *Jane Eyre*, which so wonderfully examines the chicaneries of the governess profession – a career choice for women that was positively exploding in the nineteenth century – became an international bestseller practically overnight, and from July 1848 the sisters were famous. At that time, rumours were going around London that all three were one and the same person, one and the same author – male, of course. To clear up this misunderstanding and divest themselves of the attendant problems, Anne and Charlotte dropped their disguises and travelled to the capital. Charlotte's publisher at Smith, Elder & Co. later remembered how these two 'rather quaintly dressed little ladies, pale-faced and anxious looking' were waiting for him at reception, where one of them, the rounder one with the glasses, thrust a letter addressed to 'Currer Bell' into his hands. 'Where did you get this?' he asked. 'You sent it to me,' Charlotte replied. The man's face must have been a picture: the most successful author on his list was a woman, and one from the provinces to boot.

He must have been asking himself the same question as when we read the sisters' books today: how could these young women, who had grown up in the middle of nowhere between a cemetery and the Yorkshire moors, and led an uneventful life, suddenly write the most beautiful novels of all time? Just like that, out of nowhere? One possible answer is provided by these miniature books, which the Brontë siblings made as children. They measure roughly two and a half centimetres by five centimetres, about the same as a matchbox, and are filled with pages of tiny block lettering. The Brontë children sewed them together out of packing material, empty sugar bags, strips of wallpaper and all kinds of other scraps (paper was expensive!) and filled them with wild stories. Most of the twenty 'little books' that still exist today – housed in the collections of the Brontë Museum in England, Harvard Library and a few private individuals – were penned by Charlotte and her brother, Branwell. Normally, history is happy to overlook the sisters of famous men (Alice James, for example, or Nannerl Mozart) but in this case it's the brother, Branwell, who has been forgotten. Although the family's hopes once rested on him, his talent sadly couldn't hold out against his addiction to alcohol. Nonetheless, he played an essential role in the development of his sisters' imaginations and writing. As Patti Smith (not only a rock legend, but also a huge fan of the Brontës) has said: 'When you come here you think of Charlotte, Emily and Anne, but Branwell gifted the sisters with the gift of the dark romance, it was a world they created together.'[1] Indeed, the three sisters' worlds didn't just come bowling out of their heads one day amid their duties as teachers and governesses, but were the result of a years-long game of writing and storytelling, with Charlotte and Branwell serving as masters of ceremonies.

Legend has it that the game developed thus: when the four siblings lost first their mother and then their two older sisters within a few years of each other, burying them in the graveyard next to the family home,

1   Patti Smith, quoted in 'Rock legend Patti Smith thrills fans at concert in Haworth's Bronte Schoolroom', the *Telegraph and Argus*, 20 April 2013, available at <https://www.thetelegraphandargus.co.uk/news/10368918.rock-legend-patti-smith-thrills-fans-at-concert-in-haworths-bronte-schoolroom/>

their father, Patrick Brontë, tried to brighten their sombre, loss-stricken childhood with little acts of attention. And so it was that he returned home one day with a group of tin figures that would change everything. The four children shared them out and began creating not just adventures but an entire world for them: the Glass Town Federation. They probably told their stories to one another and acted them out before writing them down. Or perhaps it was the other way round. The tiny books that held the products of their imagination were based on a magazine that Charlotte deemed 'the best publication in existence' and sought to emulate with her in-house *Blackwood's Young Men's Magazine*. The editor's name was given as 'the genious C.B.'. The magazine's choice of subjects and stories was eclectic; it included 'military conversations', poems, fiction and practical guides, such as 'How to Curl One's Hair' by 'Monsieur Whatsthereason'. The children must have spent most of their time in these dream worlds, alongside characters like Colonel Naughty, Captain Bud and Charlotte's alter ego, Lord Charles Wellesley, successfully escaping their grey reality. Many episodes and elements that appear in their later novels were already to be found here: the tree outside Cathy's window in *Wuthering Heights*, for example, or the burning house in *Jane Eyre*. These 'little books', which once numbered nearly a hundred, are said to be the matrix of the mysterious Brontë world.

Charlotte seems to have been the first to step out of this dream world and talk her sisters into publishing their work. Branwell, however, never completely resurfaced from the Glass Town they'd created together, and died just a year after the surprising success of *Jane Eyre*. At that time, it was this novel that was regarded as the family's mysterious stroke of genius; *Wuthering Heights* was too wild and rebellious for the critics, who declared it 'tasteless'. It took a few decades and the opinion of Virginia Woolf to correct this view on one of the most beautiful novels ever written. In April 1916, writing in *The Times Literary Supplement*, she told readers: 'Hers [Emily's] is the rarest of all powers. She could free life from its dependence on facts; with a few touches indicate the spirit of a face so that it needs no body; by speaking of the moor make the wind blow and the thunder roar.'

ANALYTICAL ENGINE

1834

In the America of the late nineteenth and early twentieth centuries, if a gentleman asked a young lady what she actually did with her life, how she spent her time, it was – rarely, but definitely occasionally – possible that this lady wouldn't reply, 'I enjoy playing badminton', or, 'I'm very good at embroidery', but instead answered: 'I'm a computer.' She didn't intend this as a futuristic joke, nor as a prophecy that there would one day be love affairs between humans and computers, like in the 2014 film *Her*. She meant it as a serious statement. She was a computer. That was her job.

The world's first computers were different to the metallic things people sit around with in cafés today. They were young, exceptionally clever, very fast and extremely precise. They wore skirts and set their hair in waves. In short, they were women. People called them 'the computers'. Nowadays when we talk about the history of computers, the first image that springs to mind is of spotty boys tinkering around in suburban American garages. But if we think back a bit further and go specifically in search of a woman, it will always be the same name that crops up: Ada Lovelace, computer pioneer of the early nineteenth century. While her father, the poet Lord Byron, was sitting out the erup-tion of a volcano in the company of his friends Percy and Mary Shelley at a villa on Lake Geneva (which allowed him to witness the creation of Mary's now world-famous novel *Frankenstein*), Annabelle, Ada's mother, was channelling all her efforts into ensuring her one-year-old daughter would not end up like her unreliable ex-husband. Instead of schooling her in literature and art, her father's fields of expertise, the girl's mother steered her into the unfeminine territory of mathematics. By the age of twelve, Ada was dreaming of one day building a flying machine. Instead, she made the acquaintance of the mathematician Charles Babbage, and participated indirectly in the development of his adding machine.

Babbage's 'analytical engine' – part of the prototype for which is pictured here – is treated as a forerunner of modern computers: a mechanical adding machine equipped with an arithmetic unit (the part shown here), memory, input and output, operated with punch cards similar to those used by the recently invented Jacquard loom. The idea was that the results would be spat out by a printer. Unfortunately, the machine was never finished. It would have been the size of a room, almost nineteen metres long and three metres high, and powered by a stationary steam engine. It was thanks to these delusions of grandeur that the American government, which had supported Babbage's early machines, stopped believing in him and what it came to consider his entirely insane inventions, and promptly dropped him. This is where Ada Lovelace comes into play again. When her friend Babbage asked her to translate a report on his 'analytical engine' from French into English, he also – knowing how clever she was – requested that she add some of her own remarks. And so the young lady inserted a few visionary comments. In her 'notes', she foresaw that Babbage's machine would be able to do more than 'just' calculations, it would also be able to process other data. At least, it would if these data were treated in a 'language' that the machine could understand: 'operations may of course be performed on an infinite variety of particular numerical values, and do not bring out any definite numerical results unless the numerical data of the problem have been impressed on the requisite portions of the train of mechanism'.[1] It was with this sentence, written in the 1840s, that Lovelace set out the fundamental principles of programming – hence she is said to have foreseen the emergence of information technology and computers.

But until we got to that stage, computers would be human and often female. At Harvard, for example, one professor of astronomy kept an entire row of these living, breathing adding-machines (albeit all-male). Legend has it that one day, Mr Pickering – for so the good fellow was called – bellowed in an attack of rage: 'Even my maid could do a better job!' Soon after, he fired his male team and hired said maid, Williamina Fleming. She was soon joined by a dozen other young

---

1 Menabrea, Luigi, 'Sketches of the Analytic Engine invented by Charles Babbage, Esq', in *Scientific Memoirs Selected from the Transactions of Foreign Academies of Science and Learned Societies*, tr. and with notes by Ada Lovelace (London, 1843). See for example <https://www.maa.org/press/periodicals/convergence/mathematical-treasure-ada-lovelaces-notes-on-the-analytic-engine>

women, who sat day in, day out on the top floor of Harvard College Observatory, analysing glass slides showing photos of the night sky. They were known as the 'Harvard computers', or 'Pickering's harem'. It was also in the USA, a couple of decades later, in the middle of the Second World War, that a group of six 'computers' – six young women – working in absolute secrecy programmed the world's first universal computer. This was the Electrical Numerical Integrator and Computer (ENIAC), a colossus weighing 27 tonnes, with 17,000 cables, which could complete approximately 5,000 calculations per second. It would take years for it to be widely recognised that the women in the photos of the computer weren't just standing there to make it look good, like the 'refrigerator girls' in fridge adverts, but because they'd been the ones responsible for getting it up and running.

In most people's ears, computers and women clearly sounded like a contradiction in terms, despite the fact that the 1960s saw several women seated at enormous computers, programming for IBM as 'senior system analysts'. Even in the 1950s, Black female computers – chief among them Katherine Goble Johnson, Mary Jackson and Dorothy Vaughan, whose stories inspired the 2016 book and film *Hidden Figures* – were responsible for the immensely complex calculations that would eventually help NASA achieve the first moon landing. *Cosmopolitan* wrote at the time that 'computer' was an ideal profession for women, with the programmer they chose to interview, Dr Hopper, explaining rather airily, 'It's just like planning a dinner [. . .] Programming requires patience and the ability to handle detail. Women are "naturals" at computer programming.'[1] Now is not the time for further discussion of the fact that women don't plan better dinner parties or have more patience per se – especially since it was the very people who thought women belonged in the kitchen who would eventually decide they probably weren't all that good with numbers. Nowadays, programming is a predominantly male profession and the world of IT chiefly one of men; women have to be 'encouraged' to venture into this particular field. Somehow, we've forgotten the fact that not just Ada Lovelace, the first person to think about programming, but also many of the first 'computers' themselves were women.

---

1   Mandel, Lois, 'The Computer Girls', *Cosmopolitan*, April 1967, available at <https://blog. adafruit.com/2021/03/12/a-1967-cosmopolitan-article-on-female-computer-programmers -history-programming-women/>

ANTI-SLAVERY COIN

1838

In the history of feminism and abolitionism – the movement to abolish slavery – the year 1851 is remembered for being the one in which a woman, an emancipated slave by the name of Sojourner Truth, more or less spontaneously took to the stage during the Women's Rights Convention in Akron, Ohio, and gave the following incendiary speech: 'That man over there says that women need to be helped into carriages, and lifted over ditches, and to have the best place everywhere. Nobody ever helps me into carriages, or over mud-puddles, or gives me any best place! And ain't I a woman? Look at me! Look at my arm! I have ploughed and planted, and gathered into barns, and no man could head me! And ain't I a woman? I could work as much and eat as much as a man – when I could get it – and bear the lash as well! And ain't I a woman? I have borne thirteen children, and seen most all sold off to slavery, and when I cried out with my mother's grief, none but Jesus heard me! And ain't I a woman?'[1]

Her words, which the ladies present received with great enthusiasm, passed into legend as 'Ain't I a Woman?' The question drew on what was then a new way of treating women: ever since establishing that ladies were frail creatures, and using their new middle-class ideals to shackle them to hearth and home, men – in a rather paternalistic gesture – had been putting about the notion that women, those fragile beings, needed especially gallant treatment. Holding open doors and helping into coats originated in this era, yet this new and supposedly caring way of behaving didn't extend to all females. Black women were treated dismissively at best, brutally at worst, with colonial fantasies

---

1   Truth, Sojourner, 'Ain't I a Woman?', speech given at the Women's Rights Convention in Akron, Ohio, 1851, available at: <https://www.nps.gov/articles/sojourner-truth.htm>

putting ideas about their sexual submissiveness into the head of many a man. *Why?* asked Truth. *Am I not a woman like any other? Don't I too deserve gallant treatment?* It was a question that confronted men with their ideological contradictions: so, they wanted to be civilised and cultivate excellent manners, but not towards everyone? How was that compatible with an honest spirit?

Now, it's probably worth adding that while these words are certainly cutting, it's unclear whether Sojourner actually uttered this famous, oft-repeated sentence. When she walked on stage that day, she wasn't holding a piece of paper or wearing a pair of glasses; she could neither read nor write. The speech she gave was entirely off the cuff. And so her words were recorded for posterity by others, in two different versions: one with and one without this sentence. The first version was published shortly after the event; it had been written down by a friend, the abolitionist Marcus Robinson, and didn't include 'Ain't I a Woman?' The second, the speech quoted here, the one we all know and which all the anthologies include as a classic of feminism, followed some twelve years later.

Back then, these words had been doing the rounds since the 1830s, on coins like the one shown here. The sentence was famous in abolitionist circles. It was derived from the male version of anti-slavery coins, which depicted a man kneeling in chains, asking – after all the lovely ideas of the Enlightenment, all those declarations of human rights – 'Am I Not a Man and a Brother?' *Doesn't the fraternity being proclaimed everywhere apply to me too? Are human rights not mine as well?* These coins were passed around between England and the USA; they were part of an anti-slavery movement powered above all by women. British women in particular had got involved in the fight at an early stage: around 1825, for example, members of the Female Society for Birmingham (formerly the Ladies Society for the Relief of Negro Slaves) made little bags which they filled with flyers and manifestos and handed out. The front of the silk bag showed a woman, a slave, feeding her children; the idea was that people would find images like this moving. Much the same as Alexandria Ocasio-Cortez recently had her political message ('Tax the Rich') printed on a dress for New York's Met Gala, the women of that era would carry their 'message bags' on evenings out at the opera or to parties. Some boycotted the sugar from plantations worked by slaves, others pinned up their hair with brooches that made political statements, wore armbands on their wrists or handed out coins like this one.

For many women – who, in the USA, became politically active in groups like the American Anti-Slavery Society (AASS), which allowed them to give speeches and advocate for something other than their families for perhaps the first time ever – joining the fight to abolish slavery sparked their later involvement in feminism. But so incensed did some of them become about the servitude of others that they quite forgot their own, idealising their lives and tending towards subtly condescending gestures. Some – no doubt unintentionally – refuted enslaved women's ability to emancipate themselves, thereby ignoring to some extent the struggles and rebellions already going on. But the longer they were involved, the clearer it must have become to them that the treatment of both slaves and women was stoked by similar ideological notions and thought-constructs. They wouldn't just have to liberate enslaved women from a life of servitude, but also free themselves from their own form of bondage (principally marriage, which Mary Wollstonecraft had already decried as a form of slavery back in the seventeenth century). It's telling that the majority of the early suffragettes were abolitionists first – and somewhat perplexing to consider how, just a century later, this fledgling feminism would mutate into an exclusively white event that completely blanked out the issue of racism.

In Truth's time, however, no one saw this divide between white and Black feminism coming. Women saw themselves united. 'If the first woman God ever made was strong enough to turn the world upside down all alone, these women together ought to be able to turn it back, and get it right side up again!' she said. 'And now they is asking to do it, the men better let them.'

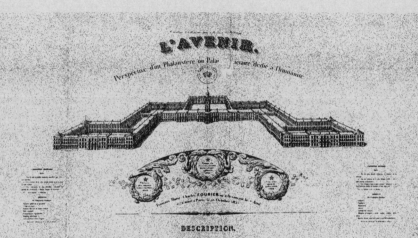

L'AVENIR.

Perspective d'un Phalanstère ou Palais ... dédié à l'humanité

DESCRIPTION.

LITHOGRAPH, *L'AVENIR.* PERSPECTIVE D'UN PHALANSTÈRE OU PALAIS SOCIÉTAIRE DE L'HUMANITÉ

c. 1840

The nineteenth century is often described as the age of feminist awakening. While the middle classes were inventing the new ideal of the housewife, and medicine was creating the myth of the lustless woman, for the first time in history it was no longer just a few individual women who insisted on equality, but whole international networks. Women had finally realised that it wouldn't be enough for them to fight alongside men for justice and human rights – they were skilfully left out of all those pretty speeches about equality and fraternity, and still treated like second-class citizens. Or, as the socialist and feminist Flora Tristan, grandmother of Paul Gauguin, put it in 1843: 'Even the most oppressed man finds a being he can oppress: his wife. The woman is the proletarian of the proletariat.' Feminism was born, at the latest, with this realisation – and gave the burgeoning socialist movement a helping hand in the struggle against an unjust power system: patriarchal capitalism.

But who actually invented the term 'feminism'? It's often attributed to the man who created this architectural and community model, the so-called *phalanstère* – a kind of XXL version of Versailles whose halls were ruled not by monarchy and hierarchy, but by egalitarianism and socialist ideals of freedom. This man's name was Charles Fourier, and he was one of the most interesting utopians of his day. It's hard to say whether he really was the first person to talk about feminism, or whether it might have been more likely that a woman gave the movement its name. What is certain is that Fourier's dream of a small town contained under one roof – which one of his students would promote as 'the future' in the advert pictured here, published after his death – clearly shows that his community model and the fight to obtain for women a new place in society were closely interwoven. 'Social progress and changes of period are brought about by virtue of the progress of women toward liberty [. . .] the extension of the privileges of women is the fundamental cause of all social progress,' wrote Fourier, a sentiment that would later find an echo far and wide.[1] Marx and Engels cited his thoughts verbatim in *The Holy Family*; Rosa Luxemburg was also fond of quoting this sentence. Even today's feminists make reference to it, explaining repeatedly, relentlessly, that no society can speak of modernity or progress if women continue to occupy an inferior place within it. During his lifetime, however, the poor man wasn't understood at all. The few people who knew of him and his architectural and social utopias didn't view Fourier as a visionary so much as a lunatic: perfectly nice, but completely insane.

He was, admittedly, rather peculiar. As a child, he would scare customers out of his parents' shop by telling them they'd be badly ripped off there and would do better to make their purchases somewhere else. As an adult, he dreamed that the sea would turn to lemonade and people would one day live on the sun. But until such time, he wanted to make the world a place in which people could live free and happy lives, instead of being trapped by lies and constraints. The *phalanstère*, a turbo-charged early version of Le Corbusier's 1927 'machine for living in', would educate a core society he christened 'harmony' and reimagine, if you like, two areas of life in particular – the most important two, namely work and love. Society, Fourier believed, should be shaped in line with human passions, not according to contrived middle-class and early capitalist norms. He argued the case for the residents of his *phalanstère* not to do the same work every day – how boring! – but instead to try something new each day and have the chance to develop their talents. Especially, however – and this is

1 Fourier, Charles, 'Théorie des quatre mouvements et des destinées générales', in *Oeuvres complètes de Charles Fourier* [OC], 12 vols (Paris: Anthropos, 1966–8), pp. 130–3. Available at: <https://www.bloomsburycollections.com/book/utopian-moments-reading-utopian-texts/ch15-women-s-rights-and-women-s-liberation-in-charles-fourier-s-early-writings>

important for us – he said that the housework and vegetable patch shouldn't always be left to women. In *A New World of Love*, he wrote: 'Harmony cannot emerge if we are foolish enough to exclude woman from medicine and science and limit her to the kitchen and cooking. Nature equipped both sexes equally with aptitude in science and art.' *Mais oui!* A couple of decades later, the British philosopher and early feminist John Stuart Mill would say something similar in 'The Subjection of Women', an essay he wrote along with his wife, Harriet. But let's stick with Fourier: in order to shatter the notion – steadily gaining traction in the nineteenth century – that there was a 'natural' link between women and the hearth, he said, children should be brought up equally. Boys should be allowed to develop their 'feminine' side, and girls their 'masculine' side. In such an extremely masculine century, this was a new and wild thought.

Less new, but still rarely voiced by a man, was his view that the classic mould of civic marriage held women back in terms of personal development. It was out of the question that something as beautiful as love should have been invented only for it to wither away in something as dull as marriage, wrote this particular bachelor, arguing that an institution which treated women like goods for sale should be abolished. Monogamy, which he saw as an insane, hypocritical concept, would be the next to go; it produced nothing but lies and frustration. In contrast to many of his contemporaries, Fourier evidently didn't see women as frigid, sexually indifferent creatures in any way; his extremely amusing and clearly very earnestly meant typology of the 'cuckolded' man laughs at the myth that says men stray more often than women because they 'must'. You know: male sex drive, nature and so on.

Charles Fourier, who was once aptly described as a cross between Rousseau and the Marquis de Sade, believed that the world would be a better place and the people in it happier if they were allowed to live and love with greater freedom. Sadly, his *phalanstère* – the building in which this revolution of living and loving was to take place – was never built in this form. The only model to be inspired by it, the *familistère*, was not a success. Nonetheless, Fourier's ideas about work and love did inspire socialists and feminists to fight for a new social order. So that, one day, this world-in-a-building might be more than just an idealist's paper dream.

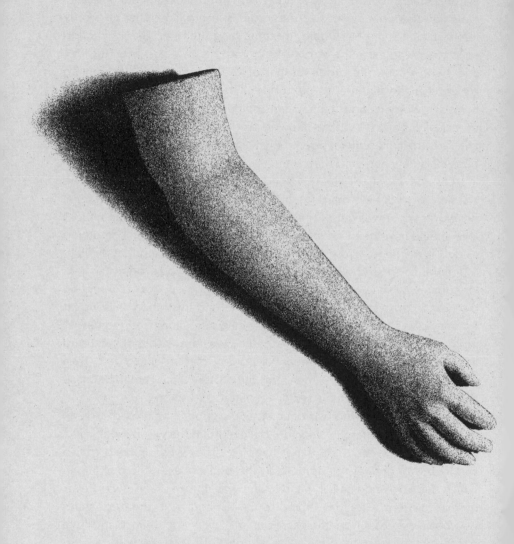

GEORGE SAND'S RIGHT ARM

c. 1847

In the early nineteenth century, if a woman wanted gently to suggest to her husband that she didn't agree with Napoleon's view that a woman was '[man's] possession, as the fruit tree is that of the gardener', and that she wouldn't be letting him order her about in future, she would simply leave a copy of a novel by George Sand lying around the house. The French novelist, who began writing under a male pseudonym in the 1830s, stirred something in the women of the era and gave the men of France, England and Germany – even America and Russia – a terrible headache. In an 1836 caricature by Honoré Daumier, we see a trouserless man in holey socks standing before his wife, who is reading a book, shouting in one last, desperate attempt to maintain his authority: 'I don't care one whit about her, your Madame Sand, who stops women mending their husbands' trousers. Either we bring in divorce or that woman gets abolished!'

Sand wrote the books that encouraged her fellow women to desert their 'duties' – *Indiana*, *Lélia*, *Little Fadette* and *The Devil's Pool* – with this very hand, her right one. This replica was made by her son-in-law, the sculptor Auguste Clésinger, in the same batch of work that also produced the left hand of Chopin, the most famous of George's lovers. Today, they lie next to one another inside a display case in the Musée de la Vie Romantique in Paris. It's as though, in a fit of romanticism, we've tried to hold on to the exact spot on the body where their genius spilled forth: playing the piano for Chopin, writing novels for Sand. And while Chopin moved people's ears, George Sand moved something very specific in society; just as her friend Gustave Flaubert's 'Bovarysme' would catch hold and give a name to the longings of middle-class housewives a couple of years later, so too did 'Sandisme' spread like wildfire. It encouraged women less towards melancholy dreaming and far more to take action: to question their place in the world, the entire gender-related distribution of roles, and perhaps to position themselves differently, become more independent and self-willed. Writing in an American newspaper, her contemporary Henry James once said that George Sand stood for a certain attitude to the world: it was his belief that anyone who read her books wanted that to say something about themselves, in much the same way as people might go around these days with a tote bag from a particular bookshop to announce their convictions. According to James, reading Sand was a bit like wordlessly saying, *I'm a socialist, transcendentalist and abolitionist*. A bit like declaring, *I'm modern and progressive*.

Because George Sand certainly was modern and progressive. She was one of those writers who didn't just inspire her contemporaries with her books, but also with her unusual lifestyle. Seeing as Aurore Dupin (as she was once known) was bored in her marriage and often had affairs anyway, in the 1820s she successfully persuaded her husband to let her spend half the year living on her own in Paris. Later, when she'd established herself as an author under the name George Sand (derived from the name of one of her lovers, a certain Monsieur Sandeau) and was selling a lot of books, she obtained a separation from her husband in a court case that was followed by the whole country. Divorce didn't exist at the time – Napoleon had abolished it with his misogynistic *code civil* – but 'George' clearly wasn't about to let a little thing like that impede her. Equally, she refused to let impractical women's clothing impede her: even though it was strictly forbidden – a punishable crime – for a woman to march around town wearing trousers, Sand somehow managed to get herself an official certificate of exemption. From then on, she was able to walk the streets dressed as a man – to perambulate, to promenade, observing others without being observed herself. Or, as she wrote in her autobiography, *Story of My Life*: 'I flew from one end of Paris to the other [. . .] I ran out in every kind of weather, I came home at every sort of hour . . . No one paid any attention to me, and no one guessed at my disguise.' In one of her lesser-known works, a play titled *Gabriel*, playing with gender roles is an important theme; her protagonist wishes to be neither man nor woman, but simply free. She/He thus spends half the year dressed as one gender and half as the other, until the world punishes her/him for taking such a liberty.

Strangely, history has condemned Sand less for her unconventional way of living than for an ostensibly feminine hobby. Her liaison with Chopin and stormy affair with Alfred de Musset – whom she in turn betrayed with his doctor as he lay mortally ill in bed – are all part of the George Sand legend and have contributed to her fame for decades. What was long held against her, however, was something quite the opposite: that she didn't just use her right hand for writing novels and practising free love, but also enjoyed making jam with it. In Paris she was George, who walked around town in trousers and smoked a pipe, but at home in Nohant she might have been more Aurore. She loved taking care of her guests and cooking for her gentle friend Flaubert. The Russian novelist Turgenev felt so at home with her that he joined in with the dancing, and even a jealous Balzac dropped in often. While he didn't think much of 'Sandisme' – a trend, he claimed, that encouraged talentless women all over the country to try their hand at writing – he never questioned George's skill as a writer of novels or as a hostess. And it was these apparently unforgivable housewifely qualities that eventually earned George Sand the nickname of *bonne dame de Nohant* (the good lady of Nohant) in France, and left her languishing for a long time in a corner of shallow, slightly-too-romantic women's literature. The fact that she'd once incited a revolution was simply forgotten, and instead she was derided as a nice little woman. People evidently resented how, despite her assumed name, she hadn't wanted to be a 'real man', but instead had used her strong right hand to cobble together a different role. A role in which jam-making, writing, trouser-wearing, pipe-smoking, wild love affairs, romance and independence were all able to co-exist, each one in no way excluding the others.

WASHING PADDLE

1850s

One of the most famous and terrifying figures in the matriarchal world of Celtic folklore is the night washerwoman. She's known as the *femme blanche*, the *lavandière* or the *chanteuse de nuit* and, according to legend, you'll encounter her at night or early in the evening near the large communal washtub that still forms the heart of almost any Breton village. A man walking past one of these granite tubs by moonlight and seeing a young woman standing there, dressed all in white, would be well advised to turn back immediately. If he doesn't, the woman will ask for help, saying she needs his strong arms to wring out her washing, claiming she's weak and helpless. Lies, all of it. Or, as George Sand tells us: One ought to avoid disturbing or observing them, because even if you happen to be two metres tall and correspondingly muscular, they will seize hold of you, beat you in the water and wring your neck as though it were a pair of stockings.[1]

Sand, who famously had a weakness for streams, swamps and similarly mystical places, and who loved a rural legend, wrote that she'd 'often heard the beating, and imagined that it was night washers'.[2] And the women she heard were probably doing their beating with an object just like this one: a washing paddle, an essential piece of kit for any country-dwelling woman. The legends about these nocturnal laundresses weren't exactly flattering: according to the ideas of the period, the night washerwomen were 'ruined' women who had murdered their children or husbands and would therefore, so people believed, never find 'eternal peace'. By night, it was said, they tried to wash the

---

1 Sand, George, *Rustic Legends: Twelve Ghostly Tales*, tr. Hannah Hoyt (Dragonet Classics, 2017), p. 27
2 ibid.

blood from their sheets – or, if you like, to wash their consciences clean – which explained why they were always to be found right there by the tub. But maybe there's also another explanation as to why the washtub and that washerwoman with her paddle became such a spooky image in the collective consciousness.

Right into the late nineteenth and early twentieth centuries – until early versions of the not-yet-electric washing machine, with their strange drums made of wood or metal, had become established – the communal washtub was an important site of female socialisation, one of the few places in the village that belonged to the women. Market, graveyard and church were mixed, but the rest of the public domain was divided by gender: bistros and cafés were male; springs, streams and washtubs female. Even in the Ancient World, the spring was the only place women were allowed to go outside their own homes – they just weren't allowed to spend any length of time there. Thanks to laundry, a couple of centuries later they had a good excuse to spend an hour or two by the water. If men wanted a chat, they went to the pub; if women were in the mood for a natter, they went off to do the laundry. Once a week at least. Of course, the physical effort required was quite different to that involved in drinking a glass of beer but, all the same, they could converse in peace.

They knelt by the tub, put their pre-soaked laundry in the water, rubbed it across their washing boards, scrubbed at stains with brushes or beat the fabric with wooden bats like this one. This particular washing paddle comes from the Loire region and is decorated with a tree and flowers; others were painted, some even engraved with short messages. Perhaps it was a sign of prosperity in misery if you possessed a particularly pretty washing paddle, but most likely only the more basic ones were used on a daily basis, while the rest stayed hanging on the walls as decoration. Whatever. You'd sit there by the water and chat. About your neighbours; about little Dupont, who really was thoroughly spoiled; about the stable boy who ran off with the baker's daughter. You complained or talked about yourself. About your dreams, your worries, your fears, your good-for-nothing husband, your unwanted pregnancy, your miscarriages, beatings, money troubles. And sometimes the laundry spoke for itself. Spots of blood gave away this or that, or at least they implied it; not for nothing does the phrase 'airing your dirty laundry' exist in one form or another in nearly every country in the world. Laundry provided glimpses of intimacy. This was doubt-less often unpleasant, but sometimes also helpful. Because the others could understand what was going on, even if you chose not to say it in so many words; because, maybe, they could help if you needed it.

It's often and eagerly said that the invention of the washing machine emancipated women by giving them more time to do other things, instead of having to kneel in the village square with lots of other women and do exhausting manual labour. And, of course, this is partly true. But it also isolated women – at least those who belonged to a certain section of society. They suddenly found themselves standing alone in front of their newfangled washing automaton; suddenly there was no one else around to laugh at the others or to confide in. Public areas were now free of their 'tittle-tattle'. To many, this seemed a good thing – men especially, for whose tastes women talked a smidge too much – but it did mean that a place for female socialising and solidarity had fallen away. Now, if a woman needed help or advice, she would actively have to go out and ask for it. The threshold of inhibition was far higher and, as you can imagine, only a few felt able to cross it. Bearing this significance of the washtub in mind, if we think back to the legend of the night washerwomen and the washing paddles they held aloft in such an allegedly threatening manner, a completely different interpre-tation suggests itself. Maybe the legend doesn't point to 'evil women' so much as to men being scared of such purely female places. Maybe those young women didn't come back as washerwomen – if they came back at all – because they wanted to get their revenge on men, but because the washtub had been one of the few places in their lives where they'd felt safe and understood, one of the few places that belonged entirely to them.

SINGER SEWING MACHINE

1851

If this book were a history of women in two objects rather than one hundred and one, its pages would contain the following items: a spindle and a needle for sewing. If we want to imagine a woman and her life in just one incisive picture that could apply virtually all the way from antiquity into the late nineteenth century, it would look much like this: a woman sitting alone, or perhaps with another woman, in a room or a courtyard, holding a spindle or sewing together pieces of fabric. Women and textile work have gone hand in hand since time immemorial. Even linguistically: ever since the sixteenth century, the word 'spinster' has been used in England to mean an older single woman, because spinning was the most obvious way for such women to earn a living.

At least, it was until the beginning of the nineteenth century. But then a fresh wind began to blow – after all, the eighteenth century had brought about revolutions not just in politics, but especially in technology. Suddenly, we had machines that did exactly what women had been doing at home for centuries, only much faster and probably also better. The spinning jenny, for example, made spinsters – female spinners – pretty much superfluous. Many women lost their job as a result, but many, too, found a new one. This time, they wouldn't be doing it within their own four walls, but in a factory. This new working environment and the rise of mass manufacturing had both advantages and disadvantages for the female population of Europe. One advantage was that it allowed them to leave the house and spend the day with others; they came into contact with other views, other stories, other ways of thinking, and thus broadened their intellectual horizons. On the less advantageous side was the fact that they were now at the mercy of their brutally minded bosses, to most of whom employees were just as much possessions as their machines were. There was also the fact that the new world of work saw them as second-class labourers: if a job was monotonous, and thus deceptively tiring, it was left to women, who would be paid remarkably badly for doing it. They were categorically excluded from joining unions, because men didn't want to have them there.

So much for the first half of this revolutionary century. The second brought with it yet another new machine, of which you see a prototype here: the Singer sewing machine, which would turn the lives of more than one woman upside down. But before that stage, before the Singer had flooded the American and European markets and lodged itself in every home as the woman's 'best friend', a small war was waged. A group of men fought over which of them was to be king of the sewing machine, the inventor of this object – or, to be more precise, of its component parts. In all seriousness, the matter went down in history as the Sewing Machine War. At some point, though, the gentlemen finally managed to agree on a shared patent, and in 1851 the Singer was finally able to embark on its meteoric trajectory. Those were the early years of mass manufacturing, which required more and more seamstresses, many of whom were employed in sweatshops. If the *New York Herald* is to be believed, working conditions back then were just as terrible as they are in fast fashion today – or, as the paper said of those seamstresses: 'We know of no class of workwomen who are more poorly paid for their work or who suffer more privation and hardship.'[1] Women must have been all the more excited about the advent of this early sewing machine: not only did it mean they could avoid the sweatshops (even though these did still exist), but they could also earn considerably more money. Or, at least, that's what a Singer advert claimed: 'Up to 1,000 dollars a year' was what you could expect to make with one. You could also save money and, above all, time: making new clothes on a machine was around three times faster than sewing them by hand, allowing Madame to do other things besides work. This was a luxury, and it explained the Singer's roaring success. Especially since the company chose to adopt a clever sales strategy: it addressed women directly and, for the first time, gave them the feeling that they

---

1 Quoted in 'The accidental Singer sewing machine revolution', by Tim Harford, BBC News website (15 January 2020). Available at <https://www.bbc.co.uk/news/business-50673541>

were what mattered here, that this machine had been invented purely for them. 'Sold only by the maker directly to the women of the family', went the advertising slogan; shops offered training courses, and Singer technicians made home visits to talk things over with the sewing machine's boss: the woman.

This must have confused more than a few men. 'Why buy a sewing machine when you can marry one?' was no doubt a common saying in male circles at the time. Some even blamed Isaac Singer – 'You're getting rid of the only thing we can use to keep women quiet for a while!' – thereby completely failing to recognise his intentions. After all, the man was anything but a feminist. Others, however – especially doctors, who had always had their suspicions about an alliance of women and machinery – were afraid for female virtue. 'Thanks to the continual movement (of the foot on the pedal), an object of this kind can trigger hysterical delirium,' they said, while others claimed: 'It triggers a genital arousal so strong that the workers have to take a break and dab at themselves with cold flannels.' But, at some stage, men's fear of being replaced by machines must have subsided, and the sewing machine became the 'most wonderful wedding gift', a must-have for any modern woman. Because, unlike the spinning jenny, the Singer brought women back into the home and allowed them to merge fully with the ideal of mother and housewife. It's hard to say whether this machine served to bind women even more closely to their state of subjugation, or whether, in giving them the opportunity to be creative and earn some money, it did emancipate them somewhat. At the very least, it gave them the feeling of enjoying a privileged relationship with modernity and progress – or, as French writer Gaston Bonheur said with hindsight: 'The fact that this machine was invented for women finally gave them sovereignty over the household. Men were still busy with their horses and carriages, their grand gestures in red trousers. The twentieth century had decided in favour of women.'[1]

---

1   Thuillier, Guy, *Pour une histoire du quotidien au XIXème siècle en Nivernais* (Paris: Mouton, 1977), p. 180, note 145

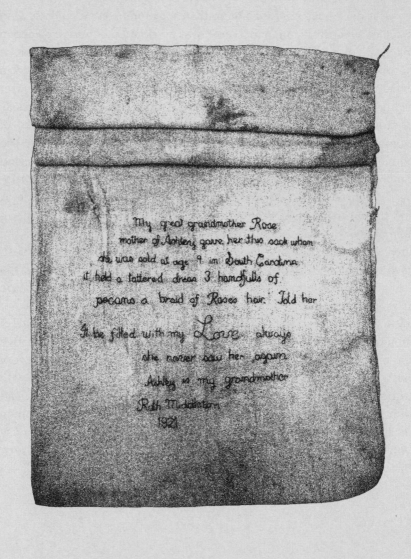

ASHLEY'S SACK

1852/1921

Of all the objects in this book, it's this one here, Ashley's sack, that is perhaps the most moving. Next to its display case in Middleton Place in Charleston, South Carolina, a former cotton plantation turned museum, there's a box of tissues standing permanently at the ready, for the simple reason that only very few visitors are able to pause in front of it without feeling emotional. When the Smithsonian National Museum for African American History & Culture in Washington, DC, had it on loan for five years, this little bag was described as the most heart-rending piece on display in a collection that isn't exactly lacking in moving objects and stories.

Ashley's sack is made of cotton and measures eighty-three centimetres by forty centimetres; it was discovered by chance among a heap of other fabric remnants at a flea market in Nashville in 2007. It is unique in relating – in an incredibly intimate and moving manner – one particularly tragic aspect of the American slave trade: the separation of families, especially mothers and children. As the words embroidered on the bag put it: 'My great grandmother Rose / mother of Ashley gave her this sack when / she was sold at age 9 in South Carolina / it held a tattered dress 3 handfulls of / pecans a braid of Roses hair. Told her / It be filled with my Love always / she never saw her again / Ashley is my grandmother / Ruth Middleton / 1921'.

It must have been the winter of 1852 when the aforementioned Rose realised she was likely soon to be separated from her little daughter Ashley. The owner of the plantation where Ashley was enslaved, Robert Martin, had just died. For enslaved people, such an event was especially fraught, as it meant that the deceased's possessions – including themselves – would be divided up. Their owner's offspring would draw lots for them or auction them off at market; the likelihood of their staying together as a family was low. It's estimated that at least one in four children was separated from their parents – father, mother, sometimes both – most of them for ever. The fear of this happening must have been ever-present, not least because those who bought and sold enslaved people used it as a means of exerting pressure – it was especially great where daughters were concerned. Not for nothing does Sethe, a character in Toni Morrison's *Beloved*, come to the unthinkable decision, reached by many enslaved people in real life, to kill her little daughter, her baby, herself, instead of having her grow up to become enslaved. How crushing must that desperation have been, how appalling the prospect of their looming fate, for someone to take a step such as this? During that time, African American women were the 'mules of the earth', as the writer Zora Neale Hurston once put it: they were abused as sex slaves, as nannies for their owners' children, and forced to produce children themselves – more human resources that could pass into their owners' possession like another tract of land. And there would have been no hesitation when it came to selling those babies for a new field or smart new dress.

Unfortunately, as is so often the case in history, there's a distinct lack of first-hand sources when it comes to the stories of enslaved women. Apart from a few exceptions like Harriet Jacobs' memoir *Incidents in the Life of a Slave Girl*, hardly any formerly enslaved women committed their life stories to paper. Most could neither read nor write, and even those who could will not have banked on anyone ever being interested in their fate. The objects that could have given us an insight into the lives of these women have also been lost or destroyed over the years. Which makes Ashley's sack all the more significant. Because in its quiet, intimate way, it tells a big story. Because it describes the strength of a mother who, despite all that fear and pain, gave to her daughter something that could act as a small place of safety. She scraped together what little she could find. Nuts, which were expensive back then. A braid of hair, the most popular personal keepsake in the nineteenth century. A dress, so she would be warm. She gave her this sack like an emergency kit for the future, and filled it symbolically with courage and love.

The brief report stitched onto the sack in brown, pink and green thread was only written decades later, in 1921, by Ashley's granddaughter Ruth. Unlike both Rose and Ashley, Ruth was born a free woman; this cotton sack, which was evidently never lost but passed down through the family along with its story, was the link that connected several generations of women. Ruth used it to record the fates of her grandmother and great-grandmother as a reminder of her family's personal history, but also to bear witness to the bigger story. After slavery was abolished in the 1860s, the wave of appeals published in newspapers swept across the USA like a roaring babel of voices. Men begging for information about their wives, brothers searching for their sisters and women for their children. They described where they'd seen them last, at which market they'd been sold to different owners, and asked for any information about them. As one Elizabeth Williams wrote, for example, in a notice about her four children: 'She has never seen the above-named children since. Any information given concerning them, however, will be gratefully received by one whose love for her children survives the bitterness and hardships of many long years spent in slavery.'[1] We don't know whether she was reunited with any of them. Rose and Ashley, we do know, never saw each other again.

---

1 Elizabeth Williams, 'Information Wanted', *Christian Recorder*, Philadelphia, 17 March 1866, quoted in DeNeen L. Brown, '"My mother was sold from me": After slavery, the desperate search for loved ones in "last seen ads"', *The Washington Post*, 7 September 2017, available at <https://www.washingtonpost.com/news/retropolis/wp/2017/09/07/my-mother-was-sold-from-me-after-slavery-the-desperate-search-for-loved-ones-in-last-seen-ads/>

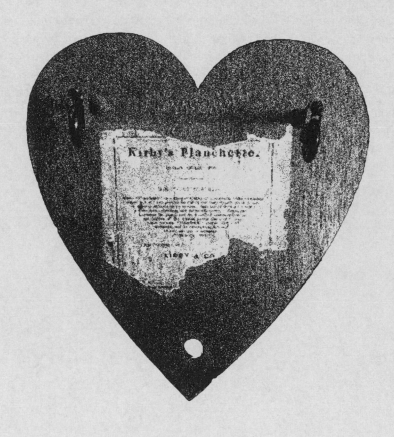

PLANCHETTE

1853

In times of unrest and general uncertainty, we look for alternative ways of living and thinking. It's always been this way. Today, there's a booming business in healing crystals; in the second half of the nineteenth century, it was objects like this one that flooded the market: so-called planchettes.

Invented in France in 1853, a planchette consisted of a heart-shaped wooden board mounted on two small castors with a pencil attached to the point of the heart, and it served to aid communication with the dead. Alone or in a pair, you put a finger on the board and waited till it began to move, as though guided by an invisible hand, to write out a (usually illegible) message. It was a mystical experience and game rolled into one, and it got people so excited that they stormed the bookshops en masse to buy their very own such object. In 1868, the manufacturer of this particular planchette, Kirby & Co., sold 200,000 of its boards in the USA in a matter of months, thereby irretrievably transforming a movement initiated by two young American women roughly twenty years before into a commercialised mass phenomenon: spiritualism.

The belief in the possibility of communicating with the dead was born in Hydesville in upstate New York. When sisters Maggie and Kate Fox initiated this movement in the 1840s, they were tapping into a development already long underway in their local region – the so-called 'burned-over district' – which had been a centre of alternative beliefs and lifestyles (such as Mormonism) since the start of the nineteenth century. For these two girls, however, it all began in quite an unspiritual fashion. In a silly children's game, they led their mother to believe that they were communicating with a man once murdered in their house. Their dialogue was conducted through a system of knocking. One knock meant yes, two knocks no, and the spirit said all manner of things that no one could verify but everyone soon believed. First the neigh-bours, then the entire district. As is so often the case, all it took was a sufficient number of people to believe it for the story to spread like wildfire and convince even the most sceptical minds of its truth. Perhaps because the girls had unknowingly touched on a sore spot: recent scientific discoveries and dramatically new ways of living had shaken religious certainties about life and death, leaving many people unset-tled. The death rate was still very high, especially among young people. The promise of still being able to speak to the dead offered some comfort and explains the enormous success of their practical joke. In 1848, when their older sister Leah – clearly an adept saleswoman – brought the two Fox sisters to live with her so they could demonstrate their 'skills' at public séances, Maggie and Kate became so famous that they started touring the United States. They made appearances in New York and Washington, DC, in Philadelphia, Columbus and St Louis, peddling, without really meaning to, a new lore that gained disciples everywhere it went. And which spawned imitations. Spiritualists mush-roomed all over America; suddenly, everyone seemed to be discovering a hitherto buried talent for communicating with the next world.

What's interesting is that most of these new saviours were women. Being a medium was a female occupation, not because it had been invented by women, but because the traits that were apparently needed for this sort of communication were held to be feminine: great sensitivity, fragility, empathy. Passivity, too – after all, people didn't mess about long with knocking, but quickly allowed spirits to start 'speaking through them'. For many women, this was an emancipatory strike: they could travel around freely, earn money and make appear-ances in public without being regarded as an 'easy girl'; they were listened to and celebrated as mouthpieces of another world. Or, as the famous suffragettes Elizabeth Stanton and Susan B. Anthony wrote in their *History of Woman Suffrage*: 'The only religious sect in the world, unless we except the Quakers, that has recognized the equality of woman, is the Spiritualists.'[1]

It may be no coincidence that the American women's movement launched by these two ladies, Stanton and Anthony, was born in the

---

1   Stanton, Elizabeth Cady, Susan B. Anthony and Matilda Josyln Gage (eds), *History of Woman Suffrage*, Vol. III (New York: Susan B. Anthony, 1886), p. 531

same summer as spiritualism. While the Fox sisters spent the summer of 1848 knocking on wooden boards, Stanton and Anthony were sitting at another table, a couple of hundred miles away in Seneca Falls. This table was where they wrote the 'Declaration of Sentiments', the manifesto they would sign along with sixty-eight other women and thirty-two men, which demanded equality between men and women and fired the starting shot for the USA's feminist movement. At the time, of course, neither group was aware of the other's existence, and at first glance they had very little in common. What could possibly unite two mature, politically active women and two recalcitrant, unprincipled teenagers? Nothing – and yet, plenty. Because even if not all suffragettes were spiritualists, almost all spiritualists were feminists. Because many people associated spiritualism as a worldview with the women's movement. Both wanted to break with the prevailing order and power structures of the patriarchy – something that manifested, for example, in no longer having need of priests to explain the world to them. Communication with a higher power was now open to everyone, thanks to objects like the planchette. Beyond this, both spiritualists and feminists revolted against slavery, against sexual violence, against the duress of motherhood, and against the oppression of women that the Church and its representatives had supported for centuries. 'Spiritualism ushered in the era of women,' a well-known spiritualist once said. And she was right. Globally, hardly any other belief system has so enthralled and empowered women, from artists to thinkers to Victorian housewives.

Yet it didn't actually bring its inventors, the Fox sisters, much happiness. After many demoralising years on the road, they dropped out of society altogether and died at a very young age, alone, impoverished and forgotten. Maggie Fox did make one attempt to set things right, at the Academy of Music in New York City in 1888. She had issued an invitation to one final séance to explain how it had all been one big joke: the noises had merely been her cracking her feet, and there had never been any conversations with the dead. Only, no one wanted to believe her. Access to the beyond and the worldview associated with it had become too important simply to let the spirits go again. And so Maggie was laughed at. 'Humbug!' cried the public, and back to their planchettes they went.

FANOOS LAMP

c. 1854

At the beginning of the coronavirus pandemic in 2020, there was a brief moment when nurses and carers were fished out of the swamp of indifference and thrust into the limelight. They were applauded and celebrated before sinking back into oblivion. More than 150 years earlier, something very similar happened in England: society was washed by a brief wave of enthusiasm for the nursing profession, but especially for the woman who had left her mark on it. This was Florence Nightingale, the famous Lady with the Lamp.

'When all the medical officers have retired for the night, and silence and darkness have settled down upon these miles of prostrate sick, she may be observed alone, with a little lamp in her hand, making her solitary rounds,' wrote *The Times* in 1855, fanning the flames of the Nightingale myth that burned so brightly across Europe: 'every poor fellow's face softens with gratitude at the sight of her'.[1] In illustrations, Florence is usually to be seen making her way through the darkness with a little oil lamp, but in reality she strode the corridors of her Crimean field hospital with this very lantern, a Turkish *fanoos*. The picture of a young lady with a lamp, sacrificing her own sleep in order to watch over wounded soldiers, cemented her image: she was thought of as gentle and maternal, the 'Angel of Crimea', a 'ministering angel', an angel full stop. She was the perfect embodiment of an ideal: the devoted woman who lives only for others.

The reality, however, was quite different. Florence was certainly caring, wrote long letters to soldiers' relatives and was one of the first people to understand that the mind plays an important role in the physical healing process. But she was also rebellious, stubborn and out for

---

1   John Macdonald, letter from Scutari published in *The Times*, 8 February 1855

power in a way that was refreshingly unusual for that day and age. When her mother – who often said despairingly that she'd 'hatched a wild swan' – opposed her wish to work in a hospital, Florence secretly set out for Germany to train as a nurse in Kaiserswerth hospital in Düsseldorf (now the Florence Nightingale Hospital). She moved to Rome to study further, ran the Institute for the Care of Sick Gentlewomen in London, and, in 1854, at the behest of British defence minister Samuel Gridley Howe, led a group of thirty-eight personally selected nurses to Constantinople to care for British soldiers wounded in the Crimean War.

In nineteenth-century England, a career trajectory of this kind was not something that could be sustained purely through gentleness and a friendly disposition, certainly not as a young woman from the upper classes. If you had a life like this, it meant you'd fought hard for it. After all, in Victorian society a lady's place was in the home, and – unless she happened to be called Emily or Charlotte Brontë – her influence on society amounted to zero. Florence could have spent her days at salons, bridge parties and afternoon teas, at balls and other chic occasions; she should have married and had children. But she evidently couldn't bring herself to lead such a life. 'I'd rather die than sit around in boring salons,' she wrote as a young girl – this despite (or maybe because of) the fact that great British thinkers like Charles Darwin and the mathematician Ada Lovelace were forever coming and going from her parents' house. She wanted something altogether different: to be a nurse. Scandalous! Wanting to take care of the sick and poor was normal and acceptable – a woman of good breeding was expected to demonstrate social engagement, but only within certain parameters. You could hand out pieces of fruit to the needy here and there, dispense sips of brandy and warm blankets, but hospitals were to be kept at a distance. Women who worked in such places were usually elderly and poor, with a reputation for selling not just their good-heartedness but also their bodies to patients. 'Nurse' didn't sound like a career choice for a young woman, but the endpoint of an unsuccessful life.

At least, it did until Florence exploded that particular cliché. After the war correspondents had written their reports, after the soldiers had sung her praises in their letters home, and after Florence's mother had engaged in some skilful PR work, the Lady with the Lamp was a new cult figure, the most recognised woman in the whole empire after

Queen Victoria. Newborns and ships were named after her, Nightingale statuettes went on sale, biographical pamphlets were handed out on the streets of London, songs were sung about her: 'Listen, soldier, to the tale of the tender nightingale.' Even the queen wrote her a letter, in which she congratulated her on being 'one who has set so bright an example to our sex'.[1]

Nightingale had indeed proved that women most certainly could achieve things if only they were allowed out of their salons. When she took over the Scutari field hospital in the Crimean War, the death rate among soldiers dropped considerably thanks to the measures she introduced. Florence had noticed, for example, that most soldiers didn't die of their wounds but instead of diseases they caught in the unhygienic surroundings of the field hospital. As a result, she and her female team introduced a few new standards of care – a great source of irritation to the male doctors. Starting immediately, patients were to be washed and given clean clothes; they were fed decent meals; rooms and equipment were regularly cleaned and aired; and, most importantly, hand-washing became mandatory. To us, all that sounds normal. No one would voluntarily enter a hospital where other rules applied, but it's Miss Florence Nightingale we have to thank in large part for this normality. At the time, she was rightly celebrated as *the* heroine of the Crimean War; even the soldiers paled by comparison. Later, she opened a school for nurses who would go on to spread her teachings throughout England and the whole of Europe over the decades that followed. Her books are still a cornerstone of nursing theory, and 12 May, her birthday, is celebrated across the world as International Nurses Day.

1 Bensons, Arthur Christopher and Viscount Esher (eds), *The Letters of Queen Victoria*, *Vol. III, 1854–1861* (London: John Murray, 1908)

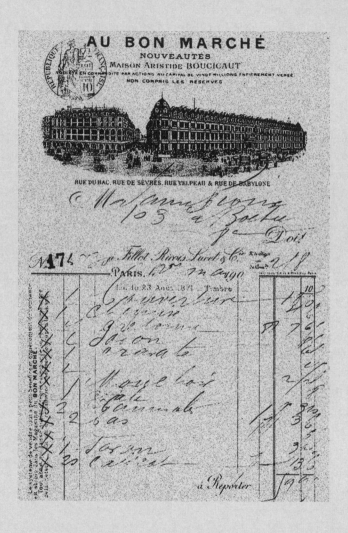

'AU BON MARCHÉ' RECEIPT

1860s

In the opening chapter of Émile Zola's famous novel *The Ladies' Paradise*, we find the following sentence: 'In the great metropolis, black and silent beneath the rain – in this Paris, to which she was a stranger, it shone out like a lighthouse, and seemed to be of itself the life and light of the city.' The 'it' referred to is a department store, Au Bonheur des Dames (The Ladies' Paradise) and to Denise, the heroine of the novel, it appears as the very thing it was to so many others in those dying years of the nineteenth century: a theatre of modernity, emblem of a dawning era in which women would be given an entirely new role – that of consumers. The prototype for this story – a story about the origins of mass consumerism, product mountains, spending sprees, but also the democratisation of shopping – was the legendary Parisian department store that issued the receipt pictured here. The goods listed on it – 'one blanket', 'one shirt', 'one tie', 'two pairs of stockings' and a couple of indecipherable items – were purchased from none other than Le Bon Marché, formerly Au Bon Marché, the first department store of its kind.

Thanks to the Industrial Revolution and new manufacturing technologies, shopping habits had undergone a gradual transformation. More people lived in urban areas, in the vicinity of shops, and were now willing to buy things from them that they would previously have made at home and used for many years. Now, they didn't make new purchases every couple of years, but shopped all the time, in a process of constant renewal. Hence the boutiques selling 'new products' that were opening up all over Europe. When Aristide Boucicaut and his wife, Marguerite (a statue of whom, incidentally, still stands in the square opposite the store), opened Au Bon Marché in 1852, they followed the principle of stocking constantly new, constantly fresh products, but also expanded on it with a few ideas that were revolutionary for the time. First, they displayed their goods instead of hiding them away in the stockroom. This meant that customers no longer had to hope the shop owner would be friendly enough to let them look at things, but could blithely touch and try on anything they wanted; if it didn't fit or wasn't quite what they were looking for, they could simply return it. Entry was free – if the customer didn't want to buy anything, she didn't have to – and it was entirely permissible simply to wander the aisles and intoxicate yourself. There were regular special offers, a delivery service and marketing flyers; it was possible to order things by post and visit during the popular 'home textiles month' put on several times a year. The *grand magasin* was a temple of consumerism – or, as Zola put it, 'the cathedral of modern commerce, light but strong, the very thing for a nation of customers'.

Today, anyone crossing Boucicaut Square in the 7th arrondissement of Paris might turn in at the gilded glass doors on the corner of Rue de Sèvres and Rue Velpeau, and enter the cream-coloured aisles studded with handbags and jewellery and hats, pausing for a moment in the middle of the building, between the stands of cosmetics, to look up at the famous criss-crossing escalators. Standing there listening to the bustle, the gentle noise of luxury, breathing in the scents of perfume and powder and bathing in the warm light of the space around you, it's possible to imagine how grand, how extraordinarily modern this store must have seemed when it opened in the 1870s. And, above all, how proud and excited the women must have been, for whom this waste-fully beautiful modernity, this call of the cargo ship of the future, had chiefly been conceived. This was new. Until then, the only public insti-tution that had made any effort to appeal to (and manipulate) women was the Church. But with the advent of department stores like Au Bon Marché, La Samaritaine, Les Galeries Lafayette and others, places had appeared in the urban landscape that functioned as intermediate spaces between indoors and out, in which women could spend time without their husbands, amusing themselves and giving free rein to their newly attained power: spending. After all, Madame had just been assigned a new task. Where most women had previously contributed to their family income by working, now the ladies of the middle and upper classes were given the job of economising. Manufacturing is male, consumption is female – this, roughly, was the ideology of the time. Or, as the American artist Barbara Kruger would aptly put it a century later: 'I shop therefore I am.' The man brought home the money, the woman had to manage it cleverly. She was a 'professional consumer', they said. Consuming was her job, her duty, the sign of her femininity. The more she bought and the more beautiful those things, the more she did for the prestige of her home and husband. Of course, we still see this today: men draping young women in all manner of expensive bags and clothes to demonstrate their own financial potency.

Seen like this, the department store culture launched by Au Bon Marché is the same as so many of the accomplishments of that century: it's impossible to say whether it helped to emancipate women, or instead might perhaps have subjected them to a new, even more insidious system of repression. On the one hand, mass consumerism and the adverts that were now almost exclusively illustrated with pictures of women gave them a new significance and visibility in the urban landscape. On the other hand, they found themselves increasingly forced to fit idealised images. They became observed objects, only ever behaving in relation to this state of being observed.

There was just one kind of female customer who wanted to be anything but seen and observed. This was an entirely new category of lady thief – namely, those ladies who could afford to buy anything but were still regularly led away by store detectives for shoplifting gloves, stockings, ties or necklaces, making them disappear into the folds of their coats. The sheer excess combined with the new appreciation they enjoyed in their role of consumer turned many women's heads; they stole not out of necessity but desire. Contemporary psychiatrists found this phenomenon particularly inspiring, and a new, supposedly women-only disorder emerged in parallel with the department store. Kleptomania: the affliction suffered by all those ladies who left Au Bon Marché with plenty of beautiful things, but without a receipt like this one.

THE KILLING OF AEGISTHUS, RED-FIGURE VASE

500 BC

In the nineteenth century, archaeologists and anthropologists started thinking about human prehistory and, in doing so, transferred the norms of the Victorian era, that 'high time' of the patriarchy, onto our past. The very notion that the gender-related division of roles and work might not have been that way 'for ever', but instead had been invented at some point – based, in other words, not on the rules of nature, but on those of humans, of men – was clearly so abstruse and laughable that they never even considered it as a possibility for research. Right from the very beginning, men had been in charge and women their subordinates – this was the (slightly exaggerated) hypothesis on which everyone, save a couple of pesky suffragettes, was able to agree. Everyone except for one oddball: Johann Jakob Bachofen.

As the nineteenth century faded away, this Swiss historian and anthropologist put forward an audacious theory: he believed in an original matriarchy. Bachofen likely had a few similarities with Charles Fourier, whom we met earlier; he too was a dreamer and a crackpot, though less congenial than the Frenchman. Because while Fourier believed in good architecture, women, equality and a sexually liberated Eldorado for all, what Bachofen was hoping to achieve with his 'mother right' – this was also the title of his book – was not at all, as feminists later claimed, to rehabilitate the original power of women, but instead to explain exactly which swamp of (non-)civilisation we'd succeeded in raising ourselves out of. In his theory – which, incidentally, never uses the term 'matriarchy' (he speaks only of 'mother right' or 'gynocracy') – Bachofen did explain, to the horror of his colleagues, that women certainly had once wielded power and been worshipped as mothers, priestesses and goddesses, but their rule had gone so badly wrong that men had taken the wheel in order to save the world from anarchy and chaos. According to him, this development took place in three phases. First came 'hetaerism', in which humans lived not in monogamous pairs but in a promiscuous muddle. Everyone had sex with everyone else and fathers couldn't be named with any certainty, so women functioned as the heads of their families and only daughters were allowed to inherit. Because men would simply pounce on women whenever they felt like it during this stage, the women eventually rebelled against them, which led to the next phase, the Amazonian one. Here, the ladies joined forces in female groups and completely excluded men – which, of course, was not a long-term solution either. And so we arrive at the third – and, according to Bachofen, the best – stage: monogamy, sedentism and agriculture. Here again, he believed, women were still in power; he found evidence of this in goddesses like Demeter, even the affiliation women had with the earth. Only, this phase didn't go well for very long either.

'The history of mankind has been shaped by the battle of the sexes,' Bachofen claimed, not entirely incorrectly. According to him, there came a point when women had so far overbid the hand of their authority that a bloody confrontation took place. This vase – which Bachofen may not mention directly (unfortunately, most of the objects to which he makes reference are no longer to be found), but which is similar to the one he does reference – is symbolic of this battle between a 'faltering' matriarchy and a patriarchy rising up against 'injustice'. On display in the collection of Greek and Roman antiquities in Vienna's Kunsthistorisches Museum, it shows young Orestes just after he's killed Aegisthus: the lover taken by his unfaithful mother, Clytemnestra. Looking at the almost Tarantino-esque spurt of blood, we can't help but think that the poor woman must have known she would be next to go. Orestes committed the gravest sin of matricide in order to avenge his father, Agamemnon. The king had fallen victim to Clytemnestra and her lover – mind you, only after he himself had 1) sacrificed his daughter Iphigenia in exchange for a favourable wind to Troy, and 2) returned from the Trojan War with his trophy mistress, Cassandra, among his spoils. Yet these details don't play any role whatsoever in Aeschylus's *Oresteia*; the monster is and always was Clytemnestra, the personification of a matriarchy gone rogue, one that was prepared to do anything to protect its endangered sovereignty. According to Bachofen, Orestes murdering his mother finally put an end to that. This was the bloody victory of the patriarchy. The originality and slight insanity of his theory lies in the fact that he didn't read this ancient myth as a legend, but as a somewhat warped, though overall faithful, record of history.

Bachofen's scientifically questionable point of view and his notion – completely wacky for the time – that women might once have had a say in things saw him heartily laughed at and mocked by his colleagues. But his idea did somehow make its way in the world: hardly any other theory trading in legends, beliefs and intuition has made such triumphant progress as that of the original matriarchy. Everyone has drawn on Bachofen: socialists (especially Friedrich Engels), National Socialists, anti-feminists, psychoanalysts. And, more than anyone, agents of the second wave of feminism. In the 1960s and 1970s, they took his idea of the original matriarchy as proof of the potential power of women, and painted the matriarchy as an idyllic form of government in which peace, free love and a life lived in harmony with nature could prevail. The fact that Bachofen hadn't meant it like this at all wasn't – and fundamentally still isn't – all that important. Regardless of whether we see him as a dreamer or just another macho-man, his theory opened the door to an idea that had seemed impossible until that point: that patriarchy is not the only system possible, the only one predetermined by nature.

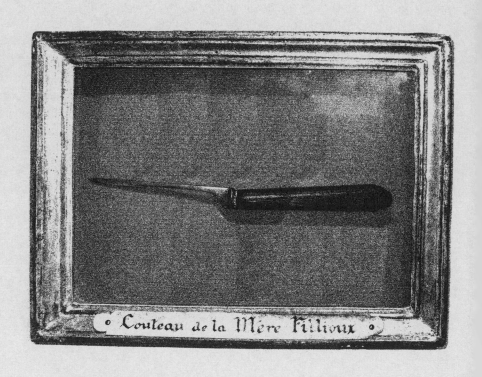

Couteau de la Mère Fillioux

KNIFE BELONGING TO
LA MÈRE FILLOUX

LATE 19ᵀᴴ CENTURY

In an interview he gave in the 1970s, the celebrated French chef Paul Bocuse, one of the fathers of nouvelle cuisine, uttered the following piece of nonsense with total conviction: 'Fire is a masculine profession; it's the magic of the fire and it's the men who make it their own. Or, as I'll often say to my friends: I don't like going to bed at night with a woman who smells of the kitchen.' What Bocuse was awkwardly trying to reinforce with this statement was the decades-old view that while women definitely did belong at the stove, they only belonged at the stove in their own home. They had absolutely no business in big kitchens, in hospitality, haute cuisine and other such culinary corners. This persuasion applied across Europe and certainly in America too, but it also held sway in Asia, where women had been banned from sushi kitchens since time immemorial because it was believed their body temperature rose to such a degree during their period that it would spoil all that expensive fish. Now, Monsieur Bocuse – who was clearly addled either by his own fame or the fumes coming from his cooking pots – had forgotten where he himself had learned his craft. Namely in the kitchen of a woman: a certain Eugénie Brazier, also known simply as 'La Mère Brazier'.

Brazier, who was a celebrity in the gourmet world of the 1930s, was one of a line of women who had shaped the culinary landscape of Lyon – and, consequently, the whole of France – since the eighteenth century, and who had ruled it since at least the second half of the nineteenth: the so-called *mères lyonnaises* (the mothers of Lyon). How motherly these ladies actually were is questionable. At that time, the word was used across France to describe any woman who ran an eating establishment, thereby feeding people like a mother would, but it was

199

in Lyon that it first became an expression of appreciation for outstanding female restaurateurs. After La Mère Guy, known as the *mère des mères*, kicked things off in the early eighteenth century – at the precise moment when increasing numbers of European women were publishing cookbooks, like Maria Sophia Schellhammer's *Die wohlunterwiesene Köchin* ('The Well-instructed Cook', first published in Germany in 1692) – it was La Mère Brigousse who stepped up to take her place at the beginning of the nineteenth century. Thanks to a very amusing idea of hers, she was also referred to as *la mère des amoureux* (the mother of lovers): instead of serving quenelles, the poached fish dumplings typical of Lyon, in their traditional elongated-boat shape, the plates she set down in front of her guests held two rounded mounds with teats. Two breasts, which – cheeky as people clearly were to Madame Brigousse – promptly became known as *tétons de Vénus*: Venus's nipples. People came from every corner of the country, a little embarrassed, a little amused, on loud stag-dos or first dates laced with innuendo, to share a pair of breasts.

The knife pictured here, which looks in its frame a little like the culinary version of René Magritte's 'Ceci n'est pas une pipe', belonged to Madame Fayolle, also known as La Mère Filloux. She opened her first restaurant a half-century after Brigousse and was one of the most famous 'mothers of Lyon'. It was she who irrevocably shaped the city's image, she whom Curnonsky – the best-known food critic of the twentieth century and the man responsible for naming Lyon the 'capital of gastronomy' – described as 'famous like Maréchal Foch, like Anatole de France, like Kipling, like Charlie Chaplin, like Mistinguett'. In France, she was also often dubbed the 'Queen of Poularde', because she perfected, if not invented, a classic of French cuisine: *poularde demi-deuil* (chicken in half-mourning). This dish involves tucking shavings of truffle under the skin of a chicken before it is poached in a bouillon. When finished, the chicken is spotted in white and black: half cheerful, half in mourning. And clearly delicious: guests came from all over France and Europe to sample the classic menu at Bistro Filloux: truffle soup, the aforementioned *poularde demi-deuil*, quenelle gratin, artichoke broth with foie gras, and praline ice cream, all washed down with Beaujolais and Châteauneuf-du-Pape.

Legend has it that La Mère Filloux used this very knife to slice open almost 500,000 chickens over the course of the years. Because, as one visitor reported: 'Madame Filloux insisted on serving her guests – who included many luminaries from the worlds of literature and politics – herself. Using a little kitchen knife, she sliced open the white of the *poularde* before their eyes.' Alice B. Toklas, Gertrude Stein's partner, wrote in her famous *The Alice B. Toklas Cookbook*: 'Mère Filloux was a short compact woman in a starched enveloping apron with a short, narrow but formidable Knife which she brandished as she moved from table to table carving each chicken.' After her death, La Mère Brazier, who had trained under Filloux and would later train Bocuse, kept the *poularde* tradition alive, which in 1933 earned her six Michelin stars. She wasn't just the first female chef, but the first chef, full stop, to be so lavishly decorated, a whole sixty years before Alain Ducasse.

If Paul Bocuse is known as the father of French cuisine, Brazier is definitely the mother of *gastronomie à la française*. Had this mother known back then that women would soon be driven out of the kitchen once more, and spoken of in such a condescending manner, she might well have brandished her *poularde* knife. And chased those men out of *her* kitchen.

REMINGTON TYPEWRITER

1874

One of the first objects most people think of in relation to women and history is this one right here. You can test that theory yourself at a dinner party. Ask which object has changed women's lives the most, and half the table will shout, 'The typewriter!' Because it created new jobs for women; because it offered them a new way of expressing themselves.

Whether that really was the case – whether this object invented in the USA in the latter half of the nineteenth century, at roughly the same time as the sewing machine, really did inspire women to record their thoughts – is doubtful. At least in its early days, the typewriter contributed less to women sharing their own thinking than it did to them taking down the purportedly brilliant ideas of men – their bosses – at top speed. However, there's absolutely no question that this machine provided women, particularly of the middle and upper classes, with entirely new opportunities to earn their own money and so gain more independence. Beyond the few socially acceptable jobs for women, like governess or teacher, the typewriter generated an entirely new line of work for those with a high-school education: secretary, shorthand typist, office worker. Or, as American historian Daniel J. Boorstin wrote, 'the typewriter [. . .] (with the telephone) helped bring women out of the kitchen into the world of affairs'.[1] Why? Very simply: because men didn't want to type on them. In 1874, when the American manufacturer Remington put its first typewriters on the market for $125 apiece, the smart little machines were a huge flop. The idea of receiving a letter that hadn't been handwritten by the author – let alone writing such a letter oneself – seemed ludicrous to most people, if not downright

---

1   Boorstin, Daniel J., *The Americans: The Democratic Experience* (New York: Knopf Doubleday, 2010)

unpleasant. Against all expectations, Remington's male clientele failed to snap up the modern contraptions. Only Mark Twain is said to have bought himself a 'new fangled writing machine', with which he wrote *Tom Sawyer* – the first novel ever composed on a typewriter. A nice anecdote, but it still didn't do much for Remington.

Until the marketing department delivered a coup: if men were going to ignore the machines, why not palm them off on women, the new queens of consumerism? Young ladies were stationed in shops to demonstrate the Remington; the message between the lines was clear: 'The typewriter is so user-friendly that even a woman can operate it.' Or, as office manager Joan says to her colleague Peggy in the TV series *Mad Men*: 'Don't be intimidated by all this technology. The men who designed it made it so simple that even a woman can use it.'[1] Can, and should. Because in some way – it was believed at the time – the typewriter seemed to have been made for women: all well-bred young ladies were raised to play the piano with at least some degree of virtuosity, so as to entertain high society at soirees. This very same skill, it was thought, stood them in good stead when it came to typing: the explanation went that men were unaccustomed to moving their fingers over a keyboard, whereas ladies were quite used to it. People even went so far as to claim there was a 'natural' link between women and typewriters. As John Harrison wrote in 1888 in his *A Manual of the Typewriter*: 'It is especially adapted for feminine fingers. They seem made for type-writing. Type-writing involves no harder labor, and no more skill than playing the piano.'[2] For women, the Remington was the easiest way to get a job – so claimed a Christmas advert in the winter of 1875.

And it was true. In the late nineteenth century, between 1880 and 1900, women and typewriters moved en masse into offices that had previously been the sole preserve of men. Industry and burgeoning capitalism were transforming the world of business and creating such mounds of paperwork that the male office staff could no longer keep up. On top of this, these gents were now aspiring to other positions: men became bosses, women secretaries. In 1880, 40 per cent of steno-typists in the USA were female; by 1900 this was 75 per cent, and by 1930 a whole 95 per cent. New technology had created a new

---

1   *Mad Men*, 'Smoke Gets In Your Eyes' (episode 1.01), 19 July 2007
2   Harrison, John, *A Manual of the Typewriter* (London: I. Pitman & Sons, 1888), p. 9

profession – only this time, even a decade after its invention, men weren't coming to complain that women were taking the good jobs away from them. After all, not a single one actually wanted to be a secretary.

In the end, as is always the case when women prove good at something, it was claimed that using a typewriter didn't require any kind of talent or skill, so the women who worked as typists didn't need to be paid particularly well. Opportunities to climb the career ladder were also few and far between, but still more and more women in blue-collar jobs and domestic employment decided to teach themselves to type, hoping to land a position as a stenotypist, which would provide them with a higher salary than a factory job and more independence than they'd have as a housemaid. Women with a high-school education started to favour the office over the classroom; the life of a secretary offered more freedom than that of a teacher. A teacher wasn't allowed to drink, smoke or consort with men, and in many countries, including the UK, was required to give up her job if she got married. By contrast, an office worker only needed to be able to type fast; no one cared about what she did in her spare time. All the same, the role still didn't offer long-term fulfilment; it was monotonous work that held women back, which was why in the second half of the twentieth century many girls were advised against learning to type, or even admitting that they could. By that time, the danger of being reduced to nothing but a typist had simply become too great.

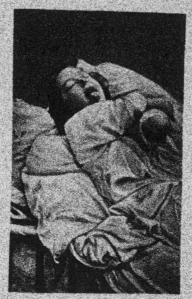

Planche XXVIII.

DÉBUT D'UNE ATTAQUE

PAGE FROM *ICONOGRAPHIE PHOTOGRAPHIQUE DE LA SALPÊTRIÈRE*

1878

On the morning of 16 August 1882, many readers of the French periodical *Gil Blas* must have choked on their croissants as they read the following lines: 'Hysterical, madame, is the word of the moment. Are you in love? Then you are hysterical. Do you feel unmoved by the passions of your contemporaries? Then you are hysterical, chastely hysterical. Are you betraying your husband? Then you are hysterical, sensually hysterical. Do you steal fabric samples from department stores? Hysterical. Are you constantly lying? Hysterical! Are you greedy? Hysterical! Are you anxious? Hysterical! Whatever you are, you are just as women have always been. Every one of us is hysterical since the good Dr Charcot – that high priest of hysteria, that breeder of hysterical ladies – began keeping nervous women in his hospital at Salpêtrière, making demons of them and driving them to madness.'[1]

The author of this text, Guy de Maupassant, was right: 'hysteria' was the buzzword in those dying years of the century. From Paris to London, Vienna to Berlin, everyone was throwing it around as though there had never been any other explanation for all the questions raised by 'mysterium woman', that 'dark continent'. If a young woman was prone to melancholy, particularly quick-tempered or particularly introverted, she was hysterical. If she was timid or distracted, people found her just as hysterical as a woman who heard voices or suffered epileptic fits. And

---

1   de Maupassant, Guy, 'Une femme', *Gil Blas*, 16 August 1882 (pp. 2–11)

any woman who uttered obscenities in her delirium was, naturally, a clear victim of hysteria. The diagnosis was so newfangled and correspondingly vague that it could be used to describe any ostensibly inappropriate outburst of feelings. That, essentially, still hasn't changed.

The word itself wasn't all that new. Even back in antiquity, scholars like Plato and Hippocrates worked on the premise that women were tormented by the uterus, the *hystera*, which roamed around in their bodies and was what made them so difficult to deal with. In the seventeenth century, the general belief was that if a woman's womb was 'undernourished' by male sperm (in other words, frustrated), it would rise up through her body and anchor itself in her head. This did not bode well. Later, hysteria was very simply defined as a 'neurosis of the female instrument of conception', and people tried using horrible smells to dispel spasms, fainting fits and frenzies – it was believed the uterus would avoid a strong stench and so return to its rightful place, like a little dog. The hysteria of the late nineteenth century was somewhat different. And it began its triumphant progress at a hospital in the 13th arrondissement of Paris: La Salpêtrière.

Jean-Martin Charcot, the hospital's head physician – the 'Napoleon of Neuroses', as he was known – was convinced that the problem lay less in the uterus than in the brain: the nerves. To prove his controversial hypothesis, the co-founder of neurology studied his (female) patients closely: he hypnotised them and triggered fits so as to make detailed sketches of their postures and contortions, the occasional onset of paralysis, closed eyelids and hands frozen into claws. Above all, however, he used the modern technology of photography to capture these symptoms on film. He wanted to prove that there was a visual schema to this affliction, and had a photo studio built in his department for exactly this purpose, where his colleague Paul Regnard would photograph the young women. It seems crazy when we consider how, at exactly the same time, photography was a medium that women were confidently adopting, and which for the first time ever allowed them to observe instead of being observed. In La Salpêtrière, you could say, the gaze had been reversed once more: here, it was men who were observing women.

This image from the plate section of *Iconographie Photographie de la Salpêtrière*, a kind of picture book on hysteria published in 1878, shows Charcot's most famous patient: Louise Augustine Gleizes. She is, as the caption tells us, at the 'beginning of an attack'. Her arms are contorted and her eyes are closed, her mouth is wide open, tongue outstretched. She's screaming, it says. In the plates that follow we will see her in poses of 'ecstasy', 'hallucination', 'eroticism', 'threat', 'mockery', 'amorous pleading' and 'crucifixion'. Visually, it's all very striking – no wonder people found pictures like these so fascinating – but the problem is that they can hardly be 'real'. To take a photo of this kind at that time, the subject would have needed to hold still for several seconds, which rather contradicts the inherent impulsivity of a fit. We can therefore assume that these photos were at least partly staged, and that Charcot's patients posed for him and performed 'being hysterical'.

Just the same as they will have done at his legendary 'Tuesday séances'. On these evenings, the neurologist paraded his patients like circus horses, with this Augustine a particular favourite. In the 1870s, she was the star of the Charcot hysteria show: Charcot would swing a shiny object back and forth in front of her eyes until her body began to tremble, her limbs contorted and she started flailing her arms and legs around in all directions. She'd scream, curse, roll her eyes, stick out her rigid tongue, throw her arms in the air, cross herself and finally sink to the floor, unconscious. Applause! It was a sensation. Curious people came from all over the world to see Charcot's pretty hysterics. Doctors like Sigmund Freud and Gilles de la Tourette sat in the audience alongside members of the public who simply wanted to enjoy the spectacle. Voyeurs, artists, fashionable *tout Paris*: from theatre diva Sarah Bernhardt to the playwright August Strindberg and even Guy de Maupassant, everyone wanted to see the 'mad women' dance. The boundary between theatre and science was extremely porous here, but the question is what role these women played in it. Could it be that they were deliberately exaggerating their poses, or assuming ones that apparently fitted their symptoms simply in order to be invited in front of the camera, or even on stage? Did they let Charcot force them into these fabricated photos simply to become famous? And does this mean they contributed to the invention of 'hysteria', an affliction for which we have a dozen specific diagnoses today? We don't know. Augustine, at least, did break free eventually. She escaped from Salpêtrière (dressed as a man!) in 1880. And, a hundred years later, the term 'hysteria' would also vanish from the manuals used in diagnosing psychological illnesses.

MARIE BASHKIRTSEFF, *IN THE STUDIO*

1881

When the creator of this image, the Ukrainian artist Marie Bashkirtseff, was twelve years old, she wrote in her diary: 'If I do not die young, I hope to survive as a great artist; but if I do, I will have my Journal published, which cannot fail to be interesting.'[1] Bashkirtseff did die young, at the age of twenty-six, but her wish was also realised: in 1887, three years after her death, her diary was published and became a cult book for her generation. The kind of book that needed to be read – and still does today. Not just because it's wonderfully refreshing, full of the cheeky, coy remarks of a young woman who moved in good society in Nice, Rome and Paris, who dreamed of an extraordinary destiny and whose deepest wish was to be recognised for the genius she was certain she possessed. But, above all, because it reveals a lot about the life and suffering of women artists in the late nineteenth century. Or, to be more precise, the women who wanted to be artists.

This picture illustrates a thought that Bashkirtseff also recorded in her diary: 'In the studio, all distinctions disappear; you have neither name nor family; you are no longer the daughter of your mother; you are yourself; you are an individual with art before you – art and nothing else.'[2] It shows a group of women studying life drawing. They're by themselves, concentrated and focused on something that has nothing to do with housekeeping or raising children. They're no longer daughters, sisters or mothers, no longer even women, merely themselves, and the easels standing in front of them are a challenge: not to remain

---

1   Bashkirtseff, Marie, *The Journal of Marie Bashkirtseff*, tr. Mathilde Blind (London, Paris & Melbourne: Cassell & Company Limited, 1890)
2   ibid.

silent but to express themselves, maybe for the first time ever. A scene like the one depicted here wasn't just a rarity at that time; in the eyes of many, it would have been scandalous. Even though women had long been permitted to take art classes – in eighteenth-century Paris, for example, at the studio of Jacques-Louis David, famous painter of historical events, or with Élisabeth Vigée Le Brun – even though they'd exhibited their work at salons, sometimes with great success, they were refused entry to art colleges almost until the twentieth century. The École des Beaux Arts, for example, only began accepting women in 1897, and even if the Royal Academy in London did take a couple of female students in the 1860s, there was one discipline in particular that continued to be denied them at all the European academies: painting nudes. Whether women should be allowed to paint a naked man or not was the number-one topic of debate in artistic circles of the day, a downright political issue that was guaranteed to dynamite any peaceful dinner party. Back then, it would be their wedding night before most young women knew what a man looked like without his trousers on, and everyone was apparently keen to keep it that way. It's telling that Marie decided to paint a boy – a child – in this picture, and to hide his penis beneath a towel. Was she trying to paint an acceptable version of reality in order to have her work exhibited at a salon? Whatever the case, she did study at one of the only art schools in Europe to allow women into life-drawing classes: the Académie Julian, which opened in 1868.

Floods of women from every corner of the earth arrived in Paris to study painting at Julian and throw themselves into artistic life in the capital. Abigail May Alcott, for example, the sister of *Little Women* author Louisa May Alcott, was one of its students, even if she did prefer to spend her time at the afternoon tea parties hosted by American painter Mary Cassatt. Käthe Kollwitz, too, spent a long time at the easels on Rue des Panoramas. A little later, they would be joined by Paula Modersohn-Becker. It's said she carefully read Bashkirtseff's diary before leaving Worpswede for Paris, eager to learn how her education would unfold: the students first drew plaster figurines before being allowed into the nude class, though Marie claimed some would simply throw themselves greedily into the real thing. Perhaps they were disappointed. Because the gentlemen were evidently only seldom naked; most of the time they were wearing underpants or, as we can see here, draped in a little cloth – or at least, they were at the Académie Julian. On the other bank of the Seine, at the Académie Colarossi, where Finnish painter Helene Schjerfbeck was studying at roughly the same time, things might have been different. The works of Camille Claudel, at least, Colarossi's most famous female student, certainly imply that they didn't set much store by cloth over there. Claudel's sculptures, which tell of her love affair and later separation from the sculptor Auguste Rodin, may be the most beautiful and heart-rending depictions ever made of passion and the pain of separation, yet they do perhaps also confirm what Bashkirtseff once claimed – namely that the milieu of art is dangerous for women. At the age of forty, Claudel was taken away from her atelier on the Île Saint-Louis and locked up in a psychiatric unit for the rest of her life. She'd been found lying among the shards of her sculptures, destroyed by her own hands; she was convinced that Rodin wanted to steal her work from her.

The Parisian art world was harsh, but it was also one of the few places in which women could be something other than mothers, daughters and wives. Berthe Morisot, who never actually attended art school, let alone a life-drawing class, was celebrated as the 'First Lady of Impressionism'; the aforesaid Mary Cassatt enjoyed international renown, perhaps in part because she devoted herself to subjects typically perceived as female: motherhood and intimacy. Even during her brief lifetime, Marie Bashkirtseff received recognition as an artist, though these days she is appreciated more for her diary, because it offers us an insight into the thoughts of women who, at the turn of the century, dared to live a different kind of life, and who refused to understand why men should be allowed to paint naked women, but women weren't allowed to paint naked men. As Anaïs Nin once said of Bashkirtseff: 'There are things [she] says that are reflected word for word here in my own diary. It's enough to make me think I am mad and that I copied them – or else that Marie's soul has been reincarnated in me.'[1]

1   Diary of Anaïs Nin, 23 September 1921, available at: <https://www.54books.de/der-wunsch-sich-selbst-zu-gestalten-ueber-das-tagebuch-der-marie-bashkirtseff/>

SAFETY BICYCLE

1889

In 1895, then-eighty-year-old women's rights activist Elizabeth Cady Stanton stated that, in her opinion, the most significant invention of the nineteenth century in terms of women's emancipation was the bicycle: 'the bicycle will inspire women with more courage, self-respect, reliance . . .' Her friend Susan B. Anthony, whom Gertrude Stein dubbed 'the mother of us all', agreed with her: 'I think [cycling] has done more to emancipate women than anything else in the world. It gives women a feeling of freedom and self-reliance. I stand and rejoice every time I see a woman ride by on a wheel . . . the picture of free, untrammeled womanhood.'[1]

From the 1890s onwards, Ms Anthony will often have had cause to rejoice. Because, back then, the streets of New York and Boston, the parks of London and Paris, and probably many other places, offered a completely new sight: suddenly, women could be seen everywhere, not just as beaming figures on the billboards advertising biscuits, champagne and household goods, but as the real thing. Real women gliding cheerfully past. Wearing short skirts over voluminous trousers, they perched on steel-framed contraptions, whipping past pedestrians at a ferocious speed with their hair billowing out behind them, no doubt inwardly rejoicing just as much as Susan B. Anthony. Nothing of the sort had ever been seen before. In the Victorian era, women had either stayed at home or hung out in the brand-new department stores. Perhaps they might occasionally have visited a museum or library, but they didn't have any business out on the streets. Not alone, at least. They could travel in carriages, maybe even take a few steps in the

---

1 Susan B. Anthony, quoted in: <https://www.womenshistory.org/articles/pedaling-path-freedom>

company of a governess or husband, but hurtling around town on their own? Possibly with no destination? No, that wasn't an option. Even early versions of the bicycle were designed so that women had to share them with men. Men had been allowed to cruise around unaccompanied on their bikes since at least the 1850s, but women were only permitted to join them on a tandem. He sat at the front, she at the back; he decided where they went and how fast, she pedalled along obediently. Until the 'safety bicycle', just like this one, was finally invented. It was indeed safer – also cheaper – and so quickly gained popularity among the middle and upper classes. A veritable cycling mania exploded in those years: everyone wanted to have a bike, everyone wanted to enjoy that feeling of freedom, of being able to move along under your own steam, of simply riding off whenever and wherever they felt like it. This was likely a new feeling even for men. For women, it was a revelation. Just imagine: after decades of being more or less locked up, they were finally able to swing themselves into the saddle, feel the wind on their face and move their body, to feel as though they were alive. It must have been overwhelming. A certain Annie Londonderry was so enthralled that in 1894 she set out from Boston without a cent in her pocket – but a revolver in her handbag – to circumnavigate the globe by bicycle. It took her nearly a year.

Of course, with the advent of this new mode of transport, fashion had to change as well. You wouldn't get far in long Victorian skirts and impractical undergarments; the fabric got tangled up in the wheels; it was dangerous and uncomfortable. Women thus reached for a garment that had already caused a stir and cries of 'Scandal!' in the USA some fifty years before: bloomers. Puffed-up trousers in the oriental style, cuffs laced tightly at the ankles – much the same as they are on today's more safety-conscious cyclists. On top, they wore a kind of short skirt and fitted blazer. American women's suffragists, especially Amelia Bloomer, editor-in-chief of *The Lily* magazine and the woman who lent these trousers her name, had attempted to instigate a fashionable reformation in 1851 and make it common practice for women to be allowed out in said bloomers, rather than having to go around in long dresses all the time. The few women who were brave enough to show themselves in public in this get-up were ogled as though they had absolutely nothing on. If they showed up as a group, newspapers like the *New York Tribune* would report in a panic: 'The Bloomers were out yesterday in force.' The conservative forces fought so stubbornly against this 'dress reform' that it essentially never happened: women in bloomers remained a minority for decades. Until the aforementioned safety bicycle came along. At that point, it was generally accepted that skirts and corsets weren't that suitable for cycling, and many cities officially authorised the wearing of trousers. There were, of course, still many stubborn opponents; as has so often been the case, many of them were doctors. Some declared that cycling would make women infertile; others were concerned – as they'd been about the sewing machine – that perpetual motion would trigger a state of sexual arousal. Still others saw it as the end of woman and the birth of a 'third sex': the cyclist.

As an activity, cycling has become prevalent in the West by now. None of us feels particularly emancipated or free these days simply because we've hopped on a bike. In other cultures, however, what we now regard as an everyday mode of transport continues to spark lively debate. In Iran, for example, women are still forbidden to cycle in public; those who do are risking an awful lot. When it came out in 2012, the lovely film *Wadjda*, the story of a Saudi Arabian girl who dreams of owning a bicycle and pedalling through the dusty streets just like the boys with whom she's friends, caused quite a furore. It was the first feature film shot in the country, and the first to be made by a woman – it was spoken of as if it were a miracle. And what happened was indeed just that: a year after *Wadjda* appeared in the cinemas, the women of Saudi Arabia were officially granted permission to ride bikes. Whether in the nineteenth or the twenty-first century, Stanton and Anthony were right: the bicycle was, and still is, the chassis of female emancipation.

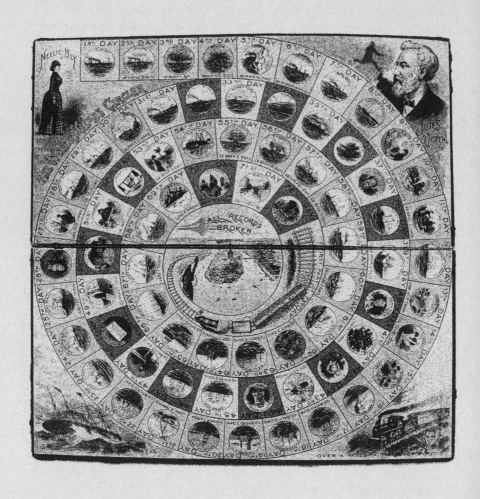

'ROUND THE WORLD WITH NELLIE BLY' GAME

1890

A couple of years ago, in her book *Flâneuse*, the American writer Lauren Elkin posited very amusingly how abstruse it is that strolling – wandering around, travelling, exploring the world with open eyes – has always been defined as a male prerogative: 'as if a penis were a requisite walking appendage, like a cane'.[1] And indeed, for a long time, those women who wanted to set out and explore the world were well advised to behave as though they did have one – a penis, that is.

Jeanne Baret, for example, who boarded the French Imperial Navy ship *La Boudeuse* in November 1766 as part of an expedition led by Louis Antoine de Bougainville, thereby becoming the first woman in history to circumnavigate the world, spent two years as 'Jean'. She bound her breasts and wore wide-legged trousers, and if ever one of the hundred-odd men on board wondered why Jean never wanted to pee in front of them, he'd explain that he was just pretty prudish. In the end, Jeanne was found out, and Bougainville – who became famous and much admired thanks to this expedition, even having a flowering shrub, bougainvillea, named after him – wrote the following wonderfully incorrect lines about her: 'She will be the only one of her sex to do this [. . .] Her example will hardly be contagious.'[2] We could make a list of all the great lady travellers who have explored the world since the nineteenth century. From Isabella Bird to Mary Kingsley, Isabelle Eberhardt, Gertrude Bell and Alexandra David Néel, to the queen of female

---

1 Elkin, Lauren, *Flâneuse: Women Walk the City in Paris, New York, Tokyo, Venice and London* (London: Vintage, 2017)
2 Louis Antoine de Bougainville, Journal, 28–29 May 1768, quoted in: <https://dangerouswomenproject.org/2016/07/27/jeanne-baret/>

travel writers: Annemarie Schwarzenbach. But that's not what we're after. This is an example that has nothing to do with either strolling or scientific research, maybe not even with serious travel writing, but which was so famous at the time, followed with such great enthusiasm thanks to the encouragement of the mass media, that it inspired countless Western women to pack their bags and strike out on their own.

Perhaps the best proof of the success enjoyed by this particular adventure, upon which American journalist Nellie Bly embarked on 14 November 1889, setting out from New Jersey with the aim of circumnavigating the globe in seventy-five days, is the board game pictured here. It was manufactured in 1890, shortly after Nellie returned home. She arrived in New Jersey on 25 January 1890 to be met by an excitable crowd. Even on the way from San Francisco to New York, as she wrote in *Around the World in Seventy-Two Days*, her train had been accompanied by scores of people. Cries went up: 'Nellie Bly's train!', 'Did you ride on an elephant, Nellie?', 'Come out here and we'll elect you governor!', 'Nellie Bly, you must touch my hand! Now you will be successful. I have in my hand the left hind foot of a rabbit!'[1] and other such ridiculous things. This woman and her trip were an absolute sensation. People talked about her, wrote about her, bet on her success, and finally created a whole board game around her so that people could simulate her adventure at home. 'Round the World with Nellie Bly' is the title on the box and, inside, the game is laid out as a race: Nellie against Jules Verne, the legendary novelist. He – or, more precisely, his novel – had given the young woman the idea in the first place. Bly had already made a name for herself as an investigative journalist for the *New York World* when, in 1887, she'd had herself committed to a New York women's psychiatry ward for ten days, exposing the inhumane living conditions to which its patients were subjected in a report entitled 'Ten Days in a Mad-House'. After that, she had felt in need of a holiday, and came across Jules Verne and his recently published international bestseller, *Around the World in Eighty Days*.

Her boss was against it at first. Having yourself locked up in an asylum without ever knowing whether you'd make it out again was OK for a woman, but travelling around the world? No. That was men's business. Eventually, though, she did manage to persuade him, and a short

---

1   Bly, Nellie, *Around the World in Seventy-Two Days*, Kindle edition, 20 July 2020

while later she was off. Looking at this game, one thing that stands out immediately is her clothing: unlike Jeanne Baret, who had to dress as a man to explore the world, Bly embarked on her adventure as a lady. She wore a long dress she'd had specially made for her trip, along with a hat and small handbag, a get-up in which she vaguely resembled a female Sherlock Holmes. Her mission: to outdo Jules Verne's fantasy in reality. Indeed, the author's home was one of the very first stops she made. The Vernes picked Nellie up from the station in the morning, and by the afternoon they were standing in front of a large map discussing her route: from Calais to Brindisi, Port Said, Ismailia, Aden, Colombo, Penang, Singapore, Hong Kong, Yokohama, San Francisco and back to New York. Verne used a pencil to mark the points at which Bly would be departing from the route taken by his fictional protagonist, Phileas Fogg, then raised a glass to her 'strange undertaking' and waved her off with a 'Good luck, Nellie Bly!'

He didn't believe she would really do it, she wrote later in her book. But in fact she completed her circumnavigation of the globe even faster than expected, in just seventy-two days. The accounts she wrote of her adventure aren't especially brilliant; Bly was a great investigative journalist but no travel writer. She lacked empathy, perhaps even simple interest; she didn't want to dive into other cultures, was simply passing through. Nonetheless, the image captured on this board is unique: that of a woman who raced clean across the British Empire in 1890 to prove something to Jules Verne and the entire world. And, contrary to what Bougainville had prophesied in the eighteenth century, the people of the nineteenth understood one thing perfectly well: this game and Bly's adventurous spirit most certainly would be contagious to other women.

CINEMATOGRAPH

c. 1900

Until not so long ago, an unspoken rule applied in the world of cinema: a woman should be seen, and not the one seeing. For a very long time, the idea that a woman could stand not just in front of but also behind the camera – and not only in independent films either, but also big-budget productions – seems to most people to have been an extremely odd one. This despite the fact that the early days of this particular art had been dominated by none other than women.

Alice Guy was perhaps the first film director in history – the first person to create a fictional story for the camera. Back in 1890s Paris, Alice worked as a secretary for Léon Gaumont, who would later go on to found the Gaumont Film Company. When her boss took her to a presentation of the Lumière brothers' brand-new *cinématographe* one afternoon, and afterwards decided he too would start marketing cine-matographs (cameras like this one) the young woman had an idea. Why should this exciting new technology, this brilliant device, be used exclusively for filming boring things like people coming out of factories or trains pulling into stations? Why not invent a story – something funny – to advertise them better? 'Do what you like, as long as my correspondence doesn't suffer for it,' Gaumont told her. 'That actually is a matter for young women.' At the time, no one believed that this peculiar new technology would eventually become 'the cinema' and a multimillion-dollar industry. People found the little films they could make now very amusing, a nice gag but nothing more. Film was new and unimportant and thus, as is so often the case, perfect territory for women.

Guy's first short, the first ever work of fiction on film, was shot in 1896 and called *La Fée au Choux* (*The Cabbage Fairy*). It was made using a camera just like this one. The film showed a woman pulling babies out of plump heads of cabbage, laughing as she did. In France, you see, there's a saying: 'Little boys are born in cabbages, little girls in roses.' The whole thing was entertaining, charming and highly successful, which in turn handed Guy a promotion: from now on, she would be responsible for Gaumont's films. She filmed the short episodic pieces that laid the foundations for the Gaumont studios' enduring success; most of them comedies, most of them about women. In 1906, for example, there was *Madame's Cravings*, in which a heavily pregnant, extremely ravenous woman tears around the city, grabbing food and drinks out of people's hands while her husband runs helplessly after her with pram and baby. In the park, she takes away a little girl's lolly; she pinches a herring pretty much straight out of a beggar's mouth; and, in a restaurant, she steals a man's glass of absinthe. Guy filmed her in close-up after each theft, swallowing her stolen goods with relish and not the least amount of shame. It was probably that same year that she filmed *The Consequences of Feminism*, a cinematic representation of a fear that had haunted men since antiquity: that of the 'upside-down world' in which women called the shots and men were their subjects who did the cooking and cleaning. The director laughs at the way society divides up roles by gender; she shows men mincing coquettishly around in front of their mirrors, ironing shirts, or drinking tea and gossiping with their friends, while their wives sit about smoking and reading the papers. When the men try to go to the park to relax after doing all that housework, they're barely able to escape the pushy advances of the ladies there. It's delicious.

Alice didn't know it back then, but her film was something of an allegory for the early Hollywood that was soon to emerge. For as long as cinema was still considered an occupation for crackpots and misfits, and the area around Los Angeles wasn't a glamorous boulevard but dusty farmland, it was often women who directed men on film sets. Guy herself even trained one of the most famous of them. After emigrating to the USA in 1910 and founding her own studio in Fort Lee, New York, alongside all the other cinema greats, she allowed a certain Lois Weber to make some films. A couple of years later, Weber would become the best-paid female director of the silent-film era and one of the most powerful names in Hollywood. She was head of her own studio, producing, filming and taking care of the editing, wardrobe and casting, sometimes even acting herself. Let's quickly remind ourselves how anachronistic this was: at that time, women weren't allowed to vote or have their own bank account, couldn't get divorced and had only recently been allowed to start wearing trousers. But shooting films with cameras like this one, generating pictures, and thereby new worlds, was something they were permitted to do. Right into the 1930s, there were more female producers and directors in Hollywood than there were male. It was a golden era. But then came 'the talkies' and, with them, the really big bucks. And as soon as the gents realised that cinema was here to stay and films could make you rich, they took the positions occupied by women and transformed a Hollywood that had been free of hierarchy – one in which any man or woman could do any job – into a professional studio business.

And because it wasn't enough to somewhat rudely show women the door, these chaps decided to rewrite the history of cinema a bit as well. Pioneers like Alice Guy and the first stories shot on film no longer appeared in this version; instead, and for a long time to come, the legend of Hollywood would read as though the film industry had been invented and raised by men. In fact, by the 1950s, just one woman sat in Hollywood among all those male directors. Her name was Ida Lupino, and in 1950 she made what was probably the first ever film about the psychological and social consequences of rape: *Outrage*. Legend has it that during those years, conferences of the Academy of Motion Picture Arts and Sciences were opened with the following words: 'Gentlemen. And Miss Lupino.'

THE HATPIN

1900

In the year 1900, a terrible fear was circulating in European and American cities. Men walked the streets with trembling knees; on public transport, instead of sitting with their legs spread wide, as they do today, they cowered meekly in their seats and secretly prayed for one thing alone: that they might be spared an encounter with a woman wearing a large hat. Because while nowadays we might look at those *chapeaux* with their liberal sprinkling of feathers, bows and artificial flowers and see nothing but a very unbecoming trend – which lent the wearer all the allure of an agitated peacock – back then people saw something else in them, namely the concealment of a dangerous weapon. The hatpin.

This image of a terrified man might be something of an exaggeration, but it was one that really did do the rounds in the media at the time. People spoke of 'hatpin peril' and 'growing danger' in cities, and were afraid of 'violent assaults committed with woman's deadly weapon'. Caricatures depicted poor chaps skewered on gigantic pins and women armed with such weapons to hunt them. What was going on? Ever since increasing numbers of women had begun roaming the streets alone and unsupervised, men had clearly taken this new presence in 'their' sphere – the public space – as an invitation to accost any young woman who happened to be walking past or sitting next to them on the bus, to pester her with questions and penetrating glances, to follow her unsolicited, even to touch her.

The women of the late nineteenth and early twentieth centuries certainly didn't look on such assaults as a game of seduction, nor as a possible form of flirting, but as an intolerable affront. They were just beginning to make public spaces their own and had no intention of letting themselves be fondled like a piece of urban furniture. And, fortunately, the fashion of the time provided an unexpected ally. In those years, it was seen as the height of chic to make your hair dramatically bouffant, padding it out with false locks or even wadded-up fabric so that it formed an enormous tower or pancake-like structure on top of your head. Simply placing the obligatory hat on top of such an edifice was impossible; it needed to be fixed in place with a particularly robust pin – up to ten centimetres in length – that bored through all the layers of hair and, it soon turned out, didn't just serve a fashionable purpose. Alongside the extremely efficient umbrella, advice books for women commended this accessory as the best tool for self-defence. If a man wouldn't leave you in peace, you should either attack him with your hatpin or wallop him with your umbrella.

In 1903, Leoti Blaker, a young woman from Kansas, opted for the hatpin. On 28 May that year, she got on a crowded bus on Fifth Avenue in New York only to realise, by the time they'd gone a few stops, that the gentleman beside her was pressing ever closer. When the bus took a sharp corner and threw the passengers into one another, the man used the opportunity presented by this brief moment of chaos to run his hairy hand over Miss Blaker's back. 'If New York women will tolerate mashing, Kansas girls will not,' she said later by way of explanation for what happened next: instead of freezing in shock and simply allowing such behaviour, Miss Blaker drew an eight-centimetre pin from her hat and rammed it into the man's arm.[1] The story landed on the front page of Joseph Pulitzer's *New York World*.

That wasn't all – ever more women were making it into the newspapers with similar stories. Like eighteen-year-old bank clerk Elizabeth Foley, who was attacked along with a colleague on Bleecker Street one afternoon. Unlike her companion, she didn't let herself be instantly felled, but flew at their attacker armed with her hatpin and sent him packing. The *New York Times* reported: 'Quick wit, feminine courage, and a hatpin put to flight a bold, daylight highwayman at Bleecker Street and Broadway'. The *Los Angeles Herald* rightly opined that men who accosted women in this way – so-called 'mashers' – were simply cowards, as 'any woman with courage and a hatpin can prove'. For a brief moment, these ladies and their hatpins were the avengers of the urban world. They were heroines who didn't need to wait for Super-, Bat-, Spider- or any other kind of man, but reached for their own

---

1 'Stuck Hatpin Into A Masher', *The Evening World*, New York, 27 May 1903, p. 3

weapons. Even at the time, cases like these sparked a debate about the safety of women on the streets, asking how it could be improved. In Nebraska, a law was passed that made men liable to a fine if they catcalled a woman 'baby doll' or 'chicken' in public.

Strangely enough, the tide turned when the suffragettes took up the subject. Women with hatpins were no longer seen as bold and quick-witted, but dangerous. Now the news was constantly reporting how a woman had accidentally stabbed her husband with a hatpin; you'd hear of innocent men who'd had their faces scratched or even an eye put out on the bus; talk turned to blood poisoning and other such dramas. Beginning in the 1910s, New York, Paris, Hamburg and other metropolises brought in new rules for hatpins: they had to be shorter, and in some cases were even prohibited; they now required a kind of weapons licence, a special permit for particularly long specimens. In Sydney, sixty women were said to have been imprisoned purely for carrying unsanctioned hatpins. Suddenly it was no longer the safety of women at issue, but rather that of others – primarily men. Less than a decade later, the matter took care of itself with the emergence of a new trend: the 'flapper'. Instead of towering hairdos and peacock hats, women wore their hair short and uncovered. The hatpin had had its day. From then on, a lady's sole defence was her umbrella.

POSTER,
'CLAUDINE AT SCHOOL'

1900

Anyone walking around Paris in 1900, inspecting the displays in bookshop windows and the posters papering the still relatively new advertising columns, would no doubt have noticed one particular name appearing quite often: Claudine. This was the year of the Paris Exposition, the first Métro line and the pardoning of Alfred Dreyfus, but if you'd pricked up your ears during the entr'act at the opera and eavesdropped on the city's fashionable residents, you would likely have heard her name above all others: *Claudine this, Claudine that, have you read Claudine yet?* Depending on who was speaking, you might have heard that it was an absolute scandal, appalling, tasteless . . . or maybe it was charming, refreshing, funny, and just wonderfully *naughty*. If you'd asked a young woman, she'd have said Claudine was fantastic: a character in whom the young women of the day could recognise themselves.

Claudine and the novel of which she was the heroine, *Claudine at School*, were *the* sensation in France in those early years of the new century. You either loved or hated her; no one was ever indifferent. At least not if they wanted to join the conversation. And yet the story itself was pretty banal: a fifteen-year-old girl from the provinces recounting her final year at school, her everyday life between wide-open fields and narrow school-benches, her pranks, friendships, dreams and first flirtations. Nothing special, then. But she relayed all this in a manner such as had never been read before: in language that was fresh and free, that sounded as though this young girl were speaking directly to the reader, as though you really were in the company of this clever, impudent teenager. More than that, the book addressed topics that weren't discussed at the time, much less written about: a very young woman's sexual desires, which weren't necessarily directed at young men, but perhaps just as much towards women. It was exciting, thrilling – but also quite the scandal.

Straitlaced society was outraged: since when had young girls been interested in sex? Homosexual sex, to boot. And, above all: since when did they learn so much about it? Were the young women of this new century no longer naïve and passive? Was the end of the 'good girl' nigh? Paris seethed with outrage while secretly swooning over this brazenly modern character. Young women were especially enthusiastic: finally, someone had written down what they really thought and felt, had captured how confusing that stage between childhood and womanhood is. Finally, someone had told the world that girls, too, had sexual feelings and absolutely weren't strangers to desire. That they wanted things, and sometimes even dared to do them. But, most of all, that even young ladies had opinions and voices. In the space of just two months, an unbelievable 40,000 copies of the book were sold, and suddenly the streets, parks and squares of Paris were filled with 'Claudines' – young women who'd squeezed themselves back into their former schoolgirl look and now walked around wearing black dresses, long stockings and the characteristic white Peter Pan collar that to this day is known in France as a *col Claudine*, thanks to this novel. There were Claudine hats, Claudine face powder, Claudine cigarettes, Claudine perfume. The patisserie La Boétie even made a Claudine cake and Claudine ice cream.

Paris was in the grip of Claudine mania. Every woman wanted to be as cheeky and liberated as she was; Willy, whose name appears so prominently on this poster as the author, was roundly celebrated for his legendary coup. But there was always one unanswered question hanging in the air: how could Henry Gauthier-Villars, aka Willy, know so much about what a schoolgirl would be thinking and doing? The answer, of course, suggested itself immediately: from his wife, Sidonie-Gabrielle Colette, known simply as Colette. At that time, Colette was twenty-seven years old; she came from a small village in the Bourgogne and had landed in Paris after marrying Willy seven years before. *Claudine at School* – as well as *Claudine in Paris*, *Claudine Married* and *Claudine and Annie*, all published to just as much acclaim over the years that followed – must surely have been inspired by her unconventional childhood. Oh, come off it. They weren't just inspired by her. She was their author.

When he first read the manuscript of *Claudine at School*, Willy thought it rubbish, but – according to Colette – when he got it back out of the drawer a year later, he cried, *'Mon dieu!* I'm an idiot!' and ran straight to the nearest publisher. Of course, at that time the general rule that had forced the Brontës, George Eliot and George Sand to write under male pseudonyms was still in force – namely that a book sold better with a man's name on the cover. And so Claudine's adventures were published as Willy's work. What happened next only exemplified the impossible situation of women writers at the time: Willy didn't just garner fame as a result of this bestseller, but also pocketed all the cash. Even after their divorce, when it had long been established that Colette was the real author, the proceeds continued to go to him, until he finally sold the series rights. Colette herself never saw a penny, and it would still be several decades before her name appeared on the front cover.

Happily, she took her revenge in the decades that followed. No one knows what Willy did after *Claudine* – most people have probably never even heard of him – whereas Colette became an icon. She was worshipped: for the autonomous life she led, for her open bisexuality, for her many marriages and scandalous affairs, and for her work as a journalist, actress and later owner of a beauty salon. But, above all, for the almost fifty novels she wrote after *Claudine*, which made her a role model for a great number of women writers in the first half of the twentieth century. No one else is quoted in Simone de Beauvoir's *The Second Sex* as often as she is – twenty-two times, to be precise. She was, de Beauvoir said, the first person to describe in her novels all the different life stages of a woman, from teenager to mature lady, and to put into words all the feelings that accompany them. Some fifty-four years later, when Françoise Sagan described how it felt to be a young woman in the 1950s in her novel *Bonjour Tristesse*, she sent one of the very first copies to her role model, Colette. She wrote: 'For Madame Colette, in the hope that this book will bring you even one hundredth of the joy your books brought me. In homage, Françoise Sagan.'

WONDERFUL HAIR GROWER

1906

We all know that hair and female identity are closely linked; not for nothing has head-shaving been a popular punishment since time immemorial, a means of stripping a woman of her dignity. But this is especially true when it comes to African American women's hair. Their curls, Afros, cornrows and braids have been made a political issue. In the 1960s, activists like Angela Davis and her proudly worn Afro pointed the way towards shrugging off the norm of 'white' – straight – hair. In the 2010s, Solange Knowles, Beyoncé's sister, sang 'Don't Touch My Hair' in protest against the molesting urge to touch that evidently still overcomes many white people at the sight of Black hair. And in almost all US states, the CROWN Act now punishes 'race-based hair discrimination'. In fact, though, the significance of African American hair didn't just arise from its contrast to 'white' hair, but goes back very much further.

Long before slavery and the arrival of Western slave traders, hairstyles had great significance in West Africa. Wearing your hair braided, decorated with beads, feathers or other accessories, piled up in a kind of sculpture or simply loose about your shoulders was a form of calling card, a way of saying who you were, where you came from, which family or tribe you belonged to. For women especially, styling and taking care of their hair was a particularly important way of getting together with other women and building community. Hair was something to be proud of – until the Europeans came and determined that these allegedly 'wild' manes weren't beautiful, but rather an expression of 'inferiority' and 'animality'. Many slaves – male and female – had their heads shaved, the significance of hairstyles was gradually lost, and their harsh lives and terrible hygiene conditions were the final straw for most women's pates.

At that time, many African American women suffered from severe inflammation of the scalp and hair loss. There were no specially developed treatments for them; in the eyes of the beauty industry, hair like theirs – curly, 'wild', different – was an aberration that no one wanted to take on. Beauty was for white women only; the others would have to shift for themselves. Until Annie Malone decided to see to her sisters' neglected heads. To give her her due, it should be said that it was she who took the first step with her hair-growing product, but it was Madam C.J. Walker, whose bestselling 'Wonderful Hair Grower' is pictured here, who realised the same idea on a rather grander scale. Because – contrary to what the Netflix series *Self Made* might claim – Sarah Breedlove (alias Madam C.J. Walker) definitely did spend a while working for Malone. As a 'Poro agent', she went from door to door selling Malone's 'Hair Grower', until she decided to establish her own brand. With historic success, as we know. Madam C.J. Walker became the USA's first self-made millionaire; her 'Wonderful Hair Grower' was a major hit, a lifesaver for many African American women. The recipe for this miracle weapon is supposed to have appeared to Madam – whose face, incidentally, is pictured on the tin – in a dream. The voice that apparently dictated the mixture then gave Madam (who was clearly also an accomplished storyteller) an additional mission: to use her beauty empire to make the lives of African American women better, easier and more beautiful, and to give them a chance at independence and personal fulfilment. Yes, we could accuse Ms Walker of partly following the beauty standards that applied at the time. While the rumour that she invented straightening irons and thereby promoted straight hair isn't actually true, she probably wouldn't have been seen going around New York City with an Afro. But that's not the point.

For the first time, thanks to this little yellow tin, Black women who were interested in beauty weren't just able to hold in their hands a product created especially for them – for their hair and their bodies – but also had new career paths open up for them. Instead of slogging away as a domestic help, farm worker or nanny, all positions that came with absolutely no possibility of advancement, they could now embark on a career as a 'Madam C.J. Walker Hair Culture Agent'. In 1910, around 20,000 young women were on the road in the USA on behalf of Madam, almost all of them African American, many from modest circumstances. It was Madam C.J. Walker's principal concern to offer women new prospects and boost their self-confidence, not only by helping them to feel beautiful, but chiefly by setting an example of how success might be hard to win yet definitely not impossible. Before she died, she decreed that her company was to be run only by women in future. When her daughter A'Lelia eventually took over, she used the fortune her mother had amassed to support African American culture even beyond matters of hair and beauty: she became one of the most important patrons of the Harlem Renaissance, that thrilling artistic and literary movement of 1920s and '30s New York and Paris, which promoted pictures of African American life beyond cliché and heteronomy. A'Lelia's legendary Dark Tower salon was the meeting place for queer, African American, liberal Manhattan; the parties held there were, as the poet Langston Hughes once wrote, 'as crowded as the New York subway'. Their hostess was known as 'the Joy Goddess of Harlem's 1920s', a woman who – just like her mother before her – understood that a confident African American culture could never be entirely separated from the politics of hair.

RADIUM CHOCOLATE

UNDATED

'The most valuable gift the world has ever received must surely be the discovery of radium by Madame Curie in 1898.' So reads a 1930s advertising flyer for the house of Burkbraun, manufacturer of 'Burkbraun Radium Chocolate' and creator of the snappy slogan: 'Bathe in radium all year round with Burkbraun Radium Chocolate'.

The Cottbus-based company had several kinds of radium-laced chocolate in its collection: drinking chocolate, whole bars and little sweet snacks that didn't just promise to taste good (they were, after all, made from 'fully ripe' cocoa beans with the radium added in such a way that it wouldn't spoil the taste) but were also unbelievably healthy: 'The secret to its quick, sweeping effect lies in the fact that the radium contained in this dark chocolate passes immediately into the blood-stream, which allows it to reach all the organs, central nervous system, glands, nerves, even the very furthest capillaries and cells.' These days we'd be thinking: *Yikes!* But at that time, people thought it was great. Since the beginning of the twentieth century, pretty much everything had been getting laced with radium: face creams, toothpaste, lipstick, powder, shampoo. There were radium suppositories to boost your 'sex power', a 'Radio-Active Eye Applicator', radioactive glasses that supposedly treated headache and vision impairments; people were encouraged to drink radium water (the glasses and bottles specially made for this still occasionally light up the odd German rubbish tip) and thermal spas offered radium baths to cure rheumatism, joint pain and similar afflictions. Even companies that couldn't afford real radium – or thought people wouldn't really notice the difference anyway – would write 'radium' on their products to make them more attractive and in keeping with the zeitgeist: there were radium cigarettes, a 'Creamy Butter' made by the Radium Brand and, yes, even condoms (which didn't actually contain any radium but still featured the word on the packet to suggest potency). Radium was the number-one health and beauty trend, a little bit like chia seeds are nowadays, only much more exciting and widely applicable.

Equally new was the fact that the name associated with this supposedly cure-all elemental force was a female one: Marie. We're all familiar with the story: it was in 1897 that Marie Curie, formerly Maria Salomea Skłodowska, a Polish émigré to France, embarked on her research in a famously dilapidated laboratory on Rue Lhomond (according to the German chemist Wilhelm Ostwald, it was a 'cross between a stable and a potato cellar'). One year earlier, the French physicist Henri Becquerel had discovered that uranium emitted radiation; Curie wanted to study this further for her doctoral thesis and, in doing so, discovered more or less accidentally that pitchblende contained other elements even higher in radiation: polonium, which was named for her homeland of Poland, and, of course, radium. It was the beginning of a historic sea-change. In 1903, she became the first woman to receive a Nobel Prize, which was awarded jointly to her, her husband and research partner, Pierre, and the scientist Henri Becquerel for their research in the fields of physics. That said, France hadn't made a single mention of her name when it put forward its candidacy for the prize, simply listing Messieurs Henri Becquerel and Pierre Curie as the scientists who had made the discovery. Fortunately, the Swedes had a considerably more feminist attitude than their southern colleagues and insisted that this misogynistic error be corrected at once. And so, to her great cost, Marie Curie became the first female 'science superstar'.

When she gave her first lecture at the Sorbonne in 1906, shortly after the death of her husband, an excitable crowd stormed the auditorium. Politicians, countesses, professors – everyone wanted to be present for the occasion. When the 'woman dressed in mourning' finally appeared, the room applauded 'long and heartily', Le Figaro reported the next day. It was a sensation, a revolution. There had always been women in scientific research, of course – many of them, even, especially in those years – but only very few were officially recognised by institutions. They usually worked somewhere in the background, in some cupboard or other, were seldom celebrated in public and generally sank into immediate oblivion. That a woman like Marie should be teaching courses and heading up a university laboratory at the beginning of the century was more than a little unusual. Unfortunately, her prominent status would soon blow up in her face: people were happy to applaud the mourning widow – they thought her strong and admirable – but as soon as it came out that she'd had an affair (with a married man; one of Pierre's students, no less) everyone was outraged. Such a famous woman! Such immoral conduct! It went so far that in 1911, when she won a second Nobel Prize, this time on her own and in the field of chemistry, she was strongly encouraged please *not* to appear at the award ceremony. Too much scandal. Too much drama. If only they'd known, she'd never have been given the prize in the first place, a colleague wrote to her at the time, to which Marie responded drily that she was being recognised for her scientific work, not for her private life.

Perhaps the Burkbraun brand, which spoke so highly of Madame Curie in its chocolate adverts, simply didn't care what a female scientist got up to in her spare time. Or maybe they hadn't got wind of the whole kerfuffle. Just as they clearly hadn't heard about the 'Radium Girls' scandal, which rocked the USA in the 1920s and shook the popularity of this new element. The girls' story was cause for immense horror: after spending months, in some cases years, coating watchfaces – of the so-called Undark brand – with radioactive paint, using the tips of their tongues to moisten the brushes as advised, and sometimes even treating their fingernails to some of the pretty, luminous polish, several of them started to glow in the dark too. A short while later, they would die of anaemia, bone fractures and other symptoms of acute radiation poisoning. It was the beginning of the end for the radium mania triggered by Marie's discovery – and also, one would hope, for the short-lived but extraordinarily popular Burkbraun Radium Chocolate.

HUNGER STRIKE MEDAL

1912

On 13 November 1913, the British suffragette leader Emmeline Pankhurst stood up in front of several hundred American women in Hartford, Connecticut, and delivered one of the most famous speeches in the history of women's suffrage. 'Freedom or Death', as it came to be called later, took stock of the situation in England. They were in the midst of a civil war, the fifty-five-year-old declared; woman were so tired of waiting for change that there was only one choice left to them: freedom or death. They would be resolute in their pursuit of hunger strikes to force the British government into making a difficult decision: do we let these women die, or do we give in? Do we give them their freedom or become responsible for their deaths?

The hunger strike medal, which was awarded to Emmeline Pankhurst in 1912 for two months of detention and starvation and is nowadays displayed in the Museum of London, is testament to this battle tactic employed by the British suffragettes. On the front of the medal are the words 'Hunger Strike', on the reverse the name of the striker. Nearly a hundred women received just such a medal between 1909 and 1914, most of them presented at the breakfast reception that would follow their release from Holloway Prison. The award, which was designed by Pankhurst's daughter Sylvia along with the 'Holloway brooch' and other 'suffragette jewellery' (all in the suffragette colours of green, white and purple), is so significant because it underlines what Pankhurst said in the USA that day: these women weren't the kind to wave around placards and politely request their rights, but soldiers to be decorated with military honours. Unlike the suffragists – who had been campaigning for women's suffrage with Millicent Fawcett's National Union of Women's Suffrage Societies ever since the 1890s, and who employed pacifist tactics, like armbands and treatises – Pankhurst and her suffragettes were convinced that nothing would ever change without attention-grabbing stunts, vandalism and, if need be, violence. Or, as she so vividly put it in Connecticut: if two babies are starving, and one cries loudly while the other waits quietly, which of the two will the mother feed first? The Women's Social and Political Union, which Emmeline and her daughters Sylvia and Christabel Pankhurst had founded in 1903, advocated for 'deeds, not words'. The women organised unannounced protests, blockades and other action, like chaining themselves to the railings of public buildings.

When all this had no effect either, they turned to more drastic measures. They'd march in their hundreds along shopping streets and, on a signal, hurl stones to smash all the windows. They blew up post boxes and later houses, bombed public buildings, cut telegraph wires, and even used axes to attack paintings on display in museums. The press spoke of 'suffragette terrorism', the activists of a climate of fear that they were creating deliberately. They staked everything on being seen and heard. They knew that trials would offer them a platform, and that arrests – especially when they were violent – could be used effectively for publicity. Hunger strikes, too.

The first woman to come up with this idea wasn't Pankhurst herself, but a certain Marion Wallace Dunlop. In July 1909, she refused to eat for days because she'd been charged as a criminal rather than a political prisoner. When the prison doctor asked what she intended to live on, she answered promptly: 'My determination.' 'Indigestible stuff,' he answered, 'but tough, no doubt.' Three days later, she was released from prison. From then on, hunger strikes became the best ploy for getting out of Holloway fast.

Only, of course, it didn't last long. The state didn't want to make things that easy for them. Instead of letting the women go, they would forcibly feed them. It must have been absolute torture: the prisoner was tied to a chair while two doctors and several wardens held her down, her mouth was forced open with a steel gap and a plastic tube pushed down her throat, through which a mixture of milk and flour could be poured directly into her stomach. If her mouth was too sore and her gums bleeding, the tube would be pushed up her nose and on into her throat; she'd often vomit the liquid, but sometimes the concoction would get into her lungs. A few women lost teeth as they fought to protect themselves. It must have been horrendous. The general public, which the suffragettes quickly informed of these goings-on, were appalled by this brutal treatment of women. Doctors got up petitions against the abuse, while some parliamentarians even resigned. The argument against women's suffrage had often been that women didn't need the vote; after all, they had men to protect them. But what were people meant to make of this new development? Was this the protection women had been promised? Seriously? At some point, the outrage became so great that the government had to think of something else instead: the Prisoners (Temporary Discharge for Ill Health) Act 1913, which British women also dubbed the Cat and Mouse Act. Women were allowed to go on hunger strike, released and then rearrested as soon as they were halfway back on their feet. Like a cat that lets its quarry run free again for a moment, before it finally finishes it off.

The prime minister and his advisors no doubt believed they would eventually get women to stop insisting on their right to vote, but that only proved how little they knew about women, said Pankhurst in her Hartford speech: 'Women are very slow to rouse, but once they are aroused, once they are determined, nothing on earth and nothing in heaven will make women give way; it is impossible.'[1] She was right. Even if employing self-harm by hunger strike as a means of protest against your own powerlessness is just as questionable as the use of violence against others, it did work in the end: in 1918, property-owning women in Britain (over thirty) were given the right to vote. Eighty years later, *Time* magazine named Emmeline Pankhurst one of the hundred most influential people of the twentieth century, writing that she 'shook society into a new pattern from which there could be no going back'.

---

1 Pankhurst, Emmeline, 'Freedom or Death', in 'Great Speeches of the Twentieth Century', *Guardian*, 27 April 2007, available at: <https://www.theguardian.com/theguardian/2007/apr/27/greatspeeches1>

ATHENA STATUETTE BELONGING TO SIGMUND FREUD

1ˢᵀ OR 2ᴺᴰ CENTURY BC

It isn't unlikely that the man who once owned this bronze statuette would have ascribed to Emmeline Pankhurst and her hunger-striking suffragettes a case of acute anorexia nervosa. For Sigmund Freud, young women who refused food (as they had been doing in growing numbers since the nineteenth century) were in fact rejecting female sexuality, rather than nourishment. Their sexuality meant – according to him – a passive acceptance of the other; their rejection of food, therefore, was a reproach to their mothers, who had failed to give them a penis and so burdened them with a lack, an insatiable hunger. We probably don't need to add that most suffragettes weren't at all anorexic. They were rebelling, yes – but against the prevailing order rather than their missing phalli. They used their bodies because no other weapons were available to them; what they envied men was power, not penises.

If we look a little more closely at this small statuette of Athena, a roughly ten-centimetre-high Roman copy of a Greek original that dated back to the fifth century BC, it quickly becomes apparent that she too is lacking weapons: in her right hand she holds a libation bowl, her chest is covered by a Medusa head (apparently to repel male desire) and she wears a helmet on her own head. Her arm is raised in a belligerent gesture, but in the place where we might expect to find a spear, there's nothing but gaping emptiness. This statuette, one of almost 2,000 pieces in the collection of antiquities that Freud began frenetically assembling in the wake of his father's death in 1896, doesn't just point to Freud's theory of penis envy, but seems also to have played a very important role for the psychoanalyst. It stood permanently on the desk in his office at Berggasse 19 in Vienna, and when he and his family fled Austria in June 1938, this Athena was one of just two objects that his friend Marie Bonaparte, the French psychoanalyst, smuggled out of the country at his request. It has stood on his London desk ever since – it's there to this very day.

We know that, like so many of his generation, Freud harboured a particular passion for the Ancient World. The names of many of his diagnoses are borrowed from ancient myths, while he liked to refer to his work as a kind of archaeology of the self. But what is perhaps less well known is that he also employed figurines like this Athena, statuettes of Isis, Osiris and Sekhmet, clay statues of Artemis and other Greek and Roman gods, during his sessions with patients.

Perhaps we should make a small digression here and situate Freud in comparison to the aforementioned neurologist Charcot. Both were similarly influential in our understanding of the female psyche, but their approaches to this subject were very different. It's beyond all doubt that Freud admired his famous French colleague: he attended one of his 'presentations' in Paris and wrote to his fiancée Martha describing how impressed he was; later, an etching showing Charcot in full flow would hang above the divan in his London office. In that picture, Charcot can be seen standing in front of a group of colleagues, while his patient droops unconsciously in the arms of an assistant; a show has clearly just ended, the doctor having used this example to demonstrate whatever he wanted to. And therein lies the difference between Freud and the French doctor: while Charcot used his eyes to look at his patients as he categorised their contortions and quite possibly encouraged them to exaggerate somewhat, Freud used his ears. He listened to women and wrote down their stories. We could even say he made them the heroines of a new genre: Anna O., Emmy von N., Lucy R., Katharina, Elisabeth von R. and Dora are all protagonists of their own novels. They don't exist through pictures taken of them, but through the words and thoughts they shared with their doctor. The subject of psychoanalysis isn't the surface but what's hidden beneath, in the subconscious – or so Freud believed. The therapist (Freud himself) was fundamentally just the person who handed the patient a spade; the digging was something she had to do herself.

A spade, or maybe a statue of Athena. The most famous story involving this object was recorded by one of Freud's patients, the

American poet Hilda Doolittle (H.D.), in *Writing on the Wall*. It was spring 1933, and H.D. had gone to Vienna on the advice of her partner to have Freud treat her case of writer's block. One day, 'the Professor' invited her not to take a seat on his famous oriental-rug-strewn divan, but instead to come into his office, where he held out this figurine to her. 'This is my favourite. She's perfect, but she's lost her spear,' he said, and left his patient alone – and somewhat confused – with this information. He knew how interested H.D. was in Ancient Greece, but why was he showing her this figurine in particular? Did he want to see how she'd react to the symbolism of Athena, this vestal goddess of war and wisdom who had issued from the head of her father, Zeus? Did he want to unsettle her? Make reference to her bisexuality? Or maybe – the most likely option, she felt – to his aforementioned gender theory, in which women suffer penis envy because of their missing 'spears'? Regardless of how he meant it, H.D. was furious. As much as she respected Freud, she didn't think much at all of his penis envy theory. The way he looked on men as the sexual norm, and women as depressed, jealous aberrations, annoyed her – just as it would annoy many female students of Freud and early psychoanalysts in the decades that followed, and garner him a reputation among the feminists of the 1970s as an enemy of emancipation. Some were so outraged that they completely forgot that psychoanalysis had been the first medical field in which women hadn't just been listened to, but had also been able to enjoy equal careers right from the off.

Doolittle continued to attend her sessions with Freud and eventually rid herself of writer's block. She never forgot the Athena episode, however. In 'The Master', she wrote, 'I was angry with the old man / with his talk of the man-strength', concluding her poem with a correction of Freud's statement that the goddess was perfect 'but' missing her spear. 'Woman is perfect.' No buts.

FIRST WORLD WAR POSTCARD

1914-18

On 16 November 1917, a certain Karl Friede wrote to his girlfriend rather grumpily from the Front: 'Tell me, why do you only write me postcards these days? Have you got so much to do that you don't have time for a letter?' Karl clearly hadn't been informed that ever since men had marched off to war, bellowing loudly and sure of their victory, and were now engaged in blowing each other's faces off, it was women who had been holding together life at home and the country in general. His girlfriend probably did have rather a lot on.

It's often said that the First World War emancipated women by helping them into new positions. This story has been told so often that it now sounds as though emancipation began less with the way that women in Germany, England, France and America came together, long before the war – around sixty years before, in fact – to fight for their freedom in every way possible, and more with how men laid waste to the world and dragged women into this madness with them. Perhaps we should be asking ourselves why the story is so often told that way. Because even if it isn't entirely wrong, it isn't entirely right, either. It isn't true that the war forced women to work for the first time; apart from a few particularly well-heeled ladies of the bourgeoisie, there'd been no point in history at which they hadn't worked. Statistics show that even before the war, the number of women in employment had increased right across Europe and that the conflict did nothing to change this. What did change were the jobs open to them. They became postal workers, train drivers or bus drivers, or worked as part of the general mobilisation in munitions factories and the metal industry. It was the completion, if you like, of the transfer of work from one gender to another: what had previously counted as a male occupation could now be done by women; the war levered out the 'women can't do that' argument, albeit briefly. Before the war, there had only been a few postwomen like the one pictured here; as far as industry was concerned, most women were employed in the textile business, while in urban areas many of them worked in service. Whether this temporary switch to the armaments industry – in which they continued to work under male supervision – really improved their living conditions and self-image is questionable. Not least because salary-matching was reversed immediately after the war and women were sent back to their 'rightful' places: back to bad pay and to oppression that only increased after the conflict ended.

There was, however, one thing that perhaps really did undergo a fundamental change, and which had a far greater existential impact for women than simply slipping into men's shoes for a couple of years. Solitude. Suddenly, there was no one there to tell them who they were, what they could do, what they should or should not. The postcards that seem to have been fired off all over the place during those years of combat do, to some extent, stand as testament to this quietness, this lack of echo and the mirror that encouraged self-reflection. The longer the war lasted, the more of these patriotic cards were produced and posted in both Germany and France. In France, the pictures were often risqué; in Germany, as it says here, the woman remained 'loyally at her post' or sat on the sofa dreaming of her soldier: 'Only one who has known longing can understand my suffering.' Over four years of war, almost 18 million postcards were sent to the Front. It's often described as the first literate war, the first one in which most people – spanning all the social classes – were able to read and write. In a time in which you could bite the dust at any moment, it was important to share your thoughts. Women were urged to write to their loved ones – husband, boyfriend, brother – as often as they could, to offer moral support and spur them on. Just no 'whingey letters'! Newspaper articles reminded those left at home only to write with cheerful news. Most letters were correspondingly trivial, but some also said things the writer might never have dared say in person. It wasn't just Guillaume Apollinaire who wrote erotic letters to his Lou; other, less poetically inclined people tried their hand at it as well. Their longing was immense, their fear probably equally so, and they had very little to lose, which briefly enabled a style of communication in which dignity and hierarchy were thrown completely overboard. Some men cunningly took to writing two letters home: one inconsequential, for the whole family to read, and the other, the more intimate, for his wife alone.

That being said, writing letters and cards had had a particular impact on women ever since the eighteenth century: it was a way in which they could express themselves as people, as the subject, and hold their own thoughts up to the light. Indeed, after the war, many women reported how they'd got to know themselves during that period of solitude. Shortly after the Armistice, a French woman wrote to the agony-aunt pages of the magazine *La Femme de France*, 'I've discovered that I have a personality and interests'. She was afraid of how this 'I' would be received by her husband. She wasn't alone in her concern. Many a woman of that time wrote that she was looking forward to her husband's return but was also afraid of how he'd react to her new self-confidence. It's just conjecture, but wouldn't it be possible to imagine that this comprehensive correspondence, this writing, also contributed – along with their jobs – to the new self-awareness felt by many women? The lady in that French magazine was, sadly, right to be concerned; many of the men who returned from the war weren't at all happy with the transformation they saw in their wives. Worse: they were scared of it. The return of many a hero was tempestuous, noted French writer Clara Malraux. It seems to have been worst in Germany, where women weren't just sent back home but also held jointly responsible for the country's defeat. It was said they'd ruined the German soldiers' morale. How? Why, by post, of course – by writing their 'whingey letters'.

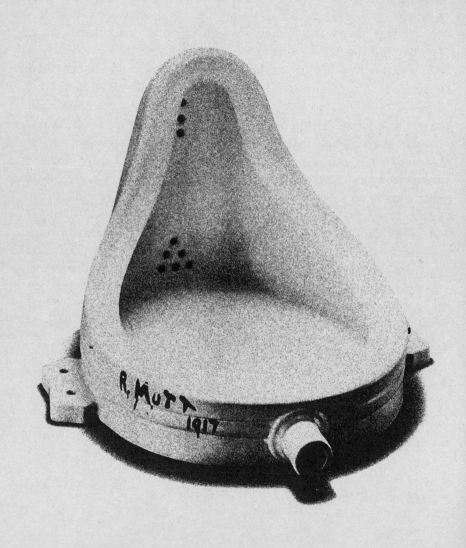

THE FOUNTAIN

1917

In March 2019, the American novelist Siri Hustvedt wrote an article in the *Guardian* under the promising title: 'A woman in the men's room'. In it, she explained rather indignantly that this object here, the so-called 'Fountain', one of the most famous works in the history of art, wasn't made, as had previously been thought, by Marcel Duchamp, but instead by a certain Baroness Elsa von Freytag-Loringhoven: 'Why is it hard for people to accept the intellectual and creative authority of artists and writers who are women? [. . .] Paintings, novels and philosophy made by men feel more elevated somehow, more serious, while works by women feel flimsier and more emotional [. . .] But what if the person behind the urinal was not Duchamp, but the German-born poet and artist Baroness Elsa von Freytag-Loringhoven (1874–1927)?'[1]

To quickly recap this legendary episode of art history: it was the year 1917, Europe was still at war, and in New York a group of artists calling themselves the American Society of Independent Artists had dreamed up a new salon with a new set of rules. Unlike the classic European salons, which were subject to strict specifications and narrow-minded notions of what constituted good art, the idea was to exhibit every work submitted, freely and uncensored. But then this piece here showed up: a urinal entitled 'Fountain', signed with the cryptic name 'R. Mutt'. At that time – long before tins of soup, artists' faeces and 'fat corners' – the idea of putting a ceramic urinal, the kind that could have been bought in any old shop, on display as a work of art was more than audacious. It was a way of laughing at art, at its creators and

---

1   Siri Hustvedt, 'A woman in the men's room', the *Guardian*, 29 March 2019, available at: <https://www.theguardian.com/books/2019/mar/29/marcel-duchamp-fountain-women-art-history>

viewers; of making them out to be idiots. A ready-made object couldn't be a work of art, decided the jury (which originally, of course, had wanted to be no such thing), and the piece was not exhibited. Scandal! Outrage! Suddenly the whole of New York was no longer talking about the art on display in the 'Big Show', but about the one piece that was missing. And that was this *pissoir*, whose 'original' version probably ended up in the bin – something that wasn't too terrible, seeing as the discussion it sparked was actually far more important than the object itself. What is art? Is it enough for someone to claim something is art? What even constitutes an artist, then, if they don't actually have to have any talent, but can simply go out and buy an object? It was a break with all the rules that had applied until that point. In 2004, 'Fountain' was voted the most influential work of the twentieth century: without this *pissoir*, we'd have had neither pop art nor conceptual art; our galleries and the works that stand or hang in them would look very different. After this work, nothing was ever the same again. After it and its alleged creator: Marcel Duchamp.

Duchamp, or Elsa von Freytag-Loringhoven? Hustvedt finds evidence for this claim – which has been put forward before – in a biography of the baroness: in a letter to his sister Suzanne, Duchamp wrote, 'One of my female friends, who had adopted the masculine pseudonym Richard Mutt, sent me a porcelain urinal as a sculpture.' There's a further clue in the fact that the shop in which Duchamp claimed (many years later) to have bought the thing never actually sold urinals like this. The inscription 'R. Mutt 1917' is also thought to look like Freytag-Loringhoven's handwriting, all the more so given the fact that she'd already been responsible for a 'readymade' work of art: a water pipe she titled 'God'. But back then, Duchamp had just 'invented' his 'Bottle Rack', so this argument isn't entirely convincing either – and, a century later, it's impossible to say who had the idea, who bought and signed the pissoir, and who ultimately sent it in. Perhaps it was the baroness. Perhaps it was Duchamp. Perhaps she'd gifted it to him and he then submitted it. Perhaps her work had inspired him. But perhaps one day someone said, 'Hey, Duchamp, you're that R. Mutt, aren't you?' and he just didn't say no. We'll probably never know for certain, and perhaps it doesn't matter anyway – the work exists, its influence too, so what does it change whether a man or a woman made it? Nothing, and yet an awful lot.

For a start, we could ask ourselves whether people would have talked about it quite so much if they'd thought a woman had made it. Might people not have laughed about it more? Might they not have said: look here, women clearly aren't made for art, they're capable of going shopping but can't produce anything themselves? For another, wouldn't it be great to know how art history might have been written if we'd thought the most 'influential' work of the new era had been made by a woman? In that case, mightn't names like Unica Zürn, Jacqueline Lamba, Leonora Carrington, Leonor Fini, Lee Miller, Dora Maar, Frida Kahlo and all the others perhaps have been recognised and well known sooner? Might they have got the same amount of exhibition space and airtime as artists like Max Ernst, Man Ray, André Breton, Hans Bellmer, Picasso and co.? It took more than half a century before the women of the avant-garde were even half recognised – recognised in the sense of being artists, not muses. And even if the case of Duchamp vs Freytag-Loringhoven doesn't seem solvable, there are enough other examples out there of women's work being ascribed to men. The Villa E-1027 in Roquebrune-Cap-Martin, for example. For decades, it was said that this beautiful house on the French Riviera had been designed by Le Corbusier. But then, at some point, it was discovered *en passant* that it was actually the work of Irish designer and architect Eileen Grey. The original assumption had been made because Le Corbusier, once a friend of Grey's, had marked the house like a dog would – artistically pissed on it, in other words: when she was out one day, he painted one of his frescoes on a wall without asking, thereby licensing himself to mess with her work, ruining the idea of a luminous white apparition above the sea, and not entirely unintentionally stealing authorship of the house for himself. As such, on the one hand it doesn't matter who bought that urinal, inscribed and submitted it – but, on the other hand, Hustvedt is right about one thing: we need to rewrite the history of art and women's place within it.

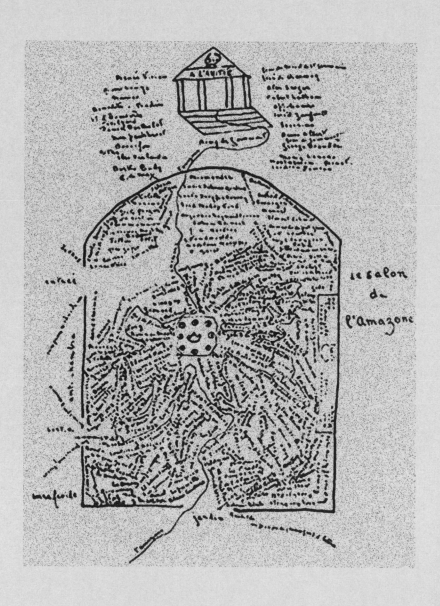

PLAN OF THE 'TEMPLE DE L'AMITIÉ', SALON OF THE AMAZON

POST-1910

Any time a war breaks out somewhere because some man or other thinks he needs to expand his zone of power, we find ourselves asking whether the world might not be better if more women were in charge than men. During the Second World War, the American novelist Charlotte Perkins Gilman was asking herself the same question, and she answered it with a novel. *Herland* is a wholly female utopia, an isolated valley in which women live by themselves, reproduce by themselves and know nothing of men, their values or the consequences of those values – thirst for power, war and oppression. The novel reads like a description of the original paradise of Wonder Woman, and speaks to a tendency of which many men have been scared since time began – and certainly since the war – and which was now becoming reality, at least in certain circles. Women no longer needed them. Not even for love.

We've already seen that from the eighteenth century onwards, (amorous) female friendships were given more space and that some, like the wonderful Ladies of Llangollen, chose to live together as a couple. In the USA, this was known as a 'Boston marriage'; in the late nineteenth century, increasing numbers of women, especially those with a university degree, were opting for this form of cohabitation. The majority of them never married but preferred to live with a female comrade. And they did this without anyone bothering about it. Not because people were so open back then, but because it didn't occur to anyone that these women probably weren't just reading and cooking together, but were also having sex. Female homosexuality was ignored for an astonishingly long time. Even when the field of sexology emerged in the mid-nineteenth century, there was interest in male homosexuality but not really in female – perhaps in part because people believed the female sex drive barely existed anyway. Why should ladies do it with each other if they didn't even want to do it with men? That just didn't make sense. It took until the end of the nineteenth century for female homosexuality to be named as such, to be studied and categorised but then, sadly, also pathologised, seen as an unhealthy divergence from the norm. On the positive side, this had the effect that many homosexual women recognised that they weren't alone and, especially in the bigger cities, especially in Paris, formed a lively lesbian subculture that only grew with the advent of the *garçonne*.

This 'visitor's floor plan' tells of that new culture and one of its most important sites: the grand and legendary lesbian salon, the Temple de l'Amitié on Rue Jacob in Saint Germain des Prés. The plan was drawn up by the salon's hostess, a certain Natalie Clifford Barney, one of the many American women striving for emancipation who lived on the Left Bank in Paris and made for much fun and furore. Djuna Barnes was a member of this group, as was Gertrude Stein, of course, plus Louise Brooks, Mina Loy and Sylvia Beach, whose bookshop Shakespeare and Company provided an intellectual home for the Lost Generation. Then there was Janet Flanner, who wrote for *The New Yorker* about all the goings-on in Paris, all the gossip and politics – pretty much anything interesting or amusing. With the help of a good magnifying glass, it's possible to find the names of all these women – who were lesbian, bisexual or simply open to anything – on this unusual map, drawn long ago by Barney's friend André Rouveyre. All were visitors to Mademoiselle Barney, the self-proclaimed 'L'Amazone'. It must have been the most wonderful bedlam, much wilder than it ever got at Gertrude Stein's on Rue de Fleurus. And this despite the fact that Natalie received her visitors in the bright light of day, always on Friday afternoons. They either gathered indoors, as indicated by the placement of the names on this sketch, or in the garden in front of the little temple – the Temple of Friendship – that still stands there today. In the middle of the room was the tea, with cucumber and roast beef sandwiches to either side, and cakes that were so good the guests wrote about them in their memoirs: meringues, éclairs, vanilla-and-chocolate cake, candied strawberries and cheese. To drink there was champagne, hot chocolate, cocktails, whisky, gin and punch.

For some unknown reason, the hostess has drawn her slow progress through the crowd: first pushing past Gertrude Stein, Alice B. Toklas and the Swiss novelist Blaise Cendrars near the entrance, then making her way over to Fitzgerald and Zelda, Isadora Duncan (who liked to perform impromptu dances that often ended with her naked), fast-driving Tamara de Lempicka, Rilke, our suffragette friend Emmeline Pankhurst, painters like Marie Laurencin, Colette – naturally – and Barney's lover at the time, the poet Renée Vivien. Sometimes she'd run into Peggy Guggenheim, Nancy Cunard or Somerset Maugham. Once, during the war, Mata Hari is said to have paraded naked through the courtyard on a white horse, though this does sound more like a legend than anything else. The discussion ran to politics, art, love, and, of course, Sappho. In order to give women the place they deserved in cultural life, Barney and her friends went on to establish the 'Women's Academy' (L'Académie des Femmes), a kind of counterpart to what was then the still entirely male Académie Française.

The focus of the salon was always on women but, unlike in Herland, men were very welcome – this hostess believed that men could do with getting to know these new women and their chic, alternative life-style a little bit better, instead of persisting in their clichéd notions. Even Marcel Proust is said to have attended once, hoping to find inspiration for Sodom and Gomorrah. Barney told him about her style of living and loving, only the writer evidently didn't really listen or look around him. In the end, he described his lesbian characters the way he preferred to imagine them. Not like the real-life women who had stood before him in the Salon de l'Amitié.

100 MPH COAT

1920

After the horrors of the war, when ten million soldiers had fallen and several hundred thousand had returned home wounded, it was high time people started living again. Hard as society might have tried to send women back to where they'd been fetched from in 1914 – subservience, in other words – it encountered resistance from the young, city-dwelling generation in particular. Thanks to the war's high death toll, many of these women would never find a husband anyway, and the city offered them new opportunities to earn their own living: as stenographers, switchboard operators, as sales assistants in the booming department stores. Why, then, force yourself into an outdated role? Hadn't women only just cast off their corsets? Why give up freedom for supposed security, which, as everyone now knew, could anyway be bombed to bits at any moment? They felt an urge to escape the stasis of family life, to dance, love, celebrate, to lose themselves in the rapture of the night. To live, then. Full throttle.

This pretty coat, which was designed in 1923 by Dornac, the Parisian fashion house on Rue de la Paix, embodies this new attitude to life *à la perfection*. It's short, shorter than coats had previously been, and – according to the standards of the time – unfeminine, well-nigh androgynous in its cut and boasting wide, baggy sleeves. The rough fabric and high collar tell us it's no coat for sitting around on the terrace waiting for something, but a coat for moving in – outdoors, maybe even out of town. Above all, though, it has a wonderful name: the *manteau 100 à l'heure*, or '100 mph coat', which points to a new *passe temps* for ladies. For the first time, it wasn't just the odd woman, but many of them who had started driving. They'd left their bicycles – along with their long braids, long skirts and subservient manners – back in the early 1900s. Now, they were modern. And what modernity meant was:

short hair, funny hats, androgynous tailoring, red lipstick, a cigarette in the corner of your mouth and, above all, speed, speed, speed.

In Scotland, Dorothée Pullinger had joined her car-building father in the family business after proving herself during the war, and, in 1921, as one of the first ever female engineers, she designed the very first car for women: the Galloway motor car. It combined some of her father's designs with the shape of the Fiat 501; a magazine described this latest model to join the brand (which, under Dorothée's management, now shared the same colours as the suffragettes: green, purple and white) as 'a car built by ladies, for those of their own sex'. Just like most things back then – and not a few today – cars were not generally designed for women's bodies. In early models, female drivers often couldn't reach either the steering wheel or pedals, or at least not both at the same time. But all that was at an end now. From now on, driving was women's prerogative too – or, as Françoise Sagan would say some fifty years later: 'I'd rather cry in a Jaguar than on a bus.'

Eileen Grey would probably have said something similar. In the 1920s, she famously – and scandalously – rattled around Saint Germain des Prés with her lover's panther in the back seat of her convertible, leaving in her wake much oohing and aahing, much staring and shaking of heads. Especially on the part of the gentlemen, to whom women's new love for cars didn't make any sense whatsoever. Maybe the rumour that women are too stupid to drive stems from this time; at least, the Berlin-based journalist Ruth Landshoff-Yorck reported in an article entitled 'The Girl with Low Horsepower' that a man would often look a proper Charlie when a woman sped past him in her car. Best to leave them with their illusions and act at least a little bit helpless, then they'd all motor gallantly to the rescue and you could race off hell for leather down your allée of men, with much whooping and shouting. This was how she described it in her column for Die Dame magazine, concluding: 'A feminine car needs to look as appetising as a baby.' Speaking of Die Dame, an iconic image of the 'new woman', one showing just such a coat as this, was painted for this very magazine: the famous Tamara in a Green Bugatti by Polish painter Tamara de Lempicka, also known as Autoportrait. The story goes that one of the magazine's editors complimented Tamara on looking so cool sitting in her car that she should definitely paint herself in it for the front cover. Lempicka clearly thought the idea was a great one, her car not so much, so she painted herself not in her yellow Renault but in a green Bugatti. We can only see a section of it in the picture, as though she's speeding past too quickly to be captured, but at her neck is the collar of a coat similar to this one. The eyes looking out of the picture are challenging and self-confident, and to this day her painting is emblematic of the 1920s woman: sitting at the wheel of her own life. Until that point, it was something only a man could have done.

A man? No, a *garçon*. The 'new woman' was young. Not for nothing were the many women now to be found strolling arm in arm down the boulevards by day, or dancing the Charleston through the clubs of Paris by night, given a new moniker by the French novelist Victor Margueritte: *garçonnes*. When he wrote his novel *La garçonne* (*The Bachelor Girl*) in 1922, he christened this new generation of women and also caused a national scandal. His National Order of the Legion of Honour was removed, and he was accused of sullying French women with his portrayal. Even feminists were outraged, judging him to have painted the emancipated woman as a sex-obsessed junkie (unlike their English and German counterparts, French women still didn't have the vote and were thus concerned about their reputation). Indeed, the novel is more amusing than excellent, but that hardly matters. Its title and the attitude to life it conveyed were exactly on point; after all, the new woman didn't just want to behave like a *garçon*, she wanted to look like one too. Josephine Baker, who drove a Delage D6, once said that when she arrived in Paris, women suddenly lost weight, cut their hair short and sped off in their chic new rides – cruising fast in their 100 mph coats.

CHANEL NO. 5

1921

The *garçonnes* might be free, might dance, smoke and drive around in cars, they might be entertaining, but, *mon dieu*, they stink! This – or something like it – is what the novelist Colette once said. As is sadly often the case with such things, this revolutionary of old didn't rub along too well with those who came after her. She, the woman whose books had encouraged the girls of twenty years before to dare to live as they pleased, had trouble dealing with the young women who were now doing exactly that. And yet her rather disdainful comment will have held a kernel of truth. While the O'Dorono brand introduced the first modern deodorants to the US market in 1919, it took until the Second World War for these small pink and blue bottles to reach Europe as well. Fortunately for Colette and the stinking *garçonnes*, at around the same time – in 1921 – a product was being developed in France that, while not a deodorant, was about to explode every code of fragrance. It was the perfume known as Chanel No. 5 – or, as people sometimes rather pompously put it, 'the scent of the century'.

In the past, perfume was a rather tricky affair. It's difficult for us to imagine just what kinds of fumes our ancestors lived with, which ones disgusted them and which ones they liked. Napoleon, for example, wrote to Josephine in 1800 after his victory at the Battle of Marengo: 'Home in three days. Don't bathe!' In the 1920s, however, people didn't think it quite so sexy if a woman didn't wash herself for days. People wore perfume, but the notes were quite different to the ones we find in perfumes today: most were one-dimensional and simply reproduced the scent of a flower. You could smell like a rose or like jasmine, like gardenia or lily of the-valley. Until one woman decided to change the perfume customs of France and, soon after, the world at large: Mademoiselle Coco Chanel. Back then, apparently, almost ten years after opening her first shop on Rue Cambon in Paris, and six years before the 'little black dress', she wanted a perfume that would make her 'smell like a woman, not a rose'. To her mind, this meant that it needed to smell more complex than a simple rose, in keeping with the new woman, who no longer just had a sweet smile on her face; but also that it needed to smell 'like freshly scrubbed skin'.

There are many legends about the creation of this perfume. One of them has Coco cruising around the south of France with her then lover, Grand Duke Dmitri Pavlovich of Russia, in the late summer of 1920, and ending up one afternoon in the laboratory of (also Russian) perfumer Ernest Beaux. Beaux had worked as a nose for Rallet & Co., former perfumer to the tsars, and, after the Russian Revolution, had been bought up along with the perfume house by a French fragrance manufacturer in Grasse. In 1913, still in the employ of the Russian empire, he had created 'Bouquet de l'Impératrice Catherine II', also known as Rallet No. 2, to mark the 300th anniversary of the Romanov dynasty. It's said that Chanel No. 5 is a variation on this, a rip-off, if you will, of his fragrant homage to Catherine the Great. Ernest Beaux, some say, had been trying to adapt 'Bouquet de l'Impératrice' to suit the French nose, and had developed ten different formulations. Mademoiselle picked the fifth one, which is how the perfume got its name. Or, as Beaux described it: 'Mademoiselle Chanel, who had a flourishing fashion house, asked me to create a perfume for her. I showed her a series containing numbers 1 to 5 and 20 to 24. She selected a few, including No. 5. "What shall we call this scent?" I asked her. Mademoiselle Chanel answered: "I will be presenting the collection on the fifth day of the fifth month, in May. So we'll leave this perfume with the number it already has. Five is its lucky number." I must admit, she was not mistaken.'

No, she really wasn't. In France, it's popularly claimed that a bottle of Chanel No. 5 is sold somewhere in the world every thirty seconds. And even if that's almost certainly exaggerated, the perfume was a hit from the word go. With its unusual blend of rose, ylang-ylang, sandalwood, jasmine and – very new and important! – aldehydes, it transformed the olfactory world of an entire century. Chanel No. 5 was a fragrant paradigmatic shift, after which nothing would ever be the same again: the 'spirit of the modern woman' was expressed in this perfume, as Vogue put it in October 1923. Especially seeing as it wasn't just the perfume that was special, but also its packaging. Instead of flowery tendrils and curlicues, instead of sweet-looking women's faces and lyrical names, here came a perfume that seemed just as mad about technology as the era in which it was created. In its angular glass bottle, it looked as though it had come straight from the laboratory, while 'No. 5' made it sound like a scientific experiment. It looked simultaneously both warm and cool, just like the modern woman herself. It's said that after liberating Paris, the American GIs fell straight on Rue Cambon to get their hands on the scent of freedom – apparently Coco Chanel was all too happy to present them with bottles of the fragrance, because she feared being judged as a collaborator. To this day, the most famous American to wear Chanel has been Marilyn Monroe, who, when asked by *Life* magazine in 1952 what she wore to bed, answered simply: 'Chanel No. 5.'

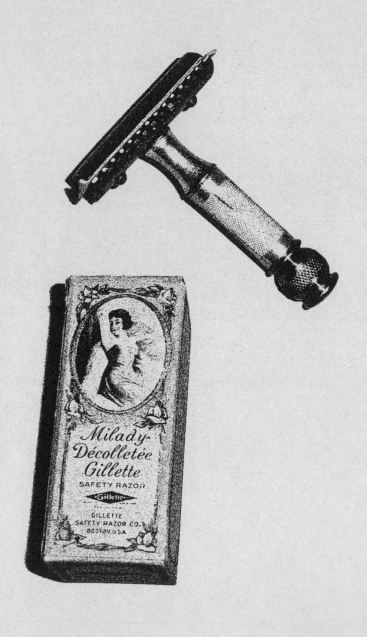

MILADY DÉCOLLETÉE GILLETTE

1920s

When *Notting Hill* hit the British cinemas in April 1999, probably no one imagined that this wonderfully schmaltzy rom-com would one day be associated with feminism. In the film, Julia Roberts professes to be a girl standing in front of a boy, asking to be loved, and even if she does play the star and Hugh Grant just a bumbling bookshop owner, it's not exactly a movie that screams emancipation. Until a couple of photos from the premiere in London were dug out of a drawer somewhere a few years ago, and Julia Roberts suddenly found herself stylised as a warrior in the fight against conventional beauty norms. Because that evening, something completely unexpected happened: when Roberts stood in front of the cinema in her sequinned red dress and waved at her fans, what we glimpsed under her arms wasn't smooth white skin but – horror of horrors – chestnut-brown hair. Today, with one in four women under twenty-five not shaving their armpits and suggesting 'Hairy January' challenges on Instagram, Roberts's 1990 underarm look is something of a statement. A challenge to the patriarchy. But, apparently, it wasn't meant that way. A little while ago, during a talk show appearance, Roberts explained that she'd simply miscalculated the length of her sleeves and hadn't banked on everything being visible.

In fact, underarm shaving for women did originate simply with a new length of sleeve. Well into the twentieth century – into the 1920s, to be more precise – hardly any garments allowed female armpits to be exposed outside the bedroom. The shortest version of sleeves covered at least a third of the upper arm, so never afforded anyone a glimpse of an armpit. No matter how often you waved at your fans, no one would see anything. It was only with the new fashion belonging to the new woman, the loose flapper dresses designed by Coco Chanel and Jeanne Lanvin – which didn't just bare legs and backs but also

271

arms, shoulders and, by extension, armpits – that the question arose: what are we going to do with this hair, then? Can we show it, or is it too intimate? It would be visible when doing the Charleston, playing tennis, swimming, driving . . . all these new hobbies that women suddenly had and which required movement and width; generous, sweeping gestures instead of restrictive sleeves. Seen like this, shaving was a side effect of fashionable emancipation, but also of the new ideal of beauty. At that time, the aim was to look more like a boy than a woman, like a creature who hadn't yet hit puberty. No breasts, no bottom and so, of course, no armpit hair.

The beauty industry and powerful fashion magazines of the time used what was in itself a short-lived trend to create a new norm and sell products. By the early 1920s at the latest, magazines like *Harper's Bazaar* were full of adverts addressing the 'problem' of underarm hair and presenting the solution: a shaving device developed specially for women, Gillette's Milady Décolletée safety razor. It served the 'modern woman' who wanted to be 'at her best', and would save her from awkward situations: 'Milady Décolleté Gillette is welcomed by women everywhere – now that a feature of good dressing and good grooming is to keep the underarm white and smooth,' read an early advert from 1917.[1] The razor was the perfect gift for the modern woman, a must-have for any lady who wanted to keep up with the times. Gillette was the best-known brand in the razor business. Around 1900, it had developed the 'safety razor' for men and supplied the American military during the First World War. The first women to shave used to borrow their husbands' razors, until the company got wind of this and conquered the market for women's razors with this chic specimen, specially made for 'Milady'. But they had to sell it, too. Not just to the handful of *garçonnes* who waved their arms in the air at 'dancings' and were soon to vanish, but to all women everywhere. And so they created pressure: from then on, the ad sections of women's magazines continually repeated how 'embarrassing' it would be if someone were to see even a single hair. The word 'embarrassing' was used conspicuously often – so often that shaving under your arms became essential, quite independent of fashion and sleeve length.

---

1   Available at: <https://commons.wikimedia.org/wiki/File:Vintage_Advert_for_the_Milady_Decollete_Gillette_Razor_-_1916_(5248628800).jpg>

And, soon after, shaving your legs did, too – a custom that estab-lished itself during the Second World War. As it was almost impossible to find silk stockings and women had to run around with bare legs, Remington made the best of the situation to see off leg hair with a special razor. In the 1950s, parallel to the invention of the bikini, there was a gradual movement towards intimate shaving, which exploded during the '80s and '90s. The basic idea was always the same: smooth, white skin comes across as clean and sexy, and therefore attractive; having hair anywhere on your body except your head is repulsive. And, loosely based on the 1920s ideal: a woman is sexy if she doesn't look like a woman, but like a little girl. In the 1960s, 98 per cent of American women aged between fifteen and forty-five reported shaving, regard-less of current trends.

Not much has changed about this 'norm' invented by the market almost a hundred years ago. When the feminist activist Gloria Steinem advocated for the 'liberated leg' in the early 1970s and declared war on the 'hairless ideal' of our culture, women only followed her for a year or two. By 1974, the New York Times was already reporting that young women were 'Back to shaving legs'. Nowadays, the same outlets carry essays with titles like 'It's Just Hair', encouraging us to celebrate our natural beauty and see our bodies as the 'wonders' that they are, 'hair and all'. Just like the accidental heroine Julia Roberts.

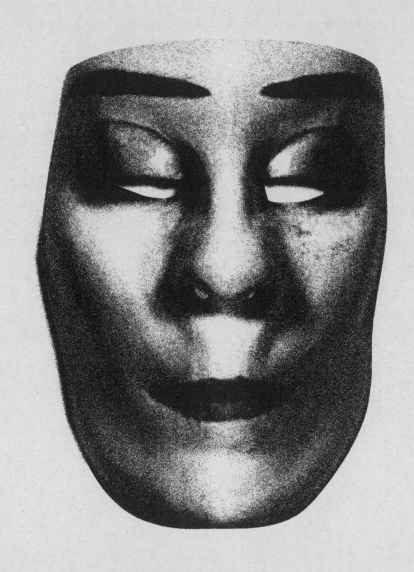

'WITCH DANCE' MASK

c. 1926

A masked figure dressed in loose clothing sits on a stage and moves to the sound of a gong. With its knees drawn up, it huddles slightly, like an animal lying in wait. It throws its arms in the air to the rhythm of the gong, one arm up, one arm down, by turns. Up, down, up, down. Almost as if it were climbing. It tenses its fingers into claws and vibrates to the rhythm of the sound waves, bending forward and slowly pushing apart its knees, as though to reveal a secret. It curls in over its spread legs, then slides clumsily on its backside to the front of the stage, where it starts turning on the spot. Faster and faster, wilder and wilder. Until it suddenly halts and, with trembling hands, casts something out into the audience.

This performance, which can be seen on YouTube in a film clip from the 1930s, goes by the title 'Witch Dance', and the figure hiding behind the mask is a woman: Mary Wigman, choreographer of this legendary show. When the German dancer performed her unusual piece for the first time in the 1910s, Suzanne Perrottet, her friend and fellow member of the Monte Verità commune, said that Mary looked ghastly that evening and, with her rough movements and terrifying mask, had stood in total contrast to the ideal image of a dancer and the rules of ballet. Indeed, ever since the advent of pointe work in the nineteenth century, and prima ballerinas à la Marie Taglioni, it had been ballet that decreed a woman should be beautiful, light-footed and delicate. A 'sylphide', then. She ought to be a passive creature, spun around mid-air by male dancers – themselves now degraded to mere lifting machines – feather-light, child-like. She might touch the floor with the tips of her toes at most. Wigman, on the other hand, crouched there like a sack of potatoes, heavy and ungraceful. She trampled, made noises, spread her legs without shame, didn't come across as pure but seemed possessed by wild desire, sexual, almost animal. Not at all like a beautifully dying swan, but something alive and challenging. The mask, which she had probably copied from her friend Emil Nolde's paintings, and which had been made for her by the artist Victor Magito, was all part of the concept. It was supposed to enable her to let go completely, to set herself free and reach the kind of ecstatic realm associated with rituals. 'No dancing without ecstasy!' was Wigman's motto. And, at some point, people grew to love her for it: when she performed at New York's Carnegie Hall in 1932, this proponent of New German Dance reportedly 'charmed' the auditorium. Back in the 1910s, however, they weren't quite ready for her. The audience hated it – or, as Mary Wigman herself recalled years later: 'People said, "This woman belongs in a mad house, not on stage!"'

But of course. A woman who didn't behave, look or move the way she was expected to, who wasn't sweet but set more store by express-ing herself than being beautiful, had always been regarded as crazy or a witch, or both. In the sixteenth century, women who danced wildly and pulled faces were burned at the stake as the devil's mistresses; in the nineteenth century, they were locked up in asylums. But in the early twentieth century, a few of them did actually succeed in getting out of there and onto the stage. Jane Avril, for example. In turn-of-the-century Paris, this young woman managed to get out of the psychiatric unit run by the aforementioned Dr Charcot and made a name for herself tread-ing the boards at the Moulin Rouge. She was the muse of Toulouse Lautrec, the 'Queen of the French Cancan', and she used her dances (which were heavily inspired by the ecstatic movements of her former comrades-in-suffering, the 'hysteria-afflicted') to prove that lots of those locked-up women weren't the slightest bit mad, but simply used their bodies to express what they couldn't say with words. And this was exactly what the fledgling discipline of expressionist dance was all about: using your body to convey what you couldn't – or weren't allowed to – say out loud. Revealing emotions that were normally suppressed for the sake of propriety, liberating yourself, rebelling against a restrictive form of being and movement. It's no wonder that this new style of dance was developed by women and is still domi-nated by female choreographers; after all, it was women who needed to free themselves from the narrow constraints of their existence. Ballet was just a reflection of a rigid norm. The dancer Isadora Duncan, for example, once said that her most important contribution had been to liberate women from their corsets – and anyone who thinks, 'Nonsense, that was Chanel', is mistaken. Even before the fashion designer, Duncan (who, incidentally, gave Chanel dance lessons) had already shown us how a female body could move if it were finally set free. Instead of being forced into a ballet corset and pointe shoes, she floated and skipped across the stages of the world, barefoot in flowing dresses, thereby laying the cornerstone of a revolution.

Duncan, of course, still looked dreamy and pretty as she did this. Mary Wigman, on the other hand, introduced something quite different with her 'Witch Dance', with her mask and her brusque movements: a wilder dimension of femininity, something raw and unfiltered. The willingness, even, to risk looking ugly. And so when the Nazis came to power, despite her unfortunately persistent attempts to be recognised by the new authorities (as late as 1936, she choreographed the opening ceremony of the Olympic Games!), she slipped down into the corner of 'degenerate art' and was banned from performing. Her picture of femininity didn't match that of Nazi Germany; she was too free, too unconventional, too different. Wigman believed a witch was a 'creature rooted in the earth, unbridled instinct, insatiable lust for life, animal and woman in one' and asked the same question some feminists pose today: 'Is there not a witch hidden inside each of us?'

TINA MODOTTI, WORKERS PARADE

1926

This object, a Polaroid photo titled *Workers Parade*, was once a gift from one woman to another. One of them, Tina Modotti, the Italian photographer, was a firm believer in communism who devoted her art entirely to this idea. The other, the Russian revolutionary Alexandra Kollontai, had helped to shape it, thereby inspiring many women to get involved in politics. Modotti most likely gave her the picture in 1926. Kollontai had just moved to Mexico after completing her first foreign posting as a diplomat in Norway, and she provided the local artists – Tina, her friend Frida Kahlo and Frida's husband Diego Rivera, plus others – with films by Sergei Eisenstein and other aesthetic novelties from the ideological motherland. Her real concern, however, was quite different, as she wrote in July that same year – who knows, maybe even with Modotti's photo in mind – in her *Autobiography of a Sexually Emancipated Communist Woman*: 'the complete liberation of the working woman and the creation of the foundation of a new sexual morality will always remain the highest aim of my activity, and of my life'.[1]

Let's rewind a few years to understand what she meant. Kollontai was twenty-six years old when she decided to leave her husband and son to study in Switzerland and familiarise herself with Marxist and feminist theories. To the Bolsheviks, with whom she increasingly sympathised, feminism sounded like the ivory-tower-dwelling members of the bourgeoisie, like women thinking from a position of privilege and failing to

---

1   Kollontai, Alexandra, *Autobiography of a Sexually Emancipated Communist Woman*, 1926, available at: <https://www.marxists.org/archive/kollonta/1926/autobiography.htm>

understand that working-class women had far more pressing concerns than the right to vote – such as a better, freer life and a more just society, changes that took place in real life and not merely on paper. It was this for which Kollontai wanted to fight, at the side of women like her friends Rosa Luxemburg and Clara Zetkin. In 1907, she accompanied Zetkin to the First International Conference of Socialist Women in Stuttgart; in 1909, they travelled together to England to support the British Socialist Party in its fight against the suffragettes. As already mentioned, the suffragettes were frowned upon. What mattered to the socialists were not women but the people, the masses, just like in Modotti's Polaroid. This was about a new solidarity.

In February 1917, when almost 100,000 female workers marched through the streets of what was then Petrograd to demand democracy and the abdication of the tsar, thus inciting a revolution, Kollontai returned from her self-imposed exile to help shape this new Russia as the 'People's Commissioner for Social Care'. The question of how women could be better supported in their essentially uncontested role as mothers was a matter of ongoing concern for female socialists, and one that was regularly discussed at their international congresses. Kollontai immediately implemented some of the points they touched on: 'One of her dearest ambitions for years has been to establish a home for convalescent mothers known as the Palace of Motherhood. This work is actually being carried out, and what few physicians remain in Petrograd are keenly interested in it. On Kollontay's suggestion, the Bolshevik Government passed a measure providing free care for sixteen weeks for women before, during and after confinement. When they leave the home they can go back if they are not well, and they are required to work only four hours a day in the factories for the first month after returning. This applies to all women, whether married or single', wrote the journalist Louise Bryant, who reported on the Russian Revolution for an American newspaper and greatly admired Kollontai.[1] And the idea behind these measures was indeed great: for one, it was supposed to make women's lives easier by ensuring that the work of raising children wasn't just left to mothers but – in a similar vein to Charles Fourier's thinking – took place in the collective, thanks to crèches, kindergartens,

---

1 Bryant, Louise, *Six Red Months in Russia* (New York: George H. Doran Company, 1936). Available at: <http://digital.library.upenn.edu/women/bryant/russia/russia-XII.html>

public canteens and so on. Another aim – again similar to Fourier – was the sexual emancipation of women. If having children no longer made life so terribly difficult and women received more support from society and the state, they could stop being so afraid of unplanned pregnancies and finally have relaxed sex. That was the thinking, anyway.

And this, in turn, would change everything. It was necessary to liberate sexuality and chuck the old-fashioned idea that women were only allowed to have one partner, in order to then burst the narrow limits of the nuclear family. So thought Alexandra Kollontai, who saw the origins of capitalist evil in the slightly claustrophobic Mum-Dad-Child version of life. This was why she advocated legalising abortion – something that was pushed through in 1920 – and, above all, a simplified divorce process. From 1926 onwards, it became possible to tell your partner by postcard that your marriage was herewith officially annulled. She thought it a good thing: marriage enslaved women and repressed their desires to the benefit of male egotism; the narrative of love thus far had encouraged women to adapt themselves to suit men's wishes, or at least to spend an unnecessary amount of time slaving away at fulfilling them. It should be possible for a woman to have sex like 'drinking a glass of water', just as simply and just as frequently – maintained the woman who was apparently the inspiration for Ernst Lubitsch's *Ninotchka*.

Love needed liberating and, alongside that, individuals needed releasing from their narrowly defined categories, she said. This was, of course, an opinion that didn't meet solely with friendly approval. Kollontai was attacked, even threatened; some actually made the accusation that her ideas about free love were – wait for it – embarrassingly bourgeois. Eventually, the men around her found her so bothersome that she was removed from the seat of power. Her views on sex and love seem to have allied her with the bisexual photographer Modotti and her friend Frida Kahlo, with whom she spent time when she was posted in Mexico. What would eventually emerge from this new sexual world was something not even they could say for certain: 'What will be the nature of this transformed Eros? Not even the boldest fantasy is capable of providing the answer to this question.'[1]

---

1 Kollontai, Alexandra, 'Make Way for Winged Eros: A Letter to Working Youth', first published in *Molodoya Gvardiya*, Vol. 3, 1923, tr. Joey Ostos, available at: <https://www.marxists.org/archive/kollonta/1923/winged-eros.htm>

LIPSTICK, 'LE ROUGE BAISER'

1927

If there's one assumption that unites all those who wear their misogyny proudly, like a particularly well-fitting suit, it's probably the following: feminists are only feminists because they're too 'ugly' to appeal to men (who are, as we know, the reference point for all things). The men who champion such views usually aren't the most attractive themselves, but that's beside the point. The idea that feminists are ugly, frustrated, frigid, that they don't take care of themselves at all, is an ancient one. Insecure alpha males reassuring themselves that even in this battle, the battle of feminism, what it all boils down to is, ultimately, their own desiring or undesiring gaze.

And so it was that, out of sheer helplessness, the suffragettes of the early twentieth century were accused of being barren or frigid or both; this was why they were so loud and embittered. Yet, at exactly the same time – in the 1910s and 1920s – a sturdy bridge was being built between the suffragettes and the blossoming beauty industry. After all, these women wanted to be seen and heard; 'discreet and invisible' was never their motto. One of the best stories in this context goes as follows: it was 6 May 1912, and the American suffragettes were marching through Manhattan, from 59th Avenue to Washington Square, chanting the usual 'Votes for women! Votes for women!' On that particular spring day, almost 20,000 women and 500 men were in attendance. All were dressed in white and, as would later be reported in every paper, the ladies wore red lipstick. Did that really need to be pointed out? Yes, because it broke with the middle-class rules of morality. In the eyes of most men, according to the *Ladies' Home Journal*, this red was a 'sign of sex and sin'. Anyone who wore red lipstick was either a prostitute or didn't have anything against being taken for one. As the crowd marched along Fifth Avenue, Elizabeth Arden, the beauty-business queen, was standing in the salon she'd opened just two years previously and, evidently, was so excited by the group that she grabbed a few of her 'Red Door' lipsticks and promptly ditched her bewildered clients, hastening outside without a word to join the protest. Granted, she did hand out a couple of lipsticks at the same time – good advertising for her brand.

Red-painted lips became a signal in those years, a way for women to tell men that in future they'd no longer give a damn about how some chap might interpret their appearance. From now on, they'd be taking back control over how they looked, and that would be as brash, as sexual, as free as they wanted. They made their mouths look so dramatic that men probably quaked simply on seeing those lips: what kind of campaign slogan would they be letting fly next? What on earth had happened to those pale lips of yore, the ones that had always been so closed and silent?

The brand represented by the object shown here only arrived on the market a few years later, in 1927, but it instantly became a cult product. The very first lipstick – Guerlain's 'Forget Me Not', which had been introduced back in the final decade of the nineteenth century – had become irretrievably associated with the idea of a permissive lifestyle thanks to its name alone, but 'Le Rouge Baiser' took things a step further. The ladies of this era, the name suggested, didn't just want not to be forgotten; no, they wanted to kiss. *Émbrassez qui vous voulez! Kiss whomever you want!* This, or something like it, was what this lipstick seemed to be calling to them, and it struck a nerve: the women of the 1920s didn't want to practise mysterious aloofness; they wanted to experiment and act out their sexuality in freedom. This lipstick promised that very thing: *Permits kissing.* Literally. How saucy.

The brand's famous advertising poster, illustrated by René Grau, showed the outline of a woman's head, a broad strip of black cloth covering her eyes; only her bright-red mouth stood out. Whatever this woman was doing, she certainly wasn't having supper with her family. The erstwhile aim of the suffragettes – to stand out to get the right to vote – had been left far behind. When it came to 'Le Rouge Baiser', a different right was at stake: the right to sex. That many men were afraid of the symbolic sexual potency of these women with their red lips is evident in the Hollywood figure of the *femme fatale*: the woman with the kohl-rimmed eyes and deep-red mouth is seductive, but also a little

bit lethal. She's changed her 'nature' and, along with it, all those charac-
teristics associated with femininity. No longer is she the personification
of gentleness, goodness and warmth, but a dolled-up, calculating minx.
Sexy, yes. But also scary.

And, as is sadly so often the case in the history of women, the
beauty industry eventually made the transition from accomplice to
enemy. Where the suffragettes and flappers of the 1920s painted courage and strength onto their lips and used beauty as a weapon for
self-empowerment, by the 1940s at the latest women were subjecting
themselves to strict beauty norms and new ideal images. From then on,
and for several generations, wearing lipstick was the opposite of a
rebellious act of self-assertion: it became the obligation of any 'decent,
well-kept' woman.

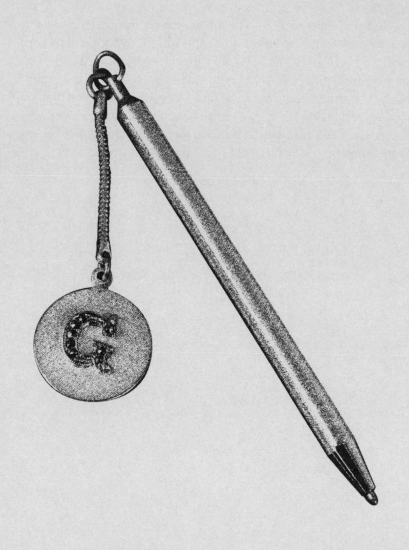

GRETA GARBO'S BALLPOINT PEN

1927

In 1934, the American film magazine *Picture Play* wrote in an article entitled 'The Battle of the Sexes': 'Though this is still a man's world, Hollywood is a woman's town, a modern Amazonia ruled by beautiful and astute women, who from their thrones of glamour unfurl their celluloid standards to the far corners of the earth.' And: 'Hollywood is a woman's town because women made Hollywood before it made them stars – and queens!'

As already mentioned, in the early years of Hollywood, women were directors, producers, camerawomen, cutters, the inventors of ways to record sound and add colour to film. What was perhaps even more important, though, was that women also wrote screenplays. Frances Marion, for example, best friend of silent-movie star Mary Pickford, was by far the best-paid scriptwriter in those early decades, well ahead of any man. The George Cukor classic *Dinner at Eight* emerged from the nib of her pen; she was the first person to win two Oscars for best screenplay, and on putatively 'unfeminine' subjects, to boot: one for the prison drama *The Big House*, and one for boxing film *The Champ*. She was also the person who wrote silent-movie star Greta Garbo's first speaking role. This film, *Anna Christie*, was advertised with the words 'Garbo talks!' and perhaps Marion wasn't an insignificant factor in the Swedish actor's successful transition – unlike many of her colleagues – from silent movies to talkies.

This beautiful gold ballpoint pen with its glittering G belonged to her – to Garbo. Admittedly, in the grand scheme of things, it isn't a terribly important part of history. But it's here to represent the influence not just of women who acted, but also of women scriptwriters: they were behind the interesting roles tailor-made for actors like Garbo. The first female characters in cinema weren't mousey, but strong and self-confident – just like the women who played them. Garbo, for example, wasn't at all willing to accept that her male co-star should earn eight times more than she did, and in 1927 she demanded equal pay. If she was going to be so obstinate, they'd send her back to Sweden, said Louis B. Meyer. *No problem; I'll be off, then*, she replied; eventually Meyer and his studio, MGM, gave in and agreed to pay her an astonishing $5,000 a week in future. Just for fun, let's imagine that Garbo signed her new contract with this very pen. Louise Brooks once said she impressed the whole of Hollywood with this move, while Samuel Goldwyn, also of MGM, noted resignedly in *The New Movie Magazine*: 'Women rule Hollywood.'

However, what he meant back in 1935 was less that women ruled as directors, writers or the recipients of giant pay cheques, and more that they were the target audience: it was women who spent their afternoons sitting in darkened rooms and identified with the characters they saw on-screen. In the 1930s and 1940s, 70 per cent of cinemagoers were women. Without them, there would be no film industry; things had to be arranged to suit them. And what they wanted to see was women. Claudette Colbert, Norma Shearer, Greta Garbo, Joan Crawford, Bette Davis, Katharine Hepburn. Just like the early days of the novel, when most stories were written for women, most of the films from Hollywood's golden era were made for them, too. Many of the films from this era, from *It Happened One Night* to *The Philadelphia Story*, are essentially 'chick-flicks': love stories in which a woman pines after a man, he pines after her, and all manner of things come between them until finally they do succeed in getting together. Yet the female characters of those years were different to what you'd expect. They were sassy, strong-willed, brave, sometimes even bad; they were incredibly quick-witted and didn't take anything lying down. If their husbands betrayed them, they betrayed them right back, like in *The Divorcee*. In *The Woman*, written by Anita Loos and directed by George Cukor, the male protagonist was so incidental that he didn't once appear on-screen, and the entire film was made with an all-female cast. Films like these might even have passed the Bechdel test, which checks whether the women in a film talk about something other than men. At least the likes of Greta Garbo, Katharine Hepburn and Bette Davis never had to sit around crying next to the phone, a tub of ice cream on hand, waiting for a call from a man who didn't love them, like so many of the actresses of the 1980s and 1990s.

And it is pretty interesting: in real life, women were beleaguered by demands and prohibitions, but what they demonstrated on the silver screen to their female audiences was a new self-awareness, intellectual freedom and independence. Because actresses fought for this, too. If their roles seemed too stereotypical or not complex enough, they'd sue the studio without further ado, as Bette Davis did in 1936. Women's roles became more one-dimensional over time, said filmmaker Nora Ephron, explaining this development with economic factors: audiences were different after the Second World War. It was no longer just women who wanted to be shown what they didn't dare demand for themselves, but men who had been buffeted by the conflict and now wanted the cinema to confirm that the old order – the clichéd bastions of masculinity and femininity – still stood. Suddenly, women were no longer witty, romantic, cool and self-confident, no longer complex but one-dimensional: sexy and murderous, or cute and naïve. They were vamps, *femme fatales* or sweet little bimbos. For a long time, very little about this changed, not even during the second wave of feminism. On the contrary, said Callie Khouri, who wrote *Thelma and Louise*: 'It's as though the feminist revolution produced on-screen characters that just got weaker and more stereotypical.'[1] That is, until recent years, which have seen increasing numbers of women take up their pens again – to write good, complex roles for their female colleagues, for example the series *Girls*.

---

1 Quoted in 'Et Hollywood créa la femme', on <https://www.wichitafilms.com>

INTERNATIONAL WOMEN'S DAY BADGE

1930

A few years back, a new day of observance surfaced on the international calendar. It was a holiday that had actually always been there, but which had long been ignored in the West: 8 March, International Women's Day. Until quite recently, most people thought of Mother's Day as the day for celebrating women. Aside from her birthday, that was the day on which you'd buy flowers, bake her a cake, write her a card whose message went along the lines of, *It's great having you as my mum.* Fathers congratulated their wives or girlfriends on having brought a child into the world and helped it along. This was all very nice, but it also didn't celebrate those women who weren't mothers, whether by choice or circumstance.

All the better, then, for a new date to exist. While commerce might view it merely as an opportunity to sell a couple of bouquets, that doesn't change anything about the fact that International Women's Day is an opportunity to recognise and celebrate women all over the world. It's about an international connection, which is standing by to fight for their rights and thump the table if those rights seem under threat. At least, that was the idea once. Nowadays, around twenty-five countries observe 8 March as a proper holiday: Armenia, for example, and Georgia, Nepal (for women only), China, Cuba, Burkina Faso, Belarus, Russia, Vietnam, Uganda, Turkmenistan and a few others. The idea of a national day off would make sense in Germany, considering that the entire thing is based on the idea of a German activist, the legendary Clara Zetkin.

It was 27 August 1910, the final day of the Second International Socialist Women's Conference in Copenhagen, when Zetkin and Käte Duncker, a Social Democrat politician, stood up in front of a hundred delegates from seventeen countries to propose a vote: for or against a day on which women across the world would turn out to demonstrate for suffrage and better living and working conditions. It was a unanimous 'Aye!', but they didn't agree on a specific date. Apparently, the Americans had been the ones to put the idea of a protest day into Zetkin's head. Two years before, in March 1908, almost 15,000 women who worked in the textile industry – including many young émigrés from Europe – had stormed the streets of Manhattan, demanding better working conditions, the right to vote, the end of child labour and higher wages. Off the back of this, the Women's Committee of the American Socialist Party had advocated for a National Women's Day in solidarity with the workers. The first such day was celebrated on 28 February 1909, with Europe following suit in 1911.

'Comrades! Working women and girls! March 19 is your day. It is for your rights,' announced Zetkin's newspaper, *Die Gleichheit* (*Equality*), on 13 March in a call for women to mobilise. That date, 19 March, had been specifically chosen to underscore the event's revolutionary ambitions and commemorate the 'March victims' who had fallen in the March Revolution of 1848 in Vienna and Berlin. Only Germany, Switzerland, Denmark, Austria and the USA took part in that first edition of International Women's Day, but Zetkin still saw it as 'the most significant rally for women's suffrage ever recorded in the history of the women's emancipation movement'. When a fire broke out in a New York factory a couple of days later, claiming the lives of nearly 150 women who worked there, the day gained even more significance and was thenceforth celebrated annually with public discussion and demonstrations.

It would require the involvement of Russian women before 8 March was fixed upon as the official date. It had been their revolt on 8 March 1917 that had set the ball rolling in the Russian Revolution – what day could be better in standing for the downfall of old systems and a spirit of female optimism? Besides the slogans demanding women's suffrage, these 'Women's Days' were also routinely celebrated with song – with lyrics about 'bread and roses'. Bread, because many women routinely went hungry; roses, because they symbolised the appreciation of women in a male-dominated society.

This Women's Day badge from the year 1930 shows that the right to vote, which German women had obtained back in 1918, was by no means the end of the story. To the activists' minds, the battlefield had only expanded: there were more rights and freedoms to be fought for yet. They'd gained in confidence and knew they shouldn't settle for less, that they could – and must – demand it all; women didn't deserve just the odd crumb of freedom and equality, but the whole package. It's evidence, too, that German women now saw themselves as serious political activists who no longer wanted to fight purely for women and female workers, but also for other causes, especially to oppose war and the fascism steadily gaining ground in their country. Three years after the women of Germany took to the streets wearing badges like this one to protest the political climate, the Nazi takeover called time on their day of demonstrations. From 1933 to 1945, Women's Day was strictly prohibited in Germany. No longer were rebellious women celebrated, not even women in general – only Aryan women and, among them, only the mothers. From then on, and for several decades to follow, the day for celebrating women became known as Mother's Day.

REVISTA SUR (SUR MAGAZINE)

1931

When Coco Chanel first paid a visit to Victoria Ocampo, she thought her very strange indeed. A rich heiress from Argentina, she was a committed Francophile and did sound interesting – she was then editor of a magazine, which was first published in 1931 in Buenos Aires – a potential client, perhaps. But one thing still wasn't quite clear to Mademoiselle: why would a lady who clearly didn't lack money choose to decorate her apartment in the chic 16th arrondissement of Paris exclusively with white furniture, cheap stuff from the department store La Redoute? The apartment Ocampo rented for a time seems to have looked a bit like this magazine cover: green and white. Green thanks to the plants dotted here and there, white thanks to the (according to Chanel) perplexingly basic furniture. White like the blinding light of South America, green like the verdant surroundings of the Argentinian capital's many parks. Not for nothing was this *revista* named as it was: *SUR* (south) was an announcement: the call of the south.

In Argentina, the magazine is famous, and its founding editor some-thing of a national heroine. There's Evita, and then there's Victoria. Two women who came from very different walks of life but both left their mark on national culture, particularly in feminist terms. Evita came from the bottom, Victoria from the top; one from the so-called folk, the Argentinian Pampas, the other from the South American oligarchy and the chic neighbourhood of San Isidro, Buenos Aires. Both advocated politically for the women of their country, both managed – each in her own way – to bring about change.

In the early days of literature, philosophy, gastronomy, fashion – pretty much anything at all that's beautiful and exciting – it was very often women who transported ideas, trends, legends or tastes from one place to another. It was women who were married off from country

A to country B because an alliance seemed advantageous, and so it was also they who carried customs and ideas in their heads and their hatboxes from old homeland to new. They were the ones who built bridges most easily, who bound countries together – rarely through grand contracts, it's true, but instead through sensory and cultural elements: a lullaby, a scent, a flavour, a certain way of dressing or viewing the world. Even before they were permitted to write themselves, women were translators. They transferred thoughts from one language to another and – even if we're sometimes too busy worshipping authors to remember this – transferral and translation are just as important, just as valuable and just as demanding as writing. After all, what is an idea or a new view of the world if it never makes it beyond the borders of its homeland? If it can't set anyone else alight? How much influence can it have then?

Ocampo, whose station in life had meant she was brought up speaking English and French fluently, must often have asked herself such questions. Why should good sentences and ideas stay locked up in one country? Why shouldn't her fellow Argentinians learn what the people of Europe were thinking and writing? Why shouldn't Europe hear new voices from the New World? Why shouldn't one nourish the other, make the world bigger and wider and more connected? *SUR* was the answer to these questions: a magazine for all those 'souls without passports'. These days, you'll sometimes read that Victoria Ocampo was a muse, but that's rubbish. If anything, she was a builder of bridges. A transatlantic *salonnière*, who brought people together and called to them across the ocean: *I think you ought to get to know each other. We should make something together.* And that 'something' was *SUR*. It was to bring together the best thinkers and writers from Europe and America, and let these very different voices enter into dialogue with one another. For the 1930s – and, on top of that, for a woman – such an undertaking seemed founded on delusions of grandeur. Yet, it worked. And the best example of this is Jorge Luis Borges.

Back in 1931, when the edition of *SUR* pictured here was still in the making, a very young Borges – himself in the making as a debut author – sat in Ocampo's snow-white home as a member of the magazine's founding editorial staff. The relationship between him and Ocampo seems to have been complicated. Her overly involved manner and almost groupie-like admiration of literary figures annoyed Borges; he got on better with her sister, the brilliantly odd writer Silvina Ocampo. Yet he knew, too, how much he owed this woman and her crazy *SUR* idea. For one thing, because she was the first person to truly believe in him and give him a job. For another, because it was through her connections that his novels reached France and, from there, the rest of Europe. You could say that Ocampo single-handedly carried that heavy man and his work across the ocean.

In return, she compelled him to carry a couple of European authors in the other direction – by translating them. The very first of these was a certain Virginia Woolf. In 1936, *A Room of One's Own* appeared in Spanish courtesy of *SUR*'s publishing arm, followed a year later by *Orlando*. Woolf also needed some time to get used to the strange Argentinian lady who talked too loudly, name-dropped constantly and wore earrings that looked to Woolf like moth's nests. But, somehow, they did find a way to connect. Woolf penned amusing letters to Ocampo in Argentina, 'land of great butterflies and vast fields', describing how she imagined life there to be: 'Every time I write I make up another picture of South America. You would no doubt be very surprised to see your house as I imagine it and arrange it.' It's hard to say whether publishing an author like Woolf really brought abrupt change to the lives of women in South America, or whether Europe's discovery of Borges actually led to anything new. Perhaps *SUR* was the crazy dream of a privileged enthusiast, but in Buenos Aires, at least, many people are united in the view that Argentinian culture – particularly today's boom in women's literature – would look quite different if it hadn't been for Ocampo and this magazine, *SUR*.

PLATE, 'THE FAMOUS WOMEN DINNER SERVICE'

1932

One of the best-known works of twentieth-century feminist art is 'The Dinner Party', an installation by the American artist Judy Chicago. A round table – or, to be more precise, a triangular table – around which sit many important women from the past: Sappho, the Amazons, Christine de Pizan, Hildegard of Bingen, Eleanor of Aquitaine, Artemisia, Elizabeth I, Margaret Sanger, Sojourner Truth, Susan B. Anthony, and so on. Each is represented by a plate featuring a painted or ceramic vulva motif. When it was first exhibited in the 1970s, at exactly the same time that women historians were setting out to narrate history from a female perspective, the installation was received as the first proper recognition of history's heroines.

In reality, almost forty years before Judy Chicago's work went on display, a certain Vanessa Bell, sister of Virginia Woolf, had done something very similar in partnership with her lover, Duncan Grant. The plate pictured here is one of fifty pieces that make up the 'Famous Women Dinner Service' of 1932, in which we find not just Woolf but also Pocahontas, Greta Garbo, Sappho (again), the ballet dancer Anna Pavlova, Sarah Bernhardt, Jezebel, the pioneering Japanese novelist Murasaki, George Sand, Christina of Sweden, Madame de Staël and her good friend Madame de Récamier, Charlotte Brontë and Catherine the Great. This unusual set of tableware has an amusing origin story: in the early 1930s, the British art historian Kenneth Clark and his wife, Jane, commissioned Bell and Grant to create a dinner service for them. The artist couple had opened their Omega workshop in London's Bloomsbury back in 1913; it was a kind of all-round arts boutique in which design, painting and happenings – art and life, in other words – melted into one another. Clark presumably expected to receive something in line with the Omega aesthetic. But Bell and Grant had something quite different in mind. Why always eat your dinner off pointlessly patterned plates? The idea was that it wasn't just *what* you ate; where you ate it from could also hold significance and spark political debate. Why not portray the forgotten heroines of history? Jane Clark seems to have been in on the idea and thought it a wonderful project; Kenneth, on the other hand, was left open-mouthed when the dinner service was finally delivered. Things hadn't turned out quite the way he'd expected, he said later, believing that this choice of motif had been Vanessa's way of publicising the matriarchy she'd established in the so-called Bloomsbury Group. It's hard to say to what extent it really was a matriarchy – this community that took its name from the neighbourhood of London where it had formed, and which consisted of Vanessa Bell, Virginia Woolf and her husband, Leonard Woolf, Duncan Grant, Roger Fry, Vanessa's husband, Clive Bell, and a couple of other peripheral figures. But the women in it did at least occupy a very different place to the one they'd have had just a few decades previously in strict Victorian society.

Possessiveness clearly wasn't an issue for them: Vanessa was married, but she lived mainly with her partner, Grant, and their daughter. Grant, who actually preferred men in the main, would often invite his lovers to move in for a while with him, Vanessa and the children. Clive, Vanessa's husband, also had his own stories to tell. And if anyone presumed to view this way of living and loving through the filter of social norms and morals, still less to judge it, that person would instantly be given a slap on the wrist: 'It seems to me at any rate rash to assume that [. . .] those who force themselves to lead lives according to convention or the will of others are more likely to be "good" (by which I mean to have good or noble feelings) than those who decide to live as seems to them best,' Vanessa Bell once wrote to an overly curious acquaintance. It's common knowledge that Virginia Woolf also had an extramarital relationship with the writer Vita Sackville-West. What's less certain is who first came up with the concept that Dorothy Parker once dubbed 'living in squares, loving in triangles'. Was it Vanessa? One of the men? Hard to say. Evidently, they were all unanimous in their view that life should be lived at one's own discretion, not according to what other people thought. And that was exactly what they all did – those women whom Vanessa painted on her plates. But quite apart from that, this dinner service – which indicates the importance of community, food and pleasure in the lives of the Bloomsbury Group – is also interesting in the context of Virginia as an author.

Woolf is sometimes imagined as an ethereal, nervy writer who didn't have a terribly firm grip on 'material life' – food in particular. Yet it's a recurring feature of her books, not just *Mrs Dalloway*. In *A Room of One's Own*, food-based situations even provide the impetus for her musings on life as a woman. Woolf describes eating a meal at a male college and another taken at a female college, noting how differently the two groups are fed. The men's lunch (on which, she finds, male writers never waste a single word, as though it's of no importance whatsoever) is extravagant: there is wine and sole, partridges, sauces, salads, potatoes, cauliflower and a pudding that 'rose all sugar from the waves'.[1] For the women, however, dinner is a bland business. Soup, soggy vegetables, stringy meat. 'One cannot think well, love well, sleep well, if one has not dined well': Woolf's adage is famous.[2] Nor can one write well: 'the luncheon and the dinner had started a swarm of questions. Why did men drink wine and women water? Why was one sex so prosperous and the other so poor? What effect has poverty on fiction?'[3] As part of the domestic (and therefore female) domain, plates have always been regarded as unimportant, as decoration, but in reality they've always been a battlefield. For a long time – and in some parts of the world, even today – men, especially young men, were served the best cuts of meat, with whatever was left then given to the women. And so, plates and what's on them were, and still are, anything but inconsequential. Vanessa and Virginia understood that early on.

---

1 Woolf, Virginia, *A Room of One's Own* (London: Penguin Classics, 2020), p. 7
2 ibid., p. 14
3 ibid., p. 19

Live Alone

AND LIKE IT

A GUIDE
FOR THE
EXTRA
WOMAN

110th to 120th Thousand

By MARJORIE HILLIS

MARJORIE HILLIS,
LIVE ALONE AND LIKE IT

1936

Even now, many people find it hard to imagine that a woman can live alone and like it. If a woman has neither husband nor wife and lives by herself, most people will look a bit awkward upon hearing this. The woman can repeat till she's blue in the face that she's chosen to be alone and even enjoys it most of the time, that she doesn't feel at all lonely but free, and people will still assume she isn't happy, but very good at hiding what's actually a deep unhappiness.

The story of the independent woman is interesting, because she hasn't long existed as a 'type'. For centuries, a woman was only someone in relation to a man: she was a daughter, sister, niece, wife – or, if she was alone, then at least a widow. A female individual without a male counterpart as reference point was unthinkable; anyone who didn't fit this pattern simply didn't exist in the eyes of society. In some epochs, women who lived alone were persecuted because they were seen as a threat to the norm; beginning in the Middle Ages, a woman who didn't want a husband or family would join a convent to escape hounding and meddlesome questions. Nuns were, if you like, the first 'single ladies' in history – even if they were, strictly speaking, 'married' to Jesus. This situation was accepted right up to the seventeenth and eighteenth centuries, when more and more people started asking whether things really had to be that way: couldn't a woman live independently of a man but still firmly within society, not somewhere on its fringes? The French philosopher Gabrielle Suchon, for example, writing in 1700 in *Du célibate volontaire*, argued that it must be possible for a woman to decide to live alone without having to shut herself up in a convent. Yet her avowal of the single life fell largely on deaf ears.

By contrast to Suchon, the author of this pretty little book, Marjorie Hillis, made the same demand two centuries later and found herself with a bestseller on her hands. *Live Alone and Like It: A Guide for the Extra Woman* was one of the most successful self-help titles of 1936, a period in which this genre of literature was already flourishing. Even President Roosevelt seems to have read it on his summer holiday; there's a photo of him laughing heartily at Hillis and her sassy suggestions. And it is genuinely amusing. We find ourselves transplanted to a period between the first and second waves of feminism, with the suffragettes and *garçonnes* on their way out; the global financial crisis of 1929 has shaken the foundations of life, and ultraconservative views are being revitalised. Into this setting walks a forty-seven-year-old woman, editor of *Vogue*, to explain cheerfully to women that they should stop pining away, stop waiting around for some hypothetical prince, and instead set about making their lives wonderful all by themselves. Her book wasn't trying to convince anyone that alone is better than together – that's something everyone should decide for themselves – but to convey the idea that a woman doesn't necessarily need a man to be happy. Life lived alone could be more fulfilling than life lived with the wrong partner, thought Hillis, an opinion that seemed to strike a chord. She sold several hundred thousand copies of her book and toured the USA dispensing pearls of wisdom on the advantages of being single.

Her arguments are as follows. Number one: If you live alone, you don't need to take anyone else into account – 'From dusk until dawn, you can do exactly as you please, which, after all, is a pretty good allotment in this world where a lot of conforming is expected of everyone.'[1] You can read, sleep, drink, dance, do whatever you like, whenever you like, and you'll also have the bathroom to yourself ('unquestionably one of Life's Great Blessings').[2] Number two: You learn to be your own cheerleader. Instead of always waiting passively for another person to do it, you should celebrate the time you spend on your own – for example, by getting all dolled up for dinner with yourself. If you do have to clean, you should do it in trousers that make you feel especially sexy; pretty but comfortable nightshirts are best worn for sleeping in. And

---

1   Hillis, Marjorie, *Live Alone and Like It: The Art of Solitary Refinement* (London: Virago, 2005), p. 80
2   ibid., p. 80

for the obligatory breakfast in bed (another of those Blessings!) you can throw on an elegant dressing gown. Hillis waved aside any objections that since no one was watching anyway, it surely didn't matter: these weren't things you did for other people – especially not for men – but for yourself. Sounds a bit like boring old 'self-care'? Yes, maybe, but then again: this was 1936. Back then, the idea that a woman could look after herself, not just other people, wasn't merely a lifestyle choice; it was well nigh subversive.

Especially as Hillis sounds a good deal funnier and more self-confident than the slightly depressing advice offered by many contemporary women's magazines. In her book, for example, she never once mentions how the woman in question (whom she never terms a 'singleton', but a 'liver-alone') might nab herself a man. And why would she? Living alone is plenty of fun already: you can host entertaining dinner parties, become an ace cocktail shaker, have breakfast in bed, run around all over New York and do only the things you actually enjoy doing. The woman Hillis was describing – with a slight touch of Dorothy Parker – sounded like a cross between Holly Golightly and Carrie Bradshaw. It just wasn't quite clear what you did about sex. Between the lines, she explained that while you could have affairs, it was best not to brag about them – the chapter 'Pleasures of a Single Bed' probably spoke for itself. Some twenty years later, in 1962, Helen Gurley Brown, who would later become editor-in-chief of *Cosmopolitan*, picked up the thread of *Live Alone and Like It* and, in her book *Sex and the Single Girl*, took a more direct approach to this rather vaguely discussed question of sex. The book became a hit and others followed, eventually also TV series like *Sex and the City* and *Girls*. Yet the single woman had been truly seen and portrayed in a positive light long before their time: way back in the 1930s, in this witty little self-help book.

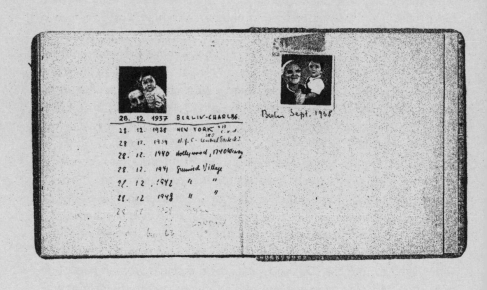

28. 12. 1937 BERLIN-CHARLBG.
28. 12. 1938 NEW YORK
28. 12. 1939 N.Y.C. Central Park
28. 12. 1940 Hollywood, 1740 Winona
28. 12. 1941 Greenwich Village
28. 12. 1942 "   "
28. 12. 1943 "   "

Berlin Sept. 1938

EXILE DIARY
OF MASCHA KALÉKO

1941-44

There was a time when talking about refugees usually meant talking about men. Young chaps who had set out to escape war, persecution or poverty and search for a better, safer life. To some extent, exile was seen as male, yet we were always aware that women most certainly made these journeys too, and that they always have done. That they too climb into boats or start walking, alone or with their children in their arms, not knowing exactly where they're going or what awaits them in those foreign lands. That they are putting themselves at the mercy of the journey and its dangers.

In Nazi Germany, beginning in 1933, women were among the very first to feel the physical effects of the new regime's politics. The sterilisation law passed in July of that year implied that there would be children for Germany – but not from everyone. Between 1933 and 1939, around 150,000 women – Jewish and Roma women, and those who were said to be either physically or mentally handicapped or the carriers of some kind of 'impurity' – were forcibly sterilised. The treatment of their bodies was a forerunner of what was to come. Now, Jewish women could prove themselves a good friend only if they ignored their acquaintances on the street and kept away from coffee mornings so as not to endanger the others; as mothers, they had to look on as their children were bullied in the school playground, hearing perhaps for the first time that they were of Jewish origin; as employees, they lost their jobs in the early months of the new regime. And perhaps this was why it was so often women who were more clear-sighted than men, quicker to urge them to flee. Or, as Marta Appel, wife of Dortmund's then rabbi, once explained: 'Is the future of our children not much more important than completely pointless perseverance in the face of Nazi ideology and crimes? All the women, without exception, were of the same opinion [. . .] while the men argued against it with varying degrees of passion. It wasn't unusual for women to show more spirit and entrepreneurship than men.'[1] According to Appel, they had less to lose – less status, less money – and so spent less time hoping that everything would come good, that the winds of this madness might yet change.

In the case of the object pictured here, it isn't quite clear who instigated the journey – possibly both the adults who appear in the photos. This book belonged to the German-Polish poet Mascha Kaléko: a diary that she began keeping for her young son, Avitar. It's read back to front, with these two pages located right at the back – at the beginning, in other words. The picture on the right-hand side, 'Berlin, Sept. 1938', shows Avitar in the arms of an elderly woman and must have been one of the very last photos taken at the family home in Charlottenburg. That same month, Kaléko, her two-year-old son – her 'little emigrant', as she called him – and her husband, Chemjo Vinaver, fled Berlin and travelled via Hamburg, Paris and Le Havre on a rusty ship to New York. Chemjo, a musician, quickly found his way back onto the stage and soon made a name for himself. As a poet in a foreign country and foreign language, things were harder for Mascha: 'Events in recent history / Took me away from Germany. / Now I sit far away, in New York, USA, / And write nothing but German poems.'[2]

Kaléko did have more to lose than her husband. In 1920s Berlin, the Berlin of the 'Romanesque Café', she'd been a star, chronicler of life in a pulsing capital city, but now, on the other side of the world, she was 'Mrs Chemjo Vinaver'.

Lots of once-independent women had a similar experience. On the run or in exile, in war in general, traditional roles are often reactivated. The punctual entries in this diary record milestones in Avitar's life. In her poem 'Homesickness', she wrote: 'I once had a beautiful fatherland / thus sang the refugee Heine. / His lay on the Rhine, / mine on the sands of the March. / We all had one once (see above!). / Consumed by plague, dispersed in the demise. / O, little rose on the moorland, / it was strength-in-joy that broke you. / The nightingales fell silent, /

---

1 Quoted in Monika Richarz, *Jewish Life in Germany: Memoirs from Three Centuries* (Bloomington: Indiana University Press, 1991), p. 356
2 Rosenkranz, Jutta, *Mascha Kaleko: Biografie* (Munich: dtv, 2012). p. 73

searched for a safe place to live, / and now the vultures cry / high above rows of graves. / Never again will it be as it was, / even if it is different. / Even if the sweet little bell sounds, / even if the swords stop clashing. / I feel, now and then, as though / my heart has been broken. / Sometimes, I feel homesick. / I just don't know what for.'

This book is both interesting and moving, trying as it does to list stations and dates on a journey taken between home – the place that had been so abruptly ripped away from them and now was probably lost for ever – and the new life that followed, a life that would always be rooted in that loss. It feels like an attempt to make that journey more tangible and so, perhaps, less brutal; as though Kaléko is spinning her son a fragile thread between Germany and America, trying to maintain a sense of origin that might otherwise get lost along the way. For refugees and those living in exile in particular, it's usually women who serve as a link to their former homeland, to their stories, food, songs and rites; women are often the custodians of a world now sunk beneath the waves. It takes great optimism to build a new life, as Hannah Arendt wrote in *We Refugees*. And it seems that women in particular displayed an incredible amount of this, and used it to motivate their families. In 1940, when a congress was convened to examine the question of 'women in exile', the German-speaking Jewish immigrant journal *Aufbau*, for which Mascha Kaléko was working by that time, wrote: 'The burden that lies on the shoulders of émigré families [. . .] is always distributed the same, and very often the heaviest share lands on the shoulders of the women [. . .] The fate of an emigrant family is very often more dependent on the wife than on the husband.'

Ständige Ausstellung
Das NAZI-PARADIES
Krieg Hunger Lüge Gestapo
Wie lange noch?

STICKER, 'RED ORCHESTRA' RESISTANCE GROUP

1942

In spring 1933, Betty Scholem wrote a letter from Berlin to her son, the German-Jewish thinker Gershom Scholem, who had emigrated to Palestine: 'It is incomprehensible to me that there aren't ten thousand, or even just one thousand decent Christians to be found, who won't just go along with it all but protest loudly.' Unfortunately, as we know, resistance to the Nazis was shockingly weak, particularly in those early years; even people who initially hoped that 'this period of terror will soon be over' had soon bowed to the regime. Nonetheless, there were still a few who preferred to risk everything than throw their principles overboard. They were Christians, Communists, Social Democrats and Conservatives; they came from all walks of life. They weren't just men, but also women.

Since the mid-1950s, when the resistance first began to be honoured as such, Germany has held an annual commemoration of the failed attempt to assassinate Adolf Hitler on 20 July 1944. The name of Claus Schenk Graf von Stauffenberg, who organised the attack, is well known; so too, perhaps, the names of Helmut Graf von Moltke, Peter Graf Yorck von Wartenburg and a couple of other men belonging to the so-called Kreisau Circle. Yet the names of the women – the wives of nearly two hundred men who were executed as traitors in the weeks and months that followed – have been all but forgotten. They were Marion, Freya, Nina, Clarita, Elisabeth, Anna, Rosemarie, Annedore. There were several dozen of them, perhaps several hundred, all of whom were informed of the plans and in some cases directly involved; they'd accepted the possibility of losing their husbands or even going to prison themselves, of being interrogated and tortured and separated from their children, who were taken away, almost without exception, to the children's home at Bad Sachsa.

When we think of resistance, we think – or at least thought for a long time – of men with weapons. We seldom consider the fact that there are many different forms of resistance, that it's just as much part of a resistance movement to conspire in keeping a meeting place secret; to design, print and distribute flyers; to take in and hide people on the run, to obtain papers for them; to maintain networks, translate, get hold of information and food and so on. Women did all this, only we rarely remember it. We hardly ever celebrate or even talk about female resistance fighters in Germany and, if we do, then only Sophie Scholl. It wasn't until 2019 that politicians from Germany's CDU/CSU and SPD parties proposed a joint motion to 'honour the women who fought in the resistance against National Socialism'. As Elisabeth Motschmann, the member of parliament who launched the initiative, explained: 'The German resistance didn't just consist of the men whose names are well known to us; it also consisted of women. Their names and their activities are largely unknown. And it is precisely this that is so unfair.' She also said: 'It's completely incomprehensible that after seventy-five years they should still lead a shadowy existence. They are among the forgotten heroines of our history.'[1]

Liane Berkowitz was one of these heroines. She was nineteen years old and still going to school when, on 5 August 1943, two days before her twentieth birthday, she was executed by guillotine in Berlin-Plötzensee. Five months prior to this, Liane had given birth to a baby girl in prison; the Reich Military Tribunal's recommendation that she should be released on the grounds of her pregnancy had been personally rejected by Adolf Hitler. The charge brought against Liane and more than a hundred other members of the Red Orchestra resistance group was 'aiding and abetting conspiracy to commit treason and aid the enemy'. More concretely, Liane and one of her comrades had spent the night of 17 May 1942 putting up roughly a hundred of these very stickers on the walls of the U-Bahn between Kurfürstendamm and Uhlandstrasse stations. 'Permanent exhibition – The Nazi Paradise – War – Hunger – Lies – Gestapo – How much longer?' the stickers read, making reference to a propaganda exhibition being shown at the time in Berlin's Lustgarten park. Titled 'The Soviet

1   Motschmann, Elisabeth, 'Ja, wir können von diesen Frauen lernen', Rede zu Frauen im Widerstand gegen den Nationalsozialismus, 28 June 2019, available (in German) at <https://www.cducsu.de/themen/elisabeth-motschmann-ja-wir-koennen-von-diesen-frauen-lernen>

Paradise', it featured images of poverty and suffering in the Soviet Union that were intended to intensify the image Germans held of their enemy. A couple of months later, in September, Liane and other members of the network were simultaneously arrested. Libertas Schulze-Boysen and her husband, Harro Schulze-Boysen, as well as Arvid Harnack, the 'founder' of what was probably Berlin's most important resistance movement, were murdered in December 1942; Arvid's wife Mildred, an American, followed in February. When Liane eventually died in Plötzensee on 5 August, thirty-four-year-old Hilde Coppi, twenty-two-year-old Cato Bontjes von Beek, thirty-three-year-old Maria Terwiel, thirty-eight-year-old sculptor Oda Schottmüller and many other women were executed alongside her.

Hilde Coppi, who had also given birth in prison, was a member of the group's innermost circle. She had got hold of the paper used to make these flyers and had been out that night in another part of Berlin, papering the U-Bahn walls with them. Cato Bontjes von Beek, meanwhile, was one of the authors of a leaflet entitled 'The People Are Troubled About Germany's Future', which proclaimed: 'All those who have maintained a sense of true values shudder as they watch the German name fall into increasing disrepute under the sign of the swastika. In all countries today, hundreds of people a day, often thousands, are being court-martialed and arbitrarily shot or hanged, accused of nothing other than remaining loyal to their country.'[1] And: 'Treat the SS with contempt! Let them feel that the people abhor murderers and spies from the depths of their souls!'[2] Their names should be remembered – the women who were active as members of this and other groups, but also as individuals; who distributed flyers like this one in an attempt to give their fellow human beings a wake-up call, and who died for their efforts. Their number may not have been great – they were far from being the majority, not even the silent one. But they existed. And in that climate of repression and turning blind eyes, their courage was all the greater.

1   Schulze-Boysen, Harro with assistance from John Sieg, 'The People Are Troubled About Germany's Future' (Berlin: February, 1942), Bundesarchiv R 58/4105, translated by Katy Derbyshire and available from the German Resistance Memorial Center, <https://www. gdw-berlin.de/fileadmin/bilder/publikationen/begleitmaterialien/Faksimiles_PDFs_ englisch/FS_14.1_ENGL_1.Aufl_RZ-web.pdf>
2   ibid.

WOMEN AIRFORCE SERVICE PILOTS INSIGNIA

1943-44

At around the same time as Mascha Kaléko and other émigrés were trying to find their feet and start a new life in New York, not long after America had entered the war, the US Air Force was realising – to its consternation – that while it had sufficient bombers on hand, it would soon run out of pilots to fly them. If all the men were away fighting on the Front, who would be left to fly the planes from factory to launch site? Who would be there to conduct test flights, carry out safety checks, break in the planes and train pilots on the latest models?

While the men were scratching their heads over these questions, failing to get any closer to an answer, two famous female pilots of the day, Jackie Cochran and Nancy Love, threw a completely crazy idea into the ring: what about training women to fly military aircraft? At that time, it certainly wasn't common for women to be able to fly planes, but nor was it entirely new. The American pilot Amelia Earhart was already a star; in 1928 she'd become the first woman to fly across the Atlantic, albeit as a passenger – or, as she put it, 'a sack of potatoes' – and in 1932 was the first female pilot to fly the same route solo. She wrote books and columns and toured the whole country; she gave talks in schools to young girls whom she encouraged to enrol at university to study 'masculine' subjects like engineering, and put off marriage until later. On the day of her own wedding, she wrote her husband a sentence so honest that it simply has to be quoted here: 'I may have to keep some place where I can go to be myself, now and then, for I cannot guarantee to endure at all times the confinement of even an attractive cage.'[1] In 1937

---

1   Earhart, Amelia, 'You Must Know Again My Reluctance to Marry', 1931, in *Letters of Note*, available at: <https://lettersofnote.com/2010/04/01/you-must-know-again-my-reluctance-to-marry/>

she flew that 'attractive cage', her marriage, for the final time, on board her Lockheed Electra. She hoped to be the first person to circumnavigate the globe by plane, but on 2 July she disappeared without trace somewhere over the Pacific Ocean. This made her legendary – and a role model for many young women who yearned for more than a cage, no matter how attractive. Perhaps it was the example she set, perhaps the time was simply ripe or the need just too great, but, at any rate, 1942 saw the creation of the first US Air Force training camps for women. Twenty-five thousand American women applied; just under a thousand successfully completed their training.

They were known as the WASPs, the Women Airforce Service Pilots, and this figure drawn by Walt Disney became their mascot. Her name was Fifinella – Fifi for short – and she had her origins in *The Gremlins*, a story by Roald Dahl. Dahl himself had been a pilot in the Royal Air Force, where 'gremlins' were technical problems, little monsters that made pilots' lives difficult. Only Fifinella, of course, was different. She was more fairy than monster; you could see that immediately. She was a mixture of angel, Superwoman and pilot, and in her role as lucky mascot she didn't just adorn the women's bomber jackets, but also the roof of their very first training camp in Texas. 'Keep them flying, Fifinella!' exclaimed a report on the WASP ladies, each of whom had 'gone into a man's world because the men needed her, gone through a tough ordeal as just a girl and come out a girl pilot with the US Army Air Force'. Just don't tell them flying isn't a job for women: 'They wouldn't believe it!' said the report. In the two years this unusual experiment lasted, the WASPs racked up almost 60 million miles with Fifinella on their chests. They flew all the military aircraft available – some seventy different models – transporting them to air bases all over the country and conducting test and practice flights. In some cases, they took on tasks for which even the men wouldn't volunteer. Flying the B-29 Superfortress, for example. This heavy bomber (the heaviest and most efficient of the war) was brand new at the time and regarded as an unsafe conveyance. Pilots had lost their lives during its early test flights; it was known as the 'widow maker', which of course meant that no one wanted to get into the cockpit. Until someone had the bright idea of having the WASPs demonstrate this four-engine monster. The message was clear: if even a woman can fly it, there's absolutely no reason you boys can't too! The gents seem to have swallowed this absurd logic at once. After two WASP ladies had carried out demonstration flights at all the air bases, the B-29 was pressed into service in May 1944. Sadly, it would later become notorious as the plane that dropped the atomic bombs on Hiroshima and Nagasaki.

But by the summer of 1945, when the atomic bombs were dropped, the WASPs were already a thing of the past. The first men had returned from their foreign tours of duty in 1944 and been amazed to find women occupying their posts, upon which the young lady pilots had been quickly but firmly shown the door. The promise of accepting them into the armed forces was never kept, and those who attempted to get jobs as commercial pilots were told in no uncertain terms that they'd be better off trying their luck as stewardesses – that was more feminine. Everyone had forgotten that the USA's war 'could not have been won' without the WASPs and Fifinella, as one general put it soon afterwards. They were simply erased from history, until the US Air Force officially began admitting women in the 1970s, prompting the papers to report that they were the 'first women to fly military aircraft'. At this point, the ladies of the 'Order of Fifinella' had had it. *We were the first. Thirty years ago!* they protested, and from then on they were gradually recalled to the public consciousness until, in 2010, they were awarded the Congressional Gold Medal, the highest civil award bestowed in the country. This was all good and important, but what actually mattered to many of these women was something quite different. As one WASP veteran said, very much in the spirit of Amelia Earhart and her need for freedom: 'We did it for love of flying.'

ROBERT CAPA PHOTOGRAPH, THE SHAVED WOMAN OF CHARTRES

1944

Perhaps this chapter ought to tell a different story. Perhaps it should be about the many thousands of women who were murdered in concentration camps like Ravensbrück, about the millions of Jewish victims of the Holocaust. Or, perhaps, about those who survived it. The ones who managed to hide, but whose hiding places, we're slowly coming to realise, weren't always granted to them out of pure humanitarianism. Yet this chapter isn't going to tell the story of the Second World War, but the story of its end; not of the undisputed victims, but of those who were also perpetrators. Of women whose bodies became theatres of conflict, of a phenomenon that existed everywhere but was particularly strong in France and which, especially in the months following the *libération*, spread like wildfire. Of which this photo by Robert Capa, *The Shaved Woman of Chartres*, is a record.

Capa was the photographer of the liberation at the time he shot this photo, in the summer of 1944. He'd landed with the Allies in Normandy on 6 June and photographed the soldiers creeping forward from their landing craft under a hail of German bullets, wading heavily armed through the sea. He'd been there for the liberation of Paris and sat in one of the vehicles processing triumphantly down the Champs-Élysées. The photos he took that day in the capital show us just what we might expect from such a moment: crowds of people flooding the streets and boulevards, or standing on balconies waving flags. People throwing their arms in the air, celebrating, laughing, embracing one another. Nurses kissing soldiers; little boys picking their noses atop American tanks. Photos of happiness, then, and of relief. Yet that August, just a couple of days before, Capa had taken quite a different photo of liberation. This one right here. It's interesting, isn't it: in one depiction – let's call it the one of 'joyful liberation' – mainly men can be seen. Policemen, soldiers, heroes crowding the streets. And in the other, the one that stood for all that was shameful and deserving of punishment – collaboration, general cowardice and (contrary to what General de Gaulle would claim, both immediately and for decades after) the fact that most French people had had absolutely nothing to do with the resistance – one saw a woman. What's more, a mother.

This photo was taken on 16 August 1944 in Chartres, less than sixty miles from Paris as the crow flies. It shows twenty-three-year-old Simone Touseau and her three-month-old baby. She has a '1944 haircut': a shaved head. Her little girl, whose dark hair forms such a stark contrast to her mother's shorn pate, was the daughter of a German soldier, a certain Erich Göz. On this day, Touseau had become a victim of the so-called *épuration sauvage*, the wild purge, which punished without trial all those who had allegedly collaborated or sympathised with the enemy. Men were simply shot somewhere behind a wall, discreetly, but women were branded. Their heads were shaved and they were paraded through the streets. This shaving business was nothing new. Hair had always been synonymous with femininity and, in turn, femininity had long been a woman's only identity. Taking her hair meant robbing her of her identity. As far back as antiquity, unfaithful women had had their heads shaved; it was the same in the Middle Ages. Witch-hunts often involved shaving women's pubic hair, to find 'the mark of the devil' or use the humiliation to force them into a confession. During the First World War, German women who were said to have had an affair with a French soldier would have their heads shaved; in Denmark and Norway, the so-called *tyskertøs* (Germans' girls) had been experiencing this treatment since 1940. But in France, the phenomenon took on hitherto unseen proportions: in the months leading up to and especially after the liberation, that summer of 1944, around 20,000 woman, perhaps even more, were subjected to this barbaric ritual.

They were dragged from their homes and had their hair cut, shaved, shorn from their bodies in front of the entire village; photos were taken of and with them, as though they were dolls. They had red swastikas daubed on their foreheads and were crammed together on trucks painted with the words *poules à boches* (Nazi whores), where they were presented to the baying crowds. They were insulted and laughed at, spat on and pelted with objects. After that, most were forced to leave the village and go into hiding for months until their hair had grown back, as Marguerite Duras describes in *Hiroshima, My Love*. The *tondues*, as they were called, were accused of one thing above all: love, or 'horizontal collaboration'. Georges Brassens once sang of a beauty who slept with the Prussian king, yet by no means all of them had slept with a 'Prussian', whether out of love or opportunism. Most of these women had simply displayed the same behaviour as most men: they weren't heroic, sometimes they were even actively cruel, but in most cases they simply had no choice if they and their families were to survive. It's telling that it should have been they who were punished so quickly, and above all so publicly, and made into a symbol of collaboration – especially when we consider how many real (male) collaborators got away without harm coming to a single hair on their head.

Many of the emotions that surged forth after the liberation came down on women's heads: shame at the capitulation of 1940, disgrace about state-level collaboration, all the fear and humiliation of the past few years, perhaps even anger at one's own cowardice or deeds. Punishing women was a way for men to restore their dented masculinity: *résistance* was given a male face, collaboration a female one. A couple of weeks after Capa published this photo as a double-page spread in *Life* magazine, the French poet Paul Éluard wrote one of his most beautiful poems to commemorate these women: 'Understand me who will / For me my remorse was / The hapless one who lay still / On the paving stone / The reasonable victim / In the ripped frock / With the eyes of a lost child / She who resembles the dead / Who have died of being desired.'[1]

---

1   Éluard, Paul, 'Understand Me Who Will', tr. George Dillon, *Poetry*, Vol. LXVII, No. 1, October 1945, pp. 8–9, available at: <https://www.poetryfoundation.org/poetrymagazine/browse?volume=67&issue=1&page=21>

THE BIKINI

1947

Essentially, it's the same thing every year. From October until, let's say, June, women's bodies are left in peace, but as soon as the sun shines for more than a couple of miserly hours a day and rising temperatures start removing layers, women find themselves deluged with advice on self-optimisation. Even in this era of so-called 'body positivity', many women's magazines just can't help suggesting 'Four Steps to a Bikini Body', and even those that no longer use terms like these still end up offering the same advice: to be a little bit cruel to yourself in summer in order to give this item its due. Enter, the bikini.

The two-piece made its debut appearance in July 1946. The setting was the Parisian swimming pool Le Molitor, where French nude dancer Micheline Bernardini modelled a new design by Louis Réard, creator of the modern bikini, and caused her contemporaries considerable horror with the flimsy fabric nothing – just three small triangles on her entire body. A couple of decades earlier, the swimmer Annette Kellerman had been arrested for effecting a public mischief by swimming in what was apparently too tight a one-piece. Even if things weren't quite so prudish any more, the bikini was still very daring. 'Explosive', you might say. At least, that's how Réard imagined it. A couple of days prior to the Molitor performance, the USA had conducted its first test of a nuclear weapon on Bikini Atoll, and the new style of bathing suit was named for this 'progress'. The garment Bernardini modelled was even printed with newspaper headlines reporting on the atomic event. It was intended to be a symbol of modernity, and of female emancipation. Nonetheless, Bernardini received strange looks – though at least she wasn't arrested – and plenty of people were against the bikini. Spain and Italy, for example, banned it completely; the Pope was outraged at the sight of women's bellybuttons; and the American magazine *Modern Girl* found it unnecessary to waste even a single word on the scrap of fabric, 'since it is inconceivable that any girl with tact and decency would ever wear such a thing'.[1] And yet, some evidently did wish to trade tact and decency for the feeling of the sun on their stomachs. Brigitte Bardot, for example, and Marilyn Monroe, Bond girl Ursula Andress, and many other stars. At the end of the 1960s, they made the 'Itsy Bitsy Teenie Weenie' bikini acceptable in polite society – the beach-based kind, at any rate. And, for a couple of decades, left swimsuits looking pretty outmoded.

This golden garment was created in 1947 for the winner of the Miss Réard beauty contest and typifies the second stage of the bikini. Because even if the saucy new style of swimwear was interpreted as a sign of emancipation for a while, it soon became apparent that it could also be used for an entirely different purpose: as a means of sexualising and objectifying women's bodies. For the pin-up girl, for example – that hyper-eroticised female figure of the 1950s, dreamed about most especially by the men who wrapped their wives in ugly kitchen aprons – the bikini was something like a work uniform. And at the beauty contests that began to materialise around this time, bikini-modelling became the supreme discipline. Here, women would parade their half-naked bodies in front of a jury made up almost exclusively of men, before trembling with nervous anticipation as they waited on the verdict. In 1951, the very first Miss World even took to the winners' podium in a bikini. And while such things were later abolished, with the candidates allowed to receive their sashes in a greater state of dress, there was still no getting around the requirement to present their bottoms in 'the triangle' – the cause of increasing distress to feminists from the mid-1960s onwards. Their protests, which remain legendary to this day, may not have been against the garment itself, but they were vehemently opposed to what it turned women into: livestock to be inspected.

That, at least, is what you might have read on the placards that took to the streets of New Jersey in advance of the 1968 Miss America beauty pageant to protest against the shameless staging of what they deemed a 'cattle auction'. One of the almost three hundred women taking part in the demonstration had even brought a sheep with her; it ran through the crowd with a Miss America sash round its neck. Other women

1   Quoted in <https://www.cosmopolitan.com/uk/fashion/style/news/a36046/100-years-of-the-bikini-evolution/>

waved signs depicting a woman's naked body divided up into cuts, like a cow at the butcher's – ribs, chuck, loin and so forth – beneath the words 'Break the Dull Steak Habit'. The famous anecdote about bra-burning also dates back to this protest, even if it does seem to be less fact than fiction: women did indeed throw their bras into trash cans, but the only thing burning was their anger.

Even more famous than that protest, however, was one that took place on 20 November 1970, when several feminists sneaked into the final of the Miss World contest, held that year in London's Royal Albert Hall. They were disguised as elegantly dressed ladies, albeit with unusual accessories hidden in their handbags: water pistols, flour bombs and a rattle to act as the starting gun. Their plan was to launch an attack during the bikini challenge – the most degrading round of all. Yet that evening the compère told one misogynistic joke after another, quickly exhausting the women's patience so that the rattle sounded much earlier than expected. Suddenly, flour and stink bombs began raining down on the stage, and furious shouts went up from the audience: 'We're not ugly! We're not beautiful! We're angry!' The young women were arrested, and that evening the first Black Miss World was elected. Interestingly, the bikini round was abolished in 2014 – at the time, it was said the competition was more about ladies' brains than bottoms – but, thanks to a decline in viewing figures, it has since been reinstated.

Meanwhile, the debates about women's swimwear trends – and, by association, their bodies – rage on. Where once it was too little fabric getting people all het up about the bikini, in August 2016 it was a case of 'too much' that ruled the French headlines: the burkini, an all-over swimsuit belonging to so-called 'modest wear', caused a summer scandal. Arrests were made on the beach, 'no burkini' signs appeared at swimming pools, and many discussions were had – the majority of their participants men. No satisfactory conclusions were reached in this way, because ultimately there can only be one answer to the question of what a woman is allowed to wear at the pool or the beach: just as much or as little as she pleases.

ALBERTO GIACOMETTI, *SIMONE DE BEAUVOIR* PORTRAIT

c. 1946

'I [. . .] gazed at the blank sheet of paper in front of me. I felt the need to write in my fingertips, and the taste of the words in my throat, but I didn't know where to start, or what.'[1] So wrote the French philosopher and author Simone de Beauvoir in *The Force of Circumstance*, the third volume of her memoirs. She was remembering an afternoon in 1948 at Café Les Deux Magots in Paris. Her friend Alberto Giacometti, who was sitting opposite, said to her, '"How wild you look!"' De Beauvoir replied, '"It's because I want to write and I don't know what".' Giacometti's answer: '"Write anything."'[2] In that moment, according to de Beauvoir, she realised she wanted to write about herself, about life as a woman. And this brief, succinct exchange between artist and novelist would result in the writing of *The Second Sex*, the book she published the following year.

Giacometti and de Beauvoir had got to know one another before the war, in the 1930s. His wild mane of hair and way of seeming 'strong as a rock' and 'freer than an elf' fascinated her just as much as his mind did. He got straight to the heart of the matter and examined things with endless patience and inexhaustible curiosity, she once said – and, in a way, these qualities are recognisable in this small sculpture, which Alberto made in 1946. It gets right to the core of his model, to the part of Simone for which she is still so admired today: her head. To her fine, sometimes stern features, her legendary piled-up hairstyle. At the time, de Beauvoir had already published three novels; she was known in certain circles, but still one revolutionary essay away from the

---

1   de Beauvoir, Simone, *The Autobiography of Simone de Beauvoir: After the War: Force of Circumstance, I: 1944–1952*, tr. Richard Howard (New York: Paragon House, 1992), p. 94
2   ibid.

international fame that would soon befall her. Nonetheless, her friend seems already to have seen her as the icon she would become. He portrayed her as we see her still: a brilliant but somewhat fierce mind, older than her years; a woman who looked down on everything with a cool, analytical manner and seldom seemed truly moved. Simone de Beauvoir was sometimes accused of being devoid of emotion, overly intellectual, out of touch with the real world. Almost in the same breath, people got worked up about the way she discussed sex so openly – or, as François Mauriac wrote to the journal *Les Temps Modernes* after *The Second Sex* was published: '"Your employer's vagina has no secrets from me"'.[1] Never before had a philosopher written about women's first periods, first sex, bodies. It was revolutionary, and shocking.

Yet in life, in contrast to her books, de Beauvoir seems to have made great efforts to appear the slightly standoffish, composed intellectual. Women lacking a body are taken more seriously – it has always been thus, and Simone doubtless knew that very well. Ever since her childhood friend Zaza had perished in the pursuit of passion, she'd understood that it was better for a woman to live at a distance, alone in her head, not letting her heart get the better of her. Whenever she and her love life are spoken of, the first figure to appear is always Jean-Paul Sartre. Sartre, her life partner; Sartre, her colleague; Sartre, that strangely brilliant man whom she met at university and never left again. Sartre the philosopher, with whom she enjoyed a lifelong, intellectually fulfilling partnership, but never passionate love. If she had 'only' ever known this deep friendship that laid claim to the head but never the rest of the body and being, then her thoughts on what it is to be a woman might have turned out quite differently. And yet *The Second Sex* is, among other things, about how 'the woman' in our societies is defined in relation to 'the man' – as the other, the second – and how it will always be dangerous for her to situate herself within this relationship. Because it automatically forces her into an old role often without her even noticing. Women of de Beauvoir's generation could go to work, study, drive a car and ride around Paris on a bike; they could be independent and have affairs, but what happened if they entered into a relationship? An intimate one, a fixed one? Could they still exist freely

---

1 Quoted in Simone de Beauvoir, *The Autobiography of Simone de Beauvoir: After the War: Force of Circumstance*, I: 1944–1952, tr. Richard Howard (New York: Paragon House, 1992), p. 187

within it, or would they once again be discreetly and insidiously forced into a position of subjugation and self-sacrifice? Unlike men, didn't women always have to make a choice: love or ambition?

While she was writing *The Second Sex*, she was probably asking herself these very same questions; she was, perhaps for the first time, properly in love – head over heels, as they say – with an American, the writer Nelson Algren. De Beauvoir met him on a trip to the USA in 1947, one year after she sat for her friend Giacometti, and fell in love on the spot. It was with him, she confided to her biographer, that she had her first orgasm; with him, she was a different woman. Anyone who thinks of Simone as the cool, casual, all-dismissing lover of Sartre will find themselves astonished by her letters to Algren. She's a different de Beauvoir. She's excitable, loving, gushing, vulnerable. Sometimes she's even corny, and harbours dreams – hard to believe, this – of domesticity. All at once, the woman who had always railed against marriage wanted to be his 'wifey', to stand at the stove and cook for him, to give him everything. Perhaps this relationship (which affected her quite differently to the one she had with Sartre) was the first time she'd personally experienced how deeply anchored those gender roles are, how difficult it is to rid yourself mentally of centuries of self-sacrifice, and how quickly even such a reflective woman can fall back into patterns that are entirely alien to her and everything she expects from life. Perhaps, in this relationship, she realised that despite all the progress they'd made, women of her day still sometimes had to make a painful choice: me or him. A truly free and egalitarian 'we' just didn't exist yet.

We know what Simone de Beauvoir chose. She refused to marry Nelson Algren, which eventually led to a breakup. 'I couldn't live only on love and happiness,' she wrote.[1] She clearly thought her love life was over. But she was wrong. A short while later she met Claude Lanzmann, seventeen years her junior, with whom she had a passionate relationship (although she wrote to Algren saying that she didn't love Lanzmann the same way she'd loved him – that kind of love was lost to her now). And yet, she was also right: men, love and lust were transient, but the one thing she'd always have was her powerful mind. Giacometti's version of the head that contained it would stand on her desk until her death.

---

1 See <https://www.radiofrance.fr/franceculture/podcasts/les-chemins-de-la-philosophie/je-ne-pourrais-pas-vivre-uniquement-de-bonheur-et-d-amour-7518835>

BASIC LAW FOR THE FEDERAL REPUBLIC OF GERMANY

1949

On 1 September 1948, when the parliamentary commission convened to commence its work on a new volume, the Basic Law for the newly created Federal Republic of Germany, with a ceremonial event in Bonn's Museum Koenig, there was an unusual guest standing in the corner. Namely, a giraffe. According to legend, this giraffe – which was usually on display in the atrium alongside several other taxidermy animals – spent the entire ceremony peering out from behind a curtain, eavesdropping on Bach's *Overture in D Minor*, Beethoven's *Leonore* overtures and the speeches that called on the sixty-five elected parliamentarians present to do their solemn duty. And no doubt that giraffe will have looked at the sea of gentlemen spread out before it and thought: *Yet again, where on earth are all the women?*

Looking at the photos taken of that day, and of the sessions held in Bonn over the months that followed, it's easy to imagine the participants were all men. It looks as though, once again, a group of tie-wearers had got together, this time to write the foundational text for a 'new Germany'. But there were women in attendance too. Four, to be exact. Their names were Frieda Nadig, Elisabeth Selbert, Helene Weber and Helene Wessel, and they were the so-called 'Mothers of the Basic Law'. We know this, even if we almost never see them in the photos. We know this because right at the start of this work, in Article 3 Paragraph 2, shortly after 'Human dignity shall be inviolable', 'Every person shall have the right to free development of his personality' and 'All persons shall be equal before the law', we find one sentence that wouldn't exist in this form were it not for Nadig, Weber, Wessel and especially Selbert. It reads: 'Men and women shall have equal rights.'[1] So simple. So succinct. And yet so hard-won. Originally, something entirely different was going to be written there, a wording that dated back to the Weimar Republic: 'Men and women shall have the same civic rights and duties.'

The words are similar, yes, but they say something quite different. Something about an individual's relationship to the state, but nothing about the balance of power between men and women. They don't rattle the bars – not even cautiously – of the legal principle laid down back in imperial times, which said that the man was the head of the family and the ultimate holder of decision-making power when it came to all life's most important questions. This was a completely anachronistic attitude that Elisabeth Selbert, lawyer and author of that far-reaching sentence, particularly wanted to see changed. As a mother of two in the Weimar Republic, Selbert had belatedly sat her school-leaving certificate and followed up with a law degree; in 1934 she had been one of the last women admitted to the Bar before the Nazis banned them from entering the profession. She'd represented people persecuted by the Nazi regime, but also often women facing a divorce, and again and again had seen 'how great was these women's fear that divorce would see them leave home empty-handed, because according to the German Civil Code they were obligated to work in their husband's shop or business without being entitled to a share of the profit or fortune they had helped to earn'.[2]

Equality was needed, one that was anchored in the foundations of the new state and that would allow women a certain independence, thought Selbert. And, as expected, she met with much outraged furrowing of brows. She was accused of holding up the entire process of writing the Basic Law with her demand, possibly even endangering it. Moreover, the German people wanted stability; this really was an inopportune moment to shake the foundations of that sacred institution: family. And, more than all this, men already felt unsettled – was it really

1   All extracts in this chapter from the Basic Law for the Federal Republic of Germany, Federal Office of Justice, tr. Professor Christian Tomuschat, Professor David P. Currie, Professor Donald P. Kommers and Raymond Kerr, in cooperation with the Language Service of the German Bundestag, available at <https://www.gesetze-im-internet.de/englisch_gg/englisch_gg.html>
2   Elisabeth Selbert quoted in 'Sie brachte die Gleichberechtigung "kurz und bündig" ins Grundgesetz', Monika Köpcke, Deutschlandfunk, 21 September 2021, available (in German) at <https://www.deutschlandfunk.de/125-geburtstag-von-elisabeth-selbert-sie-brachte-die-100.html>

necessary to unsettle them yet further? Even Frieda Nadig initially thought her SPD colleague's suggestion unrealistic. As a specialist in family law, she knew that the paragraph in question sounded unassuming, but that rewording it would necessitate an entire raft of new laws. The two other ladies, Helene Weber – who had been the first woman to work as a ministerial councillor in the Weimar Republic and was dismissed by the Nazis in 1933 for 'political unreliability' – and particularly Helene Wessel, were against it at first. The first motion was rejected with eleven votes to nine; the second also failed to pass. It didn't look good for our equal rights, but Selbert didn't let up. And because her colleagues didn't want to listen to her, she told the public instead: she spoke in factories and to women's groups, made speeches on the radio, wrote articles in newspapers and explained to women exactly what was at stake for them. She did this until the parliamentary commission was flooded with letters. Women (and perhaps even a couple of men) advocated so strongly for Article 3 Paragraph 2 that in January 1949 the parliamentarians reluctantly voted in favour of the new wording. The fundamental tenet of equal rights was set down in the Basic Law as inalienable, and laid the foundations of everything that was to follow.

It would still be a long time before equality was actually achieved; to all intents and purposes, we still haven't reached it yet. To this day, women in Germany earn roughly 18 per cent less than men; to this day, most domestic and caring work falls to them. Perhaps this is partly because the 'Mothers of the Basic Law' did fight for equality, yet hardly anyone was interested in implementing it at first. In the early years of the Federal Republic, economic advancement seemed more important to most people – including most women, by the way – than women's rights. It took until 1957 for a law to be passed decreeing that a woman could work without her husband's agreement, even against his will. After the reunification of Germany in 1990, a commission was once again formed to work on the Basic Law, and expanded on Paragraph 2 of Article 3 with a decisive, yet still not fully realised, sentence: 'The state shall promote the actual implementation of equal rights for women and men and take steps to eliminate disadvantages that now exist.'[1]

1 Federal Republic of Germany, Federal Office of Justice, tr. Professor Christian Tomuschat, Professor David P. Currie, Professor Donald P. Kommers and Raymond Kerr, in cooperation with the Language Service of the German Bundestag, available at <https://www.gesetze-im-internet.de/englisch_gg/englisch_gg.html>

DAILY NEWS

NEW YORK'S PICTURE NEWSPAPER

4¢

EX-GI BECOMES BLONDE BEAUTY

Operations Transform Bronx Youth

A World of a Difference

FRONT PAGE OF
THE *DAILY NEWS*

1 DECEMBER 1952

In 1952, Mr and Mrs Jorgensen received a surprising letter from Denmark, in which they read the following sentence: 'Nature made a mistake which I have had corrected, and now I am your daughter.'[1] The letter was signed 'Christine'. The Jorgensens will surely have needed a couple of minutes to understand what was going on. Until that moment, the couple from the Bronx thought they had a daughter and a son: Dolly and George. George had travelled to Copenhagen the previous year, ostensibly to visit an aunt and establish himself as a photographer, but now the Jorgensens were learning that he'd made the trip with quite a different goal in mind. George was now Christine; their son had become a daughter. As a child, George had once asked his mother why he couldn't be like Dolly, why he wasn't also a girl. Now, after twenty years of doubt and self-directed anger, it was high time to correct that.

Back then, in the early 1950s, in the midst of the testosterone-heavy, hero-worshipping post-war era, this was something new. Sexology – particularly the research conducted by German doctor Magnus Hirschfeld – had named and studied the existence of 'intermediary sexes', or, as he called it, a 'third sex'. In the 1920s, Hirschfeld's Institute for Sexual Science in Berlin offered a haven for anyone who felt themselves to be 'different': homosexual, transsexual, bisexual. But operations were still experimental, dangerous and correspondingly rare. In 1930, Hirschfeld's colleague Kurt Warnekros had carried out gender-affirming surgery on the Danish painter Lili Elbe, but his patient

---

1   Letter from Christine Jorgensen to her parents, 1952. Quoted in several media outlets online, including <https://www.nationalgeographic.com/history/article/how-historians-are-documenting-lives-of-transgender-people>

had since died of complications. And even if there had been a couple of other cases, they weren't well known among the general public. Especially not in the USA, where sexology was only just taking its first slow, soft-footed steps thanks to an institute established by Alfred Kinsey, and where such topics weren't generally talked about. In this context, Christine Jorgensen's letter was so sensational that it couldn't remain a private matter. Even before she returned home, the news had been leaked, which meant that the young woman landed in all the newspaper headlines a good seventy years before Caitlyn Jenner appeared on the cover of *Vanity Fair*. 'Ex-GI Becomes Blonde Beauty' wrote the *New York Daily News* on 1 December 1952, as can be seen here; inside, the paper printed Christine's letter to her parents (the reporter having led them to believe it was in their daughter's interests to publish first-hand information). Alongside the article and letter, readers could see 'before and after' photos: George the GI, Christine the glamorous beauty.

It's telling that this headline makes use of two stereotypes to help the 'transition' from one gender to another seem more spectacular: the GI, who was the personification of masculinity in post-war America, versus the 'blonde beauty', the cliché of pin ups and Hollywood attraction. According to this portrayal, Christine had propelled herself from the definitively closed category of 'man' into its opposite: 'woman'. The idea that these categories didn't always have to be clearly demarcated, but could instead be more fluid, was one people hadn't grasped yet. In an interview she gave in 1957, Jorgensen herself answered the question, 'Are you a woman?' as follows: 'You seem to assume that every person is either a man or a woman . . . Each person is actually both in varying degrees.'[1] The narrative put forward by the papers – the business with the military, for example – was completely exaggerated in any case: it sounded as though Christine had been a GI who'd set off one day to rescue Europe and returned after VE Day a woman. In reality, it hadn't been like that at all. But the break seemed far sharper and more interesting portrayed that way.

When Christine finally landed in New York a couple of weeks later, crowds of people turned out to greet her at the airport. Fans, reporters, curious onlookers – the 'blonde beauty' was a sensation. She was

---

1   Christine Jorgensen, in 'Christine Jorgensen Reveals', interview from 1957, available at: <https://www.youtube.com/watch?v=nZfVvLFdEqs>

forced to hold an impromptu press conference and, just in case she'd ever been under the illusion that she would be able to lead a 'normal' life as a young woman, that day in February 1953 doubtless showed her that no such thing would be happening any time soon: 'I was surprised that everyone seemed very interested in my life . . . time went on and I realized this was an important step in the eyes of the world.'[1] Her story was no longer merely her own; suddenly, it belonged to everyone. She usually gave a loose answer to intimate questions and requests for details about her genitalia. Watching those interviews now, it's painful to see how directly she was asked about the most intimate parts of her body. Yet it also seems that these questions weren't asked out of voyeurism or any desire to shame her publicly, but out of the wish to shed light on something that most people at the time couldn't comprehend yet. Jorgensen became a mouthpiece. She took every opportunity to explain her story – in 1967 she even wrote it all down again in *Christine Jorgensen: A Personal Autobiography* – and she used her media presence to create a language for the perception of both one's physical body and one's self, words that hadn't existed until then. Her popularity isn't just credited with helping lots of people to accept themselves, but also with advancing research, like that of the American transgender pioneer Harry Benjamin. In the 1970s, when 'gender' gradually started becoming a topic of conversation, Christine gave a lecture at UCLA in which she said: 'We didn't start the sexual revolution but I think we gave it a good kick in the pants!'[2]

---

1   Christine Jorgensen. quoted in 'From GI Joe to GI Jane: Christine Jorgensen's Story' (National WWII Museum website, 30 June 2020), at: <https://www.nationalww2museum. org/war/articles/christine-jorgensen>
2   Interview with Christine Jorgensen, quoted in 'Christine Jorgensen: 60 years of sex change ops' (BBC News website, 30 November 2012). Available at: <https://www.bbc. com/news/magazine-20544095>

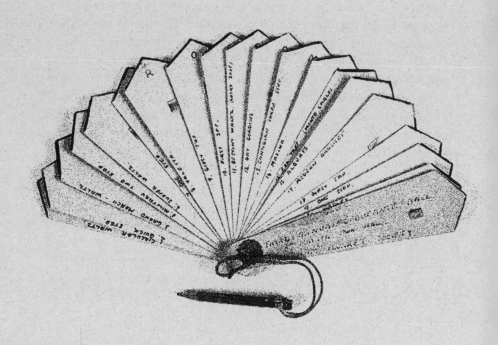

DANCE-CARD FAN

1950s

In 1939, the British novelist and painter Leonora Carrington wrote a short story so bizarre that it simply has to be told. Its title is 'The Debutante', and it goes something like this. On the day of her debutante ball, a young girl can be found at the zoo, standing by the cage belonging to her friend, a hyena, and complaining: 'What a bloody nuisance [. . .] I have to go to my ball tonight.' The hyena is surprised; she'd love to go to such an event. 'I don't know how to dance, but at least I could make small talk,' she says.[1] And so the pair come to an agreement: the hyena will take the young woman's place. The girl squeezes the animal into her ball gown, teaches her how to walk in high heels and conceals her paws in a pair of gloves – but what to do about her face? They even find a solution for that: the hyena kills the chambermaid (good timing; she was hungry anyway) and 'borrows' her face. It's all going swimmingly, but then the hyena commits a faux pas at the event. While the girl is sitting calmly at home in her room, reading *Gulliver's Travels*, the hyena announces somewhat cryptically at dinner: 'So I smell a bit strong, what? Well, I don't eat cakes!'[2] Upon which she tears off her borrowed face, gulps it down and leaps clean out of the window.

Carrington's story is somewhat disturbing but, in its exaggerated way, it engages with something many young women must have felt in the face of the ball-going tradition that had been practised since the eighteenth century. Just as the girl dresses up her friend, the hyena, so too did mothers force their daughters into a role that maybe didn't suit them at all: that of feminine perfection. Her costume had to be just right, but what

---

1   Carrington, Leonora, 'The Debutante', in *The Debutante and Other Stories* (London: Silver Press, 2017), p. 1
2   ibid., p. 4

was going on behind the façade didn't matter – just as long as the girl didn't behave like the hyena and destroy the pretty picture. Certainly, one or the other would have liked to show her 'true face' or leap out of the window, but most of them kept quiet and let it all wash over them.

This object, a fan that doubles as a dance card, speaks to this particular rite of passage, which turned young women into something akin to zoo animals. It dates back to the 1950s and comes from New Zealand, but fans like these had existed since the nineteenth century. They were often grander and more elaborate in appearance, made of ivory or sometimes even gold; sometimes they took the form of a little book, sometimes a piece of jewellery. The idea was for a young woman to note down the name of every man with whom she agreed to dance, and then at the end of the night she and her mother would also be able to check exactly which young fellow it was with whom she'd executed such a lovely foxtrot or waltz.

The 'debutante' tradition hardened into a mandatory rite of passage among the upper classes from the late eighteenth century. Because young women weren't allowed to inherit, it was important they didn't fall in love with a cute stable boy, but with a well-regarded gentleman. And to ensure this did in fact happen, each season the young women of marriageable age would be put together in a room along with said gentlemen in the hope that something would happen during the dancing. Imagine it like the dance version of speed dating: you had barely five minutes to make a convincing impression, and were up against plenty of other young, rich, attractive women. You had to make a serious effort if you hoped to stand out and have any suitors at all – whose names you could put down on your dance card, of course – for which reason mothers went to crazy amounts of expense and spent weeks terrorising their daughters with the rules of etiquette and advice on how to bewitch a man. Unlike on her wedding day, en route to the altar, it was a young woman's mother who got to lead her into a ball. Men arrived alone, of course. They weren't polished to a high shine like the finest family silver; they didn't need to please, but were there to inspect the latest goods and make their choice. Or not. A man could drift around the debutante balls for as long as he wanted; a young woman, on the other hand, ought to have been sold off after just one season if she didn't want to feel she was past her use-by date and end up with the moniker 'old maid'.

Originally, the debutante ball was an affair reserved for nobility, yet the tradition survived long beyond the decline of the aristocracy. Particularly in the USA, where the financial elite enthusiastically continued to conduct such ceremonies, which most young women described as tormenting and hopelessly stressful. Eleanor Roosevelt, for example, whose so-called 'coming out' took place in 1902 at the Waldorf-Astoria in New York, hated the experience: she felt completely stupid and went home early. Edith Wharton found it a 'long cold agony of shyness'. A little later on, balls became an opportunity for ambitious families to achieve fame through their daughters: Brenda Frazier, for example, who was the first internationally famous debutante, a so-called 'celeb-utante'. She was a kind of It-girl for the late 1930s: rich – no, nouveau riche – and famous for being famous. The ball her mother organised for her was apparently so spectacular that Frazier even made it to the cover of *Life* magazine. Alas, it didn't bring her much happiness. She became addicted to alcohol and drugs and, having spent more or less her entire life ill in bed, died relatively young; she once described her 'debut' as 'a horror'. But that didn't matter. In the 1940s and '50s, enthusiasm for the bride parade only increased; in some circles, the tradition continues, apparently now more than ever.

Funnily enough, this special dance card from May 1956 does have a name written down for every dance, yet not a single one is a man's. Instead, they're all women's. Perhaps there was a latent Leonora Carrington inside this particular debutante – or, who knows, a hyena making a stand against ceremony.

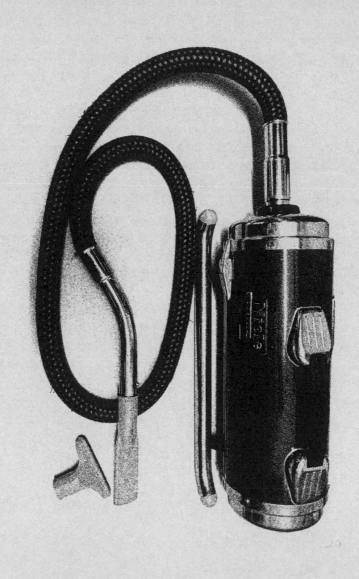

MIELE 'MODEL A' VACUUM CLEANER

1951–61

In 'how to' guides for 1950s American housewives, which nowadays may read to us like parodies, women are nudged towards an end-of-day scenario that looks something like this: when her husband returns home in the evening, like a hunter of old to his cave, she should greet him at the door, elegantly dressed and prettily made-up, offer him a smile and a drink, and ask him how his day was. The one thing she absolutely must not do, is trouble him with her trivial thoughts and concerns. He's spent the whole day working, after all. She has not.

This scene is exaggerated, of course, but reality wasn't all that different. Our clichéd image of the housewife's existence was daily life for many women in the 1950s. In Germany and the USA in particular, especially in the lower-middle-class milieu, many women spent most of their time occupied with housework, childcare and entertaining their husbands. After women across the globe had taken an active role during the war, the end of the conflict saw them kindly but firmly packed off back to their homes, and a social framework created to keep them there. Even women who studied at university found themselves tying on an apron no later than graduation. In part, this was because interesting jobs were rarely accessible to them, and tax laws such as income splitting for married couples were conceived in such a way that if the woman worked, it would result in greater outlay than income. And in part, too, because the eighteenth-century housewife ideal had been revitalised and given a fresh new look. From now on, being 'allowed' to stay at home was termed 'progress'. The women who had fought for independence at the beginning of the century were pitied. What greater luxury than being a housewife? The argument was simple, even plausible, and is still used by some young women on social media today, who give themselves fully over to these traditional roles as 'Trad-Wives'. Women had always had to work – even the well-heeled ones had had to order their servants about – but now, for the first time, they were able to do what women supposedly like doing best: namely, lazing around.

The seemingly intractable belief that housework isn't actually work is partly to do with objects like this one, Miele's 'Model A' vacuum cleaner, also known for the slogan 'Mummy does it with Miele'. The fact that it used to be hard work running a household was surely something everyone could agree on: it was physical labour to wash clothes and wring them out, while sweeping and scrubbing an entire house or whipping egg whites without an electric whisk almost resembled a Pilates class. But now, things were different: thanks to legendary 'household helpers' like this one, that little bit of cleaning, wiping, washing and cooking would take care of itself. It was a pleasant pastime – no, better yet, it was *fun*. It was all but impossible to escape the deluge of adverts showing a woman embracing her vacuum cleaner, a brand-new fridge, washing machine or other such home electronic as though it was a lover. It evidently didn't occur to many people that you'd have to be very lonely and also a bit sad to smooch with your vacuum cleaner. Instead, the understanding was that women were happy because they now had machines to do everything for them, like a good friend.

The association between women and household gadgets as the very picture of modernity was nothing new. It went back to the 1920s. An advertising poster from this period touted the very first vacuum cleaner, a certain Vampyr made by AEG, with the following slogan: 'A housewife, but still every bit the lady'. It showed the actress Edmonde Guy sporting a cool cropped haircut and golden pyjamas under a red shawl, pictured against an elegant interior background as she held said vacuum cleaner, which looked like a metal tapir. The message it aimed to convey was: vacuum cleaners and emancipation go hand in hand. We still hear it said today: household electronics liberated women; they finally had more time for their own interests. And, in part, this was indeed true. Yet these machines also considerably devalued the work women did around the house and created new, higher standards. Perfection was now a must – or, in other words, anyone who failed to keep up a gleaming home and equally gleaming appearance despite all this 'help' was simply lazy. 'Few tasks are more similar to the torment of Sisyphus than those of the housewife,' wrote Simone de Beauvoir.[1] How true. If Sisyphus had also had people telling him that a little bit of rolling-a-boulder-up-a-hill wasn't exactly a big job – a doddle, in fact – he would no doubt have been sad, or angry, or both.

And it was much the same for housewives. In the late 1950s, an international survey established that Western women were deeply unhappy, with those in Germany unhappiest of all. The astonishment was great. How could this be? They had everything, didn't they – petticoats, pretty children, husbands, houses, front gardens and all these brilliant electronics. What more could a woman want? Their answers simply went unheard or were played down as what we'd call a first-world problem. Women said they felt lonely and empty; they had the sense that they were useless and didn't really exist. In her book *The Feminine Mystique*, Betty Friedan described how American suburban housewives were running en masse to see psychiatrists because they felt vaguely uneasy, torpid and melancholy, and couldn't work out why. They also believed they had everything a 'normal' woman could wish for, and so were ashamed of not being content. Friedan dubbed this 'the problem that has no name'. Her now-controversial essay became the cornerstone of nascent second-wave feminism. Others, like the Italian feminists behind the 'Wages for Housework' campaign of 1972, approached the problem from a different angle: they demanded wages in exchange for housework, saying that women didn't fundamentally have anything against caring and domestic work – after all, someone had to do it – but the problem was that everyone was acting as though these jobs weren't work, because work was remunerated. And so they needed a salary. Not having one was effectively saying that these jobs, the caring they did, weren't essential to society or economic progress, that life would still function if they weren't done. This much is clear – or at least it should be: the much-vaunted Economic Miracle of 1950s Germany would never have happened were it not for all those housewives who did the vacuuming for free.

---

1   de Beauvoir, Simone, *The Second Sex*, Vol. II, Part II, tr. Constance Borde and Shelia Malovany-Chevallier (London: Vintage, 2011), p. 487

TUPPERWARE

1950s

In the life of a woman, as a Dr Oetker advert from the 1950s would have it, there are two questions: 'What shall I wear? And: What shall I cook?' The advert showed a very young woman – thirty at most – sweeping into a kitchen, laden with shopping bags. With her long skirt and neat dark-brown bob, she'd clearly achieved the purported life goal of all women: she'd landed herself a husband. But, the advert warned, 'Anyone who thinks she can rest on her laurels has another think coming: a man wants to be won over anew each day.' Can you guess how? Freshly baked cake, of course. Because: 'Cake will soften a man's heart, so no matter if her new dress costs an extra 100 marks.'

We know that the lives of housewives in the 1950s and early 1960s were dominated by monotony and melancholy and at first glance, this object, the Tupperware box, might appear to be just one more nail in the coffin of female freedom – yet another thing that kept women chained to their kitchens and only really helped to answer the third question in their lives: 'What shall I do with the leftovers?' We all remember these pastel-coloured plastic tubs from childhood. From the kitchens of our grandmothers or very ambitious mothers – the women who started getting ahead with lunch right after breakfast, standing at the stove still in their dressing gowns. Tupperware was an accessory for the housewife and, looked at this way, doesn't exactly scream independence and emancipation. But in fact it was the opposite of the vacuum cleaner – not a camouflaged tool of oppression, but a rather unprepossessing element of emancipation.

Or at least it was for the women of 1950s American suburbia. To appreciate this, we must quickly rewind to the beginning: it was shortly after the Second World War, and Earl Tupper, a plastics manufacturer from Massachusetts, had just bought up all the plastic left over from the conflict, thinking that an idea for what to do with it was bound to occur to him at some point. And, after a few months of trials and experiments, it did: Mr Tupper found himself holding his very first piece of 'Tupperware'. A feather-light bowl with a lid that came off with a 'Tupperware burp' and which pressed out excess air – all made from pastel-hued plastic. Tupper patented his invention, designed a small collection and in 1949 introduced it to the market as the 'Millionaire Line'. As a young man, he had vowed to be a millionaire by the age of thirty; it was a goal he hadn't yet achieved, and at first it looked as though that wasn't about to change. In design terms, people found Tupperware interesting, modern, practical; in keeping with the times. They praised its clean lines and fresh colours, but no one actually wanted to have it in their kitchen. The tubs gathered dust on shop shelves, until Brownie Wise arrived on the scene and turned Tupper's flop into an incredible success story.

Brownie – who apparently shared her name with a cake on account of her big brown eyes – was a single mother in her mid-thirties who had proved herself capable of selling almost anything as a door-to-door sales rep of household goods. Working for Tupper, she developed her natural marketing talent into a system. Everyone is familiar with 'Tupperware parties': events at which women got together over cocktails and canapés to have the benefits of Tupperware demonstrated and explained to them. They'd drink a bit, chat and, at the end of the day, high on the lovely afternoon they'd just had, head home with a long Tupperware order form or even a couple of items already tucked under their arm.

In a short space of time, Wise had sold so much Tupperware that production couldn't keep pace. Mr Tupper, on the other hand – who was no sales genius himself but clearly recognised one when she was in front of him – made the young woman general manager of 'home parties' and then allowed Wise to talk him into completely forgetting homeware shops and instead concentrating all their energies on the parties. This is where the emancipatory aspect finally comes into play: it wasn't just Brownie Wise who became such a successful businessperson that she was the first woman to make it onto the cover of *Business Week*. Many other women followed suit. All over the USA, ladies who had been sitting around bored and depressed in their kitchens started to work as freelance Tupperware party hosts. They earned money – more money than they could have in the other jobs open to them – and managed to combine work and family life, kick-starting a revolution that was so quiet and seemingly in keeping with their role that barely any husbands protested. Apparently, there was even the occasional gent who quit his own job to join his wife's Tupperware business. Simply because it was so lucrative.

Now, at first glance, Brownie Wise and her Tupperware ladies certainly weren't the embodiment of the feminist dream. The items they sold continued to bind women to home and kitchen – but thanks to Wise, who had given them a job, money and newfound self-esteem, they were able to fill those spaces with new meaning. Tupperware women didn't have to bake their husbands a cake every time they wanted a new dress; they didn't have to mollify them or beg for anything. If they wanted a new dress, they simply went out and bought it.

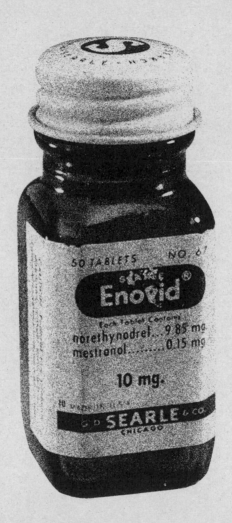

'ENOVID' CONTRACEPTIVE PILL

1957

The story of this object, which officially hit the market in the USA on 18 August 1960 as the very first contraceptive pill – 'Enovid', manufactured by Searle & Company – begins in two places. One in 1951, at a dinner party in New York, at which Planned Parenthood founder Margaret Sanger turned to biologist Gregory Pincus between the main course and dessert and asked somewhat abruptly, 'What do you think it would cost to develop a contraceptive pill?' And thus initiated both a line of research and its end product.

The second took place almost forty years beforehand, in 1914, with the publication of an eight-page pamphlet under the excellent title *The Woman Rebel*. Sanger, who was already well aware that the right to vote was doubtless important, but that women would only be truly free when they had control over their own bodies, and particularly their fertility, wrote it to speak out against the ignorance being used as a tool to repress young women, and to advocate for sex education for girls. Apparently, it was in this rebellious pamphlet that the term 'birth control' made its first appearance. Alas, it existed only for a few issues before falling victim to the Comstock Act, which prohibited the dissemination of information about contraception. In 1916, when Sanger opened the world's first contraceptive clinic in Brooklyn, New York, she didn't just give advice to women but actually pressed contraceptive diaphragms into their hands; shortly afterwards, she was sued in a headline-grabbing trial. Yet at the aforementioned dinner party in 1951, all this must have seemed very long ago. By that time, Planned Parenthood had been successfully and legally offering advice to women in the USA for several years; the next year, the organisation and its concept of family planning would expand internationally. Nonetheless, Sanger continued to dream of a contraceptive medication that would reliably protect women against unplanned pregnancies – and, that evening, she got Mr Pincus on board. He, in turn, teamed up with gynaecologist John Rock, and thus did Enovid hit the market in 1957.

Not as a contraceptive pill, however. Enovid was initially sold as a medicine for treating acne and menstrual cramps; the contraceptive aspect was a side effect. Even when the Pill finally admitted what it really was – namely 'birth control' (a combination of words that some found 'highly offensive') – it was initially only prescribed to married women and, moreover, only to those who already had children. Women would not be allowed to escape their 'natural' role that easily; only later, from the late 1960s, would the Pill give the baby boom the *coup de grâce*. Yet even in 1961, when the Federal Republic of Germany found its pharmacies stocked with the first German version of the Pill, Anovlar, *Stern* magazine described it as 'a historic day'. And it was. It was a female revolution. Perhaps the most important in history. Until then, women had had few options if they wanted to have sex but not children. They could choose between abstinence, sponges dunked in crocodile dung and inserted into the vagina, or amulets that warded off pregnancy. They could wash themselves out with the bidet we met earlier, or explain to men that condoms absolutely weren't a means to 'castrate' them, nor an attack on their masculinity, and hope they'd see it that way too. They could crouch down and sneeze, or put off the problem to another day and, in the very worst case, pay for that brief moment of forgetting themselves with an illegal abortion and their life.

Now, thanks to this little pill, reckless abandon was no longer equivalent to mortal danger. Now, for women as well as men, sex could be something that bore no consequences, something light and carefree. For the very first time in human history, sexuality and fertility were no longer intrinsically linked, and the fear of setting an unstoppable train of events in motion no longer omnipresent. It's hard to imagine today, but that feeling of freedom must have been overwhelming. Part of this was that women's bodies no longer had to be their enemies. They were no longer something that 'thwarted' them, as the writer Annie Ernaux once put it, which prevented them moving forward. 'Enjoying sex' and 'having ambition' were no longer contradictions. In that first year alone, 400,000 vials of Enovid were sold over the counter; when the price dropped in 1963, the number of women taking it rose to 2.3 million and continued to increase into the 2000s. Much to the chagrin of the Church. For centuries, it had been telling everyone – but especially women – that sex was a sin that could only be committed if it resulted in a child, and now this little bottle had undone all that laborious convincing. In 1968, Pope Paul VI condemned birth control through contraception in the encyclical *Humanae Vitae*, because, he said, it encouraged extra-marital sexual intercourse and would contribute to a 'general lowering of moral standards'.[1] Was that true? Definitely! And it was a good thing, too. To hell with moral standards, which only applied to women anyway.

Sadly, the history of the Pill also has its dark side. After Sanger and her friend Katharine McCormick, a biologist, had encouraged Pincus and Rock to explore the subject of contraception, the scientists quickly came to the conclusion that it would be necessary to trick the body into believing it was pregnant in order to prevent a 'new' one, and this ultimately led them to the artificial production of progesterone, the pregnancy hormone. Now, it just needed to be tested on someone. And this is where things become unpleasant. In 1950s America, no one wanted to know about contraception; it was out of the question that American women should be used as guinea pigs. It was, however, considered OK to use the populations of other countries. Around that time, the exploding birth rate in Puerto Rico, an unincorporated US territory, posed such a problem that even forced sterilisation wasn't off the cards – trialling the Pill there looked downright mild by comparison. No doubt many women volunteered in the hope that they would then be exempt from sterilisation, but, while this may well have been the case, they had no idea what they were letting themselves in for. They weren't informed that they were taking part in a trial, nor were they told they could expect unknown side effects. Three women died after taking what was a very high dosage at that point, and many others suffered depression, nausea and other 'side effects' that were later swept quickly under the carpet. None of this changes the significance of the Pill. But it's a sad reminder that the emancipation of some women all too often comes at the cost of others.

1   Pope Paul VI, *Humanae Vitae*, given at St Peter's, Rome, 25 July 1968, available at: <https://www.vatican.va/content/paul-vi/en/encyclicals/documents/hf_p-vi_enc_25071968_humanae-vitae.html>

HANNAH ARENDT'S BROOCH

UNDATED

A few years ago, readers of *The New Yorker* were presented with an amusing anecdote about the philosopher Hannah Arendt and her views on feminism. The author of this particular article recounted a story she'd been told by her professor. It was at the beginning of the 1970s in Chicago, and Arendt was teaching political theory at the university, where said professor was one of her students. One day, the two found themselves in the lift together – looking at the floor, not saying anything, as you do in a lift – until Arendt noticed the Chicago Women's Liberation Movement pin on her student's jacket. She apparently gestured at the badge, pulled a face and proclaimed in her German accent: 'This is not zerious!'

The pin pictured here, a brooch made of gold, pearls and three diamonds, doesn't stand for a movement – certainly not the feminist one, of which the philosopher didn't think much – but for Arendt herself. If we wanted to exaggerate a little, we could say it's the most famous brooch in the history of women's philosophy. It was apparently Hannah Arendt's favourite piece of jewellery, and she wore it on 28 October 1964 for one of her most famous appearances: on the TV show *Zur Person* with Günter Gaus. The recording, which is over an hour long, has been viewed more than a million times on YouTube; hardly any other interview with an intellectual has viewing figures that high. When Arendt made her appearance, the show had been running for more than a year. Willy Brandt had taken to the couch before her, but she would remain the only woman ever to be interviewed on the programme. 'Hannah Arendt, you're the first lady to be portrayed in this series. A lady with a profession some might regard as a masculine one. You are a philosopher,' said Gaus by way of introduction, before moving straight on to his first question: 'In spite of the recognition and respect

355

you've received, do you see your role among philosophers as unusual or peculiar because you're a woman?'[1]

Anyone who tends to picture Hannah Arendt as a person who smoked a lot, thought deeply about complex concepts like totalitarianism and freedom, and coined the phrase 'the banality of evil', gets to see her as a human being in this interview. She radiates a marvellous authority but also compelling charm. She isn't a philosopher, she says, just to set things straight; her field is that of political theory. And yet: 'You say philosophy is generally considered a masculine occupation. It need not remain a masculine occupation. It is possible that one day a woman will be a philosopher.' She herself knew at the age of fourteen that philosophy was the field for her; it was reading Kant that made her realise what she wanted to get out of life: understanding. Understanding through thinking, understanding through writing: 'For me the question was, either I study philosophy or I drown myself.'

Even if she was, as she put it, 'old-fashioned', and thought there were things a woman shouldn't necessarily do – at least not if she valued being 'feminine' – such as 'give[s] orders', she herself had never set much store by such seemliness. 'I always did what I wanted to do. I didn't worry that it was a man's job. I never gave it any thought in that respect,' she said there in the studio. And the whole time, this brooch was glinting on her lapel. Here, we see Hannah Arendt as a thinker, but also as a woman of her time. Not just because of this accessory, but also because of her amusing way of examining her nails while she speaks, as though she's sitting in a nail salon. We can see immediately that she isn't one of those intellectuals who think they somehow need to erase or hide their femininity and appear as masculine as possible in order to be taken seriously. Yet we can also see that, unlike Simone de Beauvoir, she wasn't someone who approached her understanding and thinking about the world from the perspective of a woman. For Arendt, her sex was a fact. Not a talking point.

And, to a certain extent, this interview, the way she appears in it, is so telling for exactly that reason: she was the only woman invited to appear on the programme, but she wasn't questioned as such. She wasn't there to talk about 'women's issues', about emancipation, equal

---

1 All extracts from the televised interview can be found here: *Zur Person*, Hannah Arendt, Full Interview (with English subtitles): <https://www.youtube.com/watch?v=dsolmQfVsO4>

rights or contraception; she was there to give her thoughts on one of the most important, difficult and complex topics of the time: reckoning with the Holocaust. Arendt was there that day because she was one of the first people to try to grasp what had happened in her former home-land, Germany; how the genocide could have happened, what mechanisms had been at work. She was there because that year, 1964, her extremely controversial report on the trial of Adolf Eichmann had been published in Germany in book form: *Eichmann in Jerusalem: A Report on the Banality of Evil*. When it appeared as a collection of arti-cles in *The New Yorker*, it met with a great deal of criticism. All kinds of accusations were made against her – some of them perhaps accurate – but despite everything (or maybe precisely because of that debate), it was her thoughts that really got the ball rolling on the process of facing up to the Shoah, to Auschwitz and the gas chambers. In her interview with Gaus, she explained what it had been like when she first learned about Auschwitz in 1943: 'It was as if an abyss had opened. We had the idea that amends could be made for everything else. Amends can be made for almost anything at some point in politics. But not for this. This ought never to have happened [. . .] Something happened to which we can never reconcile ourselves.' Reconciliation was impossible, but one could at least try to understand it. Her articles and the debate she sparked, as well as this interview, created a semantic basis for that reckoning – words with which to make the unthinkable somehow think-able. So it would never again be possible simply to push it aside and drown it in silence.

THE MINIDRESS
1966

In the second half of the nineteenth century, there was a particular saying in Washington, DC. You could recognise the return of spring by two things: Congress being recalled to the capital, and the sight of Susan B. Anthony's red shawl on the streets. The red shawl was her hallmark as a woman, but it was also an emblem of the first wave of the women's movement. In 1960s England, however, emancipated Britons threw their ladylike shawls into a corner along with their petticoats and curling rags, and announced themselves with a different garment: a particularly short skirt, the mini. The discussion around who invented this not-very-fabric-intensive item, whether it was the French designer André Courrèges or Britain's Mary Quant, has still not abated. Both brought out collections featuring above-the-knee skirts and dresses at roughly the same time; both caused equal amounts of shock and excitement. But Quant's design became more famous than Courrège's 'space age' look, and her name went down in fashion history as that of the woman who invented the miniskirt for her friends.

Perhaps it was because, as Quant once said, British women had better legs. French women had the advantage in all other areas – they had great breasts, beautiful waists and good bottoms – but when it came to legs, the British were unbeatable. The Chelsea girl had 'the best legs in the world', she said, and the 1960s were indeed the decade of the leg, if you will. Whereas breasts, waists and bottoms – the parts of the body that shone in the 1950s, thanks to stars like Marilyn Monroe, Sophia Loren and Brigitte Bardot – had been very important, the 'swinging sixties' turned their noses up at ample womanliness and sex appeal in hourglass form, and instead got all enthusiastic about androgynous shapes. The new role model, just-turned-sixteen-year-old Lesley Hornby, better known as 'Twiggy', was young, thin, almost gangly – and not at all 'feminine'. She wasn't mysterious but cheeky, not imposing but approachable; she was cheerful, funny and, above all else, extremely free. Perfect for the mini. Because a skirt like this wasn't made for stalking around in. With a miniskirt on your hips, you were meant to dance, jump, run, whatever, just not be ladylike. Anything but that. The same year Twiggy was declared the 'face of 1966' as the first teenage model in history, Quant showed her increasingly short hemlines at a fashion show in Paris. Pictures taken of the event captured a really rather empty room and baffled faces; at the dinner that followed, in the famous restaurant Maxim's, the entire room fell silent when Quant's troop appeared in their minidresses. One of her colleagues once said: 'I never knew whether they were shocked, disgusted or impressed.' If he'd asked Coco Chanel, she'd have given him a clear answer: the miniskirt was, according to Chanel, absolutely repulsive.

That might have been the view in Paris, but London loved the garment. It loved Quant, too. Later that year, while the French were badmouthing British 'bad taste' and lack of elegance in the wake of this performance, the queen bestowed the Order of the British Empire on Mary. When she went to accept it, the thirty-two-year-old wore this very dress, standing out in the crowd of black-clad, besuited and behatted, tie-and-fur-wearing ladies and gentlemen. But no one said a thing. No one was scandalised – perhaps because they knew her look was the future. Ever since Quant, a qualified art teacher, had opened her first boutique, Bazaar, on the King's Road in London and quickly realised that the clothing she wanted to sell didn't even exist, she'd been conquering the hearts of the Chelsea set and the capital's nascent youth movement with clothes she designed herself. Quant used new and largely unfamiliar materials, like jersey and PVC, in bright colours – red, purple, yellow – and offered not just clothes in her shop, but also a lifestyle. The music that played there was different to that in other shops, and the place looked different, too. The interior of her third boutique was designed by Terence Conran, who turned it into a kind of living room. You could go in the evening for a drink and a chat; everything was young, fresh and modern. Perfect for the mods, but also for young women who were fed up of making themselves out to be more serious and grown-up than they were. Now that women, thanks in part to the Pill, no longer expected to be having their first child at the age of twenty, they could stay young and free of responsibility for longer, and they dressed accordingly. More youthful and active-looking, with shorter hemlines, brighter colours. The mini-dress was the garment of the sexual revolution.

Unfortunately, the mini went the same way as so many items of clothing before and after it. At first, it gave women new freedom, the chance to feel young and have fun, but then the male gaze degraded it to something that became the exact opposite. In its early years, for example, newspapers regularly ran reports on how some man or other had driven into the car in front of him because he'd apparently seen a woman in a miniskirt getting out of it: *You see, Mr Policeman, it really wasn't my fault; it was the miniskirt.* Later, short skirts were used with increasing frequency as an explanation for harassment or even rape: *Why were you out at night dressed in such a short skirt? Didn't you provoke him even just a little bit?* In the early 2000s, Amnesty International found that over a quarter of sexual assault victims were deemed complicit if they'd been wearing a miniskirt. For the simple reason that not much fabric and lots of skin seem to be equated to sexual availability. We don't know what Mary Quant thought about this sad distortion of her life-affirming creation.

ARETHA FRANKLIN, 'RESPECT'

1967

Germaine Greer, the activist and feminist author – about whom Mary McCarthy complained in a letter to Hannah Arendt that she was an 'absurd Australian giantess' – once gave an interview in which she said, on the subject of music and feminism: 'Every generation has to discover Nina Simone. She is evidence that female genius is real.' Every movement needs its own sound, something that was true even of the suffragettes: in the 1920s, working women sang songs about bread and roses on their protest marches. In the '60s, the civil rights movement – the Black Panthers in particular – was accompanied by the frenzied piano and furious vocals of Nina Simone. In 1964, in 'Mississippi Goddam', she sang, 'You don't have to live next to me, just give me my equality', lyrics that referenced the murder of African American civil rights activists and Martin Luther King's non-violent movement in the same breath.

Simone, whom Toni Morrison once credited with saving all their lives, roused an incredible fighting spirit – in part because she herself had a great desire to mete out the blows. Almost ten years her junior, Aretha Franklin, whose profile we see here, used her music to convey a different feeling: that of community. At least, that's how the activist Angela Davis described it shortly after Franklin's death: 'She brought a feminist dimension, before the emergence of Black feminism, to our consciousness with "Respect" [. . .] her contributions to the creation of a kind of yearning for freedom [. . .] Aretha was the best manifestation of soul [. . .] her music helped to produce communities, helped to allow us to feel a part of something larger than ourselves.'[1]

---

1 TV interview conducted by *Democracy Now!* with Angela Davis: 'Angela Davis: Aretha Franklin "Will Forever Animate Our Sense of Collective Desire for Change"', 23 August 2018, available at: <https://www.youtube.com/watch?v=l8ztMFh0trY>

And indeed, at the end of the 1960s, anyone who set any kind of store by freedom and equality had this record, 'Respect', propped up against their wall or playing on their turntable – but so too did those who believed in soul and civil rights. Even the story behind the song is brilliant: it wasn't originally Franklin's, but Otis Redding's. The version he recorded in 1965 is that of a passive-aggressive husband explaining to his wife that she may certainly cheat on him when he's away, but when he comes home she's to show him a bit of respect. 'I heard Mr Redding's version of it. I just loved it. And I decided that I wanted to record it,' Aretha once said in an interview. 'And my sister Carolyn and I got together. I was living in a small apartment on the West Side of Detroit. Piano by the window, watching the cars go by, and we came up with that infamous line, the "Sock it to me!" line. It was a cliché of the day.'[1] You might need to listen to it quickly to remind yourself what she's referring to. She added that expression, which was one the girls in her community were using on the street, changed another couple of lines, expanded the whole thing, including spelling out the word 'respect' in a bold way, and thus transformed a not-at-all-feminist song into the anthem of the strong woman.

In her version, it isn't the husband telling his wife she's got what he needs – she knows that herself. What she wants isn't his permission to be 'allowed' to cheat on him; she wants respect – 'just a little bit'. When the song was released on Atlantic Records in 1967, it immediately became a hit, made Franklin instantly world-famous and didn't just empower others, but also the singer herself. In her first successful single, 'I Never Loved A Man The Way I Love You', she'd sung about a violent relationship she couldn't escape – like so many women (including Nina Simone) – because, well, she loved the guy, her husband, Ted White (or at least she believed she did). But now, with her sisters Carolyn and Erna in the background, she was singing about the one thing every woman should demand for herself: respect. Clearly, it was also a little bit about 'sexual attention', just as Aretha Franklin's songs were so often about power, sex and the body. In this case, however, that wasn't so important. Because the song was initially heard less as a feminist outcry and much more as the successor to 'Mississippi Goddam': as a

---

1   Aretha Franklin, The 'Fresh Air' Interview, NPR, 16 August 2018, available at: <https://www.npr.org/2018/08/16/638355847/aretha-franklin-the-fresh-air-interview>

hymn of the civil rights movement and a clear demand for respect for her people. This wasn't far wrong. Aretha had known Dr Martin Luther King since childhood, as a close friend of her father's; as a young woman, she'd accompanied him to several events and sung for him. Nonetheless, she meant 'Respect' more as a 'male–female thing', she once said, as her contribution to the gender debate. But, after all, one didn't have to exclude the other.

The song accompanied both the broader political movement and the emergence of Black feminism, just as Aretha herself accompanied both. Less explicitly than Nina Simone, perhaps, but no less intensively. When Angela Davis was arrested in 1970 for her supposed involvement in a shooting at a courthouse in California, the children of East Germany sent her postcards of roses, Nina Simone visited her in prison with a giant red balloon, and, at a press conference, Aretha publicly offered to pay Davis's bail, no matter how high it was: 'My daddy says I don't know what I'm doing. Well, I respect him, of course, but I'm going to stick by my beliefs. Angela Davis must go free. Black people will be free. I've been locked up (for disturbing the peace in Detroit) and I know you got to disturb the peace when you can't get no peace.'[1] Two years later, Franklin recorded 'Young, Gifted and Black', a song that Simone had written for her friend Lorraine Hansberry, a playwright who died tragically young, and in doing so went further than 'Respect'. Now she was saying to young African American men and women: *You don't need to wait for the respect of others; the future belongs to you, and you can reach out and take it.* It seemed only logical and fitting that it should be Franklin who stood on the podium in Washington in 2008 to use her voice to accompany the inauguration of the first African American president in US history. And, a couple of years later, she would get that very same president, Barack Obama, to sing 'You Make Me Feel Like A Natural Woman' with tears in his eyes. That, however, is a story for another time.

1   Aretha Franklin in *Jet* magazine, 1970, quoted in various articles online, including <https://www.democracynow.org/2018/8/17/angela_davis_remembers_aretha_franklin_who>

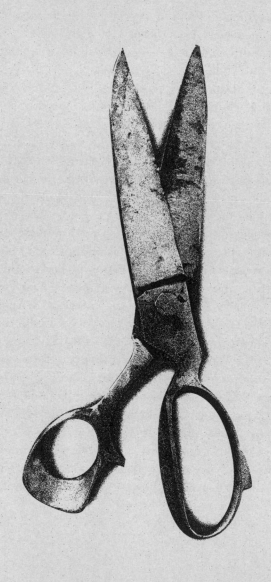

SCISSORS

1970s

In the history of women, scissors – much like needles and spindles – have played a special role. You could say they were closely entwined with the lives of women right from antiquity to the second half of the twentieth century, and were always within reach. In the Victorian nineteenth century, for example, most ladies carried around a small, prettily decorated pair on their so-called 'chatelaine' – a kind of multipurpose chain, the woman's Swiss army knife. Later, they often simply wore their scissors around their necks, so as to be ready for all eventualities: just in case something needed to be sewn, cut or otherwise repaired.

Seen in this light, for many centuries this object was not an attribute of emancipation. It implied domesticity and discretion, women who worked away in the background, whom no one saw but without whom nothing would really sit right. It remained that way until the 1960s, but it was really the 1970s that saw scissors become increasingly rare in a housewifely context and much more prominent in another: body and performance art. Hardly any other artistic movement had given women so much say – or, at least, been one in which they had so much to say. It was about roles, about bodies, about the question of who was actually looking at whom and what their gaze did with the person being looked at, how she or he behaved in that context, and also what their reaction said about the person looking at them. Women turned the tables on all this with their new artistic direction: the so-called male gaze had transformed their bodies into objects, and they were going to use them accordingly. As a canvas, as a material. They displayed them, bared them, hurt themselves or let themselves be hurt, pre-empting, as it were, the constant threats posed to them as women in the public space. And thereby shook up the order of the sexes. They ripped off all those outer layers and broke with the classic image of a pretty, clean, silent femininity that sat around waiting for someone to do something to it. Women now did things to themselves, often less than pleasant things. Their bodies were no longer those of muses, but active bodies that confronted their audience with themselves.

One of the most famous performances to make use of scissors took place in 1964 at a small theatre in Kyoto. A young woman – she was thirty-one at the time – sat on the stage in a black costume, with one of these cutting implements before her. The audience had been informed of the rules: viewers were allowed to come up one at a time, cut off a piece of her clothing and take it with them. The whole thing would go on until the artist, a certain Yoko Ono, decided it was over. On films made that day, we can sense that the audience initially feels uncomfortable: people giggle nervously and cut off little pieces of fabric, gently and carefully. But then things start gathering pace: shyness makes way for a kind of arousal, the pieces become bigger, the laughter dies away, the audience grows more self-confident, and some start prowling around Ono as she sits there motionless on stage, as though she is their prey. In the end, a clearly agitated young man cuts away her entire vest and snips the straps of her bra, so that Ono is left sitting with her arms crossed over her chest, fragile, clearly affected and very close to tears. She seems to feel attacked, yet she is both victim and perpetrator here. She has contrived and directed this game, made the entirely conscious decision to put herself through this.

A similar thing – only far more extreme, and involving a more intense loss of control – happened ten years later, in 1974, when then-twenty-three-year-old Marina Abramović issued an invitation to a six-hour-long performance, *Rhythm 0*. 'There are 72 objects on the table that one can use as desired on me [. . .] I am the object. During this period I take full responsibility,' read the instructions for the audience.[1] The objects included water, wine, bread, roses, knives, shoes, handcuffs, razors, olive oil, grapes and a pistol loaded with a single bullet – but also various pairs of scissors. Much the same as with Yoko Ono, the audience was initially gentle and hesitant, handing her water and roses, but after a short time the mood changed completely and the participants all but flipped out, as Abramović would often recount later. They cut her

1 Abramović, Marina, *Rhythm 0*, Studio Morra, Naples, 1974, quoted at <https://www.tate.org.uk/art/artworks/abramovic-rhythm-0-t14875>

clothes and pressed rose thorns into her belly, one man sliced her throat and drank her blood, she was laid out on the table with a knife planted between her legs, and one person even reached for the revolver before the gallery owner ripped it out of his hand and nearly caused a brawl. When, after six hours of existing like a doll, the artist finally moved of her own accord and tried to approach the audience, people simply fled. They ran away because they couldn't bear her gaze, because they'd shown a side of themselves they possibly hadn't known existed, or at least had never before revealed in front of other people.

In these very different performances, Abramović and Ono used scissors and other sharp objects to address what society does with women's bodies when it's allowed to, and pointed out the desire for violence that simmers just below the surface and is usually stifled with silence. In 1974, the Brazilian artist Anna Maiolino made this silencing the subject of a photo series, in which we see her cutting off her tongue with a giant pair of scissors. It would be possible to mention many more examples of artists using scissors in a concrete way, like Ana Mendieta – who died under suspicious circumstances in 1985 when she fell from the thirty-fourth floor of her New York apartment building – and her work *Facial Hair Transplant* (1972). But also of women for whom the pair of scissors, the cut, was more metaphorical, in that they were simply lacking their clothes – like Hannah Wilke in *S.O.S. – Starification Object Series*, Carolee Schneemann in *Interior Scroll*, or the Austrian artist Valie Export, who sat in front of a camera with her legs spread for 1969's *Action Pants: Genital Panic*, having cut away the crotch of her jeans so as to give a good view of her (hairy) vulva. Scissors are an expression of fragility and aggression, Export once said in relation to her scissor sculpture, *Doppelganger*. For the artist Louise Bourgeois, meanwhile, they were a symbol of femininity and a means of cutting yourself free from everything that causes one pain. A tool, then, with which to liberate oneself.

But can she type?

GOLDA MEIR POSTER

c. 1970

In 1979, in an interview conducted just a few days before she was elected prime minister of Great Britain, Margaret Thatcher was asked how she thought her gender would affect her chances of success. The answer she gave didn't make reference to Queen Victoria, Elizabeth II or other similarly powerful British women, but to a woman who was also given the 'iron' moniker and who shaped the image of female heads of state in the twentieth century: the former prime minister of Israel, Golda Meir, who had died just the year before. She'd led her country through one of the most difficult periods of its young history, said Thatcher. She'd been 'marvellous', a fantastic prime minister and a role model for all women who came after her. After her, it would never again be a problem for a woman to attain such a position of power.

Today, we know this not to be true, and in some ways this poster suggests that women already sensed it then. Perhaps a few individual women – like Meir, like Thatcher, like a couple of others – would come to power, but would that really change anything for 'women'? Would they not be seen as exceptional personages, while women, no matter how competent they were, continued to be reduced to inferior roles? Wouldn't it just end up again and again with people saying, *It's nice you have so many diplomas and good ideas but, tell me: can you type?* The poster pictured here is the design of a certain Linda B. Muller, who created it for the USA's National Organization for Women. It was immensely popular with feminist groups and put in several thousand appearances across the USA, especially at universities. It shows an image of Golda Meir, one of the most powerful women in the world at the time, only the third woman in history to become a democratically elected head of government (after Sirimavo Bandaranaike and Indira Gandhi) and a founder of the state of Israel. At first glance, with her hands resting on her bag, her necklace, brooch and entire countenance, she looks more like a friendly old lady – not for nothing was Golda known as the 'Grandmother of Israel'. By contrast to many other powerful women – such as Thatcher – Meir had somehow succeeded in coming across, not as a monster or an unnatural phenomenon, but someone who inspired sympathy. At least until the Yom Kippur War, which would cost her her position three years after this poster was first displayed. According to a 1970 survey, Meir was then the most popular woman in the USA. Not because she was the friendly lady she appears to be in this picture, but because she was, first and foremost, a tough-as-nails politician with a very clear agenda.

Nixon, for example, recounted how she once turned to him after a joint press conference, casually crossed her legs, lit a cigarette and said, 'Now, Mr President, what are you going to do about these planes that we want and need very much?' The acrimonious battle she fought with the Austrian Chancellor Bruno Kreisky is well known; and as foreign minister, she persuaded John F. Kennedy to assure her that the USA and Israel had a 'very special' relationship, comparable only with that of the USA and Britain. 'There is only one thing I hope to see before I die, and that is that my people should not need expressions of sympathy any more,' she said. The world wasn't necessarily anti-Semitic, but it did stand back and watch when Jews were under attack, as had been proved by recent history; this was why the Jewish people needed their own country. 'Someday when history will be written, it will be said there was a Jewish woman who got the money which made the state possible,' said David Ben-Gurion, so-called father of the nation of Israel. He was referring to the fundraising tour of 1948, with which Golda Meir collected $50 million in a matter of weeks to defend Israel against the Arab states. When Ben-Gurion read out the declaration of independence of the state of Israel on Friday, 14 May 1948 at the Tel Aviv Museum on Rothschild Boulevard, calling on the twenty-five representatives of parliament in attendance to sign the founding charter of the new nation, Golda was one of them. She is said to have wept fiercely as she put her name to the document.

Meir was apparently greatly amused by this poster, which the American women's organisation must have sent to her in Israel. She was pleased to be a role model, even if she wasn't interested in feminism. When the Italian journalist Oriana Fallaci asked her about the women's movement, Golda asked with some confusion: 'Do you mean these crazy women who burn their bras [. . .] and hate men?' Like many powerful women who had fought their way to the top more or less on their own, she didn't have much time for the movement, but she still admitted that a woman usually needs to be at least twice as good as a man. Most of all, though, she spoke often about a more intimate and therefore seldom addressed challenge: being a mother who wanted more than the life she was offered in that role. She often felt bad, she said, because she was one of those women who just 'couldn't stay at home'. Because life as a housewife and mother wasn't enough for her, because she wanted to be part of something bigger. It required a 'superhuman effort of will' to face the 'accusatory stares' of one's children but still leave the house to go to work. And in this, Golda was perhaps addressing the greatest difficulty in many women's lives. Somehow, most of them would always find a way to cope with men's machismo and their desire to reduce them to typists. The really difficult battle was one that many fought – and still continue to fight – with the voices inside themselves: the guilty conscience telling them their place is anywhere but out in the world and right at the top.

le nouvel

OBSERVATEUR

la liste des 343 françaises

qui ont le courage

de signer le manifeste

« JE ME SUIS FAIT AVORTER »

MAGAZINE COVER, LE NOUVEL OBSERVATEUR, 'MANIFESTO OF THE 343'

5 APRIL 1971

Anyone who happened to stop at a French news kiosk on the morning of 5 April 1971 will have soon found themselves wide-eyed and staring. 'I've had an abortion' reported one headline. Or, to be more precise: 'The list of the 343 French women who had the courage to sign the "I've had an abortion" manifesto.' Said list included several famous names: novelists Françoise Sagan, Marguerite Duras, Violette Leduc and Monique Wittig, actors Catherine Deneuve, Jeanne Moreau, Bulle Ogier, Delphine Seyrig and Anne Wiazemsky. The film director Agnes Varda, and her colleague from the theatre, Ariane Mnouchkine. The philosopher Simone de Beauvoir and her sister Hélène, lawyer Gisèle Halimi, the singer Brigitte Fontaine, and many others. People read the names of these prominent French women, but among the 343 who were 'outing' themselves they may also have discovered the name of a neighbour or colleague, their children's teacher, their husband's secretary, the baker, their cleaner. Because, as Halimi said in an interview at the time, 'All women have abortions. Even politicians' wives and ministers' lovers. Absolutely all of them. Just no one says it – so we're saying it now.'

The words they were saying in *Le Nouvel Observateur* had been written by Simone de Beauvoir at the behest of both the magazine and the feminist group Mouvement de libération des femmes, MLF for short. They went as follows: 'One million women in France have abortions every year. Condemned to secrecy, they do so in dangerous conditions, while under medical supervision this is one of the simplest procedures. Society is silencing these millions of women. I declare that I am one of them. I declare that I have had an abortion. Just as we demand free access to contraception, we demand the freedom to have an abortion.'[1] A bit like #MeToo today, the manifesto demanded that people stop looking away: this problem, according to the signatories, didn't just affect a couple of individuals, but society as a whole. It was a way for women to slam down onto the breakfast tables of middle-class households a subject that had been hitherto discussed only in whispers and say: *Stop the hypocrisy! You can't ignore this any longer. We're in 1971 – the state has got to do something.* It was out of the question that these women should keep aborting their pregnancies alone, with knitting needles, coat hangers, or – as in East Germany – *Schallwäscher* (vibrating clothes-washing devices that were a precursor to electronic washing machines), and possibly dying as a result. It took courage to say all this. Not just because these women were risking their reputations – and, in the case of the artists, their popularity and therefore their jobs – but because they were making themselves liable to prosecution. What they were admitting to having done was illegal in France, West Germany and many other Western countries; it was punishable with fines or even imprisonment (1943 was the last time a woman was executed for aiding abortion).

But what were these punishments compared to the fear, helplessness and loneliness of their situation? What was money or prosecution in comparison to the dangers of an illegal abortion or the breach that an unwanted child created in the life of a young woman? When the writer Annie Ernaux accidentally got pregnant in 1963, it was as though her body was telling her: *That's it, despite all your efforts, you're not getting any further.* In *Happening*, she describes the traumatic abortion during which she almost bled to death, and the horrifying feeling of being entirely at the mercy of your own body. It was exactly this that the manifesto hoped to take measures against: 'Our wombs [. . .] belong to us,' wrote the women of the MLF a couple of pages after the aforementioned list, and turned the phrase 'A child – if I want, when I want' into a motto that was soon echoing through the streets of Paris and Berlin. On 6 June 1971, two months after this issue of *Le Nouvel Observateur* hit the newsstands, the German magazine *Der Stern* published a list of 374 women's names under the headline 'We've had an abortion!'

1   *Le Nouvel Observateur*, 5 April 1971, quoted in <https://daily.jstor.org/the-manifesto-of-the-343/>

Instigated by Alice Schwarzer, the list included Romy Schneider, Senta Berger, Veruschka von Lehndorff and many more. They admitted to having contravened Paragraph 218 of the German Criminal Code and demanded that the law against abortion be repealed.

Few single issues of a magazine have ever had so much influence on the lives of women as this one. It was this that put the right to bodily autonomy on the political agenda in France: three years after the so-called 'Manifesto of the 343', on 26 November 1974, health minister Simone Veil stood up in front of the Assemblée Nationale and presented her draft for an abortion law. She addressed a room that consisted almost exclusively of men, saying in her opening remarks that she considered this a great pity, before explaining to them, 'Abortion is not a decision that any woman takes lightly; it is always a personal tragedy', yet the several hundred thousand women who were mutilated each year by illegal abortions could no longer be ignored. Veil, who was herself an Auschwitz survivor, was accused of wanting to put foetuses into 'gas chambers'; her front door was daubed with swastikas. But she wasn't to be intimidated. She forced through her law, the so-called Loi Veil, which made it legal to have an abortion in France up to the twelfth week of pregnancy. In Germany that same year, the law was changed to move in this direction, though even to this day Paragraph 218 still hasn't been entirely removed: terminating a pregnancy is theoretically still illegal and only 'tolerated' up to the twelfth week, following a consultation.

More than fifty years after the manifesto gave society a wake-up call, the right to abortion still isn't guaranteed and is regularly contested – particularly in times of crisis. In Poland, what was already a very restrictive abortion law was tightened a few years ago to such an extent that it is now practically prohibited; in Texas and Oklahoma, the antiquated 'heartbeat law' has applied for some time, meaning that a termination is only permissible before the foetus develops a heartbeat – which usually happens even before a woman knows she's pregnant. In 2022, the US Supreme Court overturned the landmark Roe vs. Wade decision, which guaranteed every woman the constitutional right to choose to have an abortion. Then again, abortion has recently been legalised in countries like Argentina and Ireland. As Alice Schwarzer said on the fiftieth anniversary of the manifesto: 'Then as now, the battle for emancipation is being staged on our bodies.'

VHS TAPE, *DEEP THROAT*

1972

Could it be that this film, the legendary 1972 porn flick *Deep Throat*, is to blame for the fact that, even to this day, many men don't know exactly where their partner's clitoris is located and, when in doubt, might guess it's somewhere in her throat? Because it's exactly this that most porn films suggest: fellatio – the blowjob, or, as it's sometimes called in honour of this classic, 'deep throat' – is the be-all and end-all of any sexual encounter, the beginning and end of the event. You can (according to these films) forget about pretty much everything else – cunnilingus, kissing, penetration, even touching – but the blowjob is a must. Not just because the man likes it; no, it'll make the woman come as well.

This idea might not be entirely wrong, but it isn't entirely right, either. And it's easy to surmise that it harks back to this porno, which is apparently the most lucrative film of all time (it cost $25,000 to make and has netted $600 million so far). In any case, it heralded the blowjob's triumphal march, and even gave the pushing-a-penis-so-deep-into-a-woman's-throat-that-she-cries practice its name: deep-throating. The story is a simple one. Linda Lovelace, a young and rather unspectacular-looking woman has a problem: she enjoys having sex, has a seemingly endless capacity for it, but she's never had an orgasm; she feels a little tingle but never hears 'bells ringing, dams busting, bombs going off'. Ms Lovelace isn't willing to accept anything less, and thus is very unhappy. Even when her friend Helen organises an orgy so Linda can find out what she likes, all that sex leaves her with nothing but a faint tingling sensation. That can't be it, she thinks, and so she makes an appointment with a physician, a certain Dr Young. This man examines her, asks her about possible traumas that might have damaged her sexual enjoyment, asks her where she feels most arousal, and finally makes an incredible discovery: Lovelace's clitoris isn't between her legs, it's in her throat! The solution is now perfectly obvious: if she wants to have an orgasm, she just needs to engage in some serious 'deep-throating' and find the man whose penis will reach the clitoris hidden at the back of her throat. She duly does this, and finally hears those longed-for 'bells ringing, dams busting, bombs going off'. Porn-film happy ending!

If you're thinking this sounds more like a comedy than hardcore porn, you're not wrong – unlike most contemporary pornos, you can't help but laugh on more than one occasion. And it was probably this very light-heartedness that helped fellatio become a socially acceptable cultural phenomenon in the early 1970s. If you wanted to join the conversation in America in 1972, there was pretty much no way around spending nearly sixty minutes in a porn cinema watching this film. Alongside the Watergate scandal, which was exploding at almost exactly the same time, this was the main topic of discussion among well-informed Americans; even a serious paper like the *New York Times* reported on the phenomenon under the headline 'Porno Chic'. Cinema seats were filled less with sleazy guys in shiny trench coats than with older ladies, students, film stars, politicians, TV presenters ... even Jackie Kennedy was spotted leaving a screening of *Deep Throat*. 'Sex was coming out of the closet,' said the writer Erica Jong. The film was part of the sexual revolution, a symbol of liberation not just for men, but also for women. After all, Lovelace did go in search of her own pleasure; after all, the film did mention the point of the clitoris (which would later be forgotten for quite some time); after all, it did say that a woman could have transcendentally good sex and shouldn't settle for less. But it also said that the key to that lies exactly where it suits men best: in the depths of her throat.

Back in 1972, it wasn't just the state that instigated criminal proceedings against the film or the conservative sections of society that took to the streets. Feminists, too, like Catharine MacKinnon, Gloria Steinem and the Women Against Pornography group, saw *Deep Throat* and the wave of porn enthusiasm that followed in its wake as a danger to women – especially as the content of successive films became cheaper and more extreme. This was partly to do with the invention of this object here, the VHS cassette, which came about soon after. From then on, people didn't watch 'dirty pictures' in cinemas alongside others, but on their own at home, far removed from any censure, where they could watch whatever they wanted. The harder, the better. It's said that if it hadn't been for porn films, this medium – the video cassette – might never have become established; at least half of the VHS cassettes sold in the 1970s and '80s showed pornographic content.

It's true that pornography had been spoken about in individual cases even before *Deep Throat* and the rise of VHS porn – Susan Sontag, for example, had written an essay about it in the 1960s – but it was only with the sensational success of this film that it became a serious socio-political topic and, above all, a feminist issue.

DESICCATOR

1977

In October 1937, the *New England Journal of Medicine* announced: 'Conception in a watch glass: The "Brave New World" of Aldous Huxley may be nearer realization.' Two researchers had just fertilised a rabbit's ovum 'in vitro', before re-implanting the embryos in their mother's womb and thereby inducing a pregnancy. If this experiment on a mammal could be successfully replicated in humans – in a woman – then embryos could soon be created outside the human body, the journal explained. Forty years and several failed attempts later, a prediction that had seemed like science fiction became reality: at 23.47 on 25 July 1978, under the supervision of Robert Edwards and Patrick Steptoe, the pioneers of reproductive medicine, the world's first in-vitro baby was born in Manchester. Her name was Louise Brown, she weighed 2.6 kilos and, the story goes, her fingertips were already flecked with ink when she was handed to her mother – the doctors had immediately taken her fingerprints so as to study this miracle.

Just as they did in the 1930s, people in the 1970s consulted Aldous Huxley. The *New York Times*, for example, wrote that while we hadn't yet arrived at the human farms of Huxley's dystopia, we were no longer that far off; not since the atom bomb had a scientific development divided opinion to the extent that the world's first 'test-tube baby' had. This was true: some saw it as a kind of realisation of Mary Shelley's *Frankenstein*; others, like *The Times*, viewed it as 'perhaps the most anticipated birth in 2,000 years', a second coming of Jesus, only this time a girl. For Israel's chief rabbi, it was 'immoral'; for Muslim clerics, on the other hand, it was absolutely fine – the parents were married, after all. The Vatican, which should really have been up for a bit of immaculate conception, wasn't at all *d'accord*, because the procedure had replaced the 'natural union of man and woman'. For couples who, like the Browns before them, had spent years trying in vain to conceive 'naturally', it presented a glimmer of hope: Louise Brown seemed to them, as the *Evening News* put it, a 'superbabe', a superhero in baby form. Her particular superpower lay in redefining reproduction and its unfair rules, but also in heralding a possible end to the fear of infertility. It's easy to forget, because the topic of contraception has been so important to the history of emancipation, but, for centuries, being infertile was nearly as terrible a thing for many women as an unwanted pregnancy: in earlier epochs, it was absolutely legitimate for a husband to ditch his wife if she couldn't 'give' him a child, and, if a couple did remain childless, the problem was always presumed to lie with the woman. In the worst case, she'd be stripped of her feminine identity and thus of her *raison d'être*: what was a woman, after all, if she couldn't become a mother? The whole thing was layered with shame and suffering, but Louise Brown's birth promised the beginning of a new era. For men and women both.

This crazy development had its origins in an unassuming vessel. It looks a bit like a jam jar – like the kind of thing you'd have in your kitchen cupboards – but is in fact the desiccator in which the ova taken from Brown's mother were fertilised with her father's sperm. This was the 'test tube' in which an embryo developed, before being implanted (along with two others) in Lesley Brown's womb – from where, if we fast-forward quickly, it emerged nine months later as Louise. As an adult, Brown has often been photographed with this jar in her hand, or leaning next to it, as in a family photo. When she turned thirty, the world's first test-tube baby wasn't just photographed with the desiccator; Robert Edwards, the doctor to whom she owed her life (Steptoe, sadly, had died by then) was also in the picture: part of a new style of family, one in which reproduction is teamwork involving ova, sperm, glassware and doctors, and in which 'family' and 'origin' have been redefined. When Edwards accepted the Nobel Prize for Medicine on behalf of them both in 2010, it was said that, in a metaphorical sense, he and Steptoe were the fathers of more than four million babies.

Their breakthrough realised a dream for many people, but of course it also threw up bioethical questions. What do we do with the embryos that don't get implanted? Are we allowed to experiment on them? And, if so, for how long? The answers to these and similar questions are often debated and negotiated anew; our stance on them changes with time.

Nowadays, it no longer seems particularly exciting or problematic that embryos should be created in petri dishes; every day, new ova are fertilised in jars like this one, with sperm from either the woman's partner or a donor. In countries where it's permitted, they may be implanted in surrogate mothers, so that even people without uteruses can have their own children. In China, scientists are currently working on growing a baby in the artificial womb of an intelligent robot. This may all sound wild, but it's particularly interesting in respect to the concept of 'woman': it's hopefully now been well established that men can be just as good 'mothers' as women, but what does it mean if the female body, which until now has always been needed, doesn't necessarily have to be the 'origin of the world' any more? If reproduction, which has shaped the way women are viewed for so long, no longer depends on them? Will they then, finally, be free? In the 1990s, films like (the really rather absurd) *Junior* imagined implanting in-vitro cells into men's bodies – in this case, Arnold Schwarzenegger's – and letting them give birth. The question was: would everything be different? Would the distribution of roles be reversed? What is for sure is that Louise Brown and her desiccator made new forms of family possible. And, despite the many warnings, neither our morals nor our humanity have suffered so far. On the contrary: the possibility of in-vitro fertilisation has made life better for very many people.

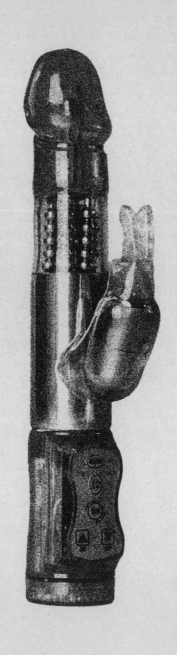

THE RABBIT PEARL

1984

This attractive-looking object also made many women's lives better, albeit in a rather different way: the Rabbit Pearl, perhaps the most legendary sex toy of all time. Its meteoric rise began in 1998, more than a decade after it was invented. When the producers of the hit series *Sex and the City* rang its manufacturer, Vibratex, to ask whether they were allowed to use the 'Rabbit' in the show, Shay Martin (who owned and ran the firm, which had been founded by her mother), only had a vague idea of what *SATC* was about, but she said yes, thereby sealing the fate of the toy. In the episode titled 'The Turtle and the Hare', Miranda extolls the virtues of the Rabbit to her friend Charlotte, who duly goes to a sex shop and buys one for herself. Shortly after, she's completely addicted, and doesn't leave her apartment for days. She does nothing any more but lie around in bed with her new toy; the orgasms are so good, she can't do anything else. This goes on until her friends intervene and take the pink contraption away again.

It's no wonder that, after this, everyone wanted a Rabbit Pearl, that marvel with two heads and a rotating ball filled with pearl-like beads. Sales of what had previously been a moderately successful product were through the roof by the very next day. It was sold by the million and copied a dozen times in various different formats; stars like Eva Longoria gave interviews in which they said they'd given all their girl-friends a Rabbit Pearl, and even Oprah Winfrey crowned it 'the Rolls-Royce of sex toys'. This attention wasn't just good for Vibratex; it also helped finally make female masturbation a little less taboo. Women could now admit to pleasuring themselves with sex toys without seem-ing extremely strange or even sick. And why should they? In part because, then as now, a widespread myth claimed a direct link between the invention of battery-powered sex toys – vibrators – and female hysteria: an illness, in other words. In this story, the first such specimens – which, unlike the Rabbit, didn't look cute but horrifying, like a cross between a hairdryer, a drill and a whisk – were invented by doctors at the end of the nineteenth century. Back then, the legend goes, neurologists used to heal their patients through orgasms, only it reached the stage at which they no longer had the inclination – or sheer strength – to satisfy these ladies manually, and so came up with an electric device: a clitoris-massaging machine. It's a good story, and many films have been made about it, but alas it seems to be a total fabrication. At least, that's what sex historian Hallie Lieberman says.

What is true is that the first vibrators weren't labelled as such, but rather as 'massage devices' that could be used to solve all manner of health issues: stomach pains, headaches, tense muscles and so on. They could be used to calm your baby or enjoy a head massage at the hairdresser's; nothing like sex or masturbation was ever mentioned. Especially not for women. Nor did these devices look like something you necessarily should (or wanted to) have in the vicinity of your genitals. There was something tool-like about them – a small sanding machine, perhaps – and they came with various attachments that could be ordered separately, most of them flat plastic discs which, if you really insisted on it, could probably provide clitoral stimulation. Until it occurred to a couple of designers that women surely needed something a little more phallic-looking for self-stimulation. Or, to be more precise, something that looked exactly like a penis. With veins, pale-pink glans, and so on. Many of these sex-toy manufacturers seem simply to have looked down at themselves and thought: *Yes, this is exactly what it should look like – how else is a woman supposed to come?*

At that time – we're talking about the 1960s and '70s here – staying true to life was clearly such a priority that the quality of the toy was all but forgotten. And, along the way, the feminist public was scared off as well: to paraphrase a campaign slogan of the time, violence is male and so are penises; as a feminist, it was unthinkable to admit that you spent your days battling the patriarchy, but by night you enjoyed pleasuring yourself with a perfectly formed plastic phallus. Dildos and sex toys were anti-feminist, the Trojan horse of the patriarchy. Until a certain Gosnell Duncan came along and rang in a new era. This man deserves to be celebrated for his contribution, especially as it had tragic beginnings: when an accident left him paralysed from the belly button down at the age of just thirty-seven, but his wife not really up for a life of total celibacy, he started looking into sex toys and was soon appalled to discover what cheap and hygienically dubious materials most of them were made from. To tackle the problem, he invented nothing less than the silicone dildo.

When he presented his invention in what was then the only feminist sex shop in New York, Eve's Garden, owner Dell Williams is said to have told him: *OK, we'll give it a go, but enough with this lifelike rubbish. Women don't want accurate-looking, flesh-coloured penises; they want something that works.* The first 'feminist' dildo made of silicone, the so-called 'Venus', accordingly looked less like a penis than a crooked finger; successive versions didn't come in beige and brown (Duncan himself was from the Caribbean and refused to accept that penises should always be white) but in pink and green and blue. To an extent, then, Williams and Duncan paved the way for the invention of the Rabbit Pearl, and thus for the slow removal of taboos around masturbation and female desire. Incidentally, the Rabbit, whose ears are supposed to stimulate the clitoris, didn't originate in the assumption that women like it cute when having sex. The design was a trick to circumvent the morality police in Japan, where the toys were manufactured. Because back then, the general rule was: producing vibrators, fine, just please not in an obviously phallic form.

DIOR 'WE SHOULD ALL BE FEMINISTS' T-SHIRT

2016

If the 1960s and '70s were the decades of second-wave feminism, and the 1980s the period in which its changes were implemented and consolidated more broadly in everyday life, then the 1990s were the decade for asking the question posed after every revolution: are things really better now? To be more precise, it was the media asking that question. Newspapers and magazines claimed that while women now had everything they'd ever wished for – the right to vote, sexual freedom, the Pill, abortion, the chance to have a career just like a man – this famous 'having it all' hadn't made them happy in the slightest. On the contrary. The modern woman was stressed, depressed, overworked and overwhelmed; her love life was either total chaos or non-existent. There was a 'shortage of men' and a 'fertility crisis'; women were lonely and alone and had made the most wonderful thing they could have in life – motherhood, all those sweet little babies – secondary to their careers. Sacrificed it, even. How sad.

As a woman in the late 1980s and early 1990s, it was probably all but impossible to pass a newspaper kiosk without having a headline or two giggle gleefully out at you: *So, how's it going with emancipation? Not so great after all, is it?* The American author Susan Faludi analysed this strange development in her book *Backlash*, finding it to be an invidious attempt to blame the women's movement for everything that could go wrong in a woman's life and to vilify feminists as some kind of bogeywomen. Possibly with a view to encouraging the ladies not to demand any more. And, as hair-raising as this might sound from today's perspective, all that power of suggestion seems to have worked rather well. As the 1990s drew to a close, and with them a century that had been very eventful from a women's rights perspective, the feminist revolution appeared to be going strong in certain spheres: theatres were staging bold plays like *The Vagina Monologues* (which would soon become much more than a celebration of the vagina, as a political movement to stop violence against women), pop was singing the praises of this new 'girl power' and neurotic figures like Ally McBeal and Bridget Jones were being celebrated as the new female ideal of imperfection. And yet, beyond these cultural representations, no one wanted to know about feminism any more. *Me, a feminist? Ugh, no!* 'Feminist': that sounded hard and hairy, it sounded loud and demanding and rough. Unlikeable, like that person who always spoils the party because she doesn't know when enough is enough. The one who doesn't see she has everything – and can have it all – if she just makes a 'small' effort and is prepared to swallow 'a little bit', and for whom it really is time to stop complaining about glass ceilings, gender pay gaps and a tiny amount of washing-up. It sounded like man-haters, like dreadful clothes, bad haircuts, dirty fingernails, uncool jobs and probably also like no sex. Or, at least, no *good* sex. She was 'far too tense' for that.

This image of the feminist as a prehistoric figure from a time long gone, decommissioned so that everyone could have a quiet life, and replaced by far-more-friendly 'girl power' or even just a more peaceable version of Woman (independent, but undemanding), clung on for a long time. A very long time. Even in the 2010s, an English study found that more than half of respondents felt that gender equality didn't really exist yet (contrary to what had been claimed in the 1990s), but still no one wanted to be deemed a feminist. The word and everything associated with it sounded unspeakably unglamorous and unsexy, until the French fashion house Dior used this T-shirt to turn it into a fashion statement and, with that, a fashion in its own right. It was autumn 2016 in Paris, the fourth day of Fashion Week. Dior, a couture house steeped in tradition, had just appointed an Italian as its head designer; the catwalk at her first show was full of long, flowing skirts, lots of see-through tulle in black, white and red, corset-style tops, low necklines and – the star of the show – a T-shirt. This one. A totally basic white T-shirt emblazoned with the words 'We should all be feminists'. A decade earlier, Maria Grazia Chiuri, as the designer was called (she has since printed other feminist phrases on tops, such as Linda Nochlin's 'Why have there been no great women artists?'), would probably have been fired for such a move. Not because of the T-shirt, but because of the words printed on it. But now the time was once again ripe for such a movement. Or at least for marketing it: anyone who wanted to wear their conviction on their chest in Dior style would have to shell out €650.

The quote was taken from a TED Talk given by the Nigerian novelist Chimamanda Ngozi Adichie in 2012. In 'We Should All Be Feminists', the author tried to paint a new picture of the movement that was so misunderstood and widely decried at the time: feminism, she said, didn't mean contesting men's place, but simply granting women equal rights and no longer drumming into girls that they had to make themselves small in order not to scare off the boys. She was for a more respectful coexistence, one that was free of fear. You could say that Ngozi Adichie made feminism socially acceptable again with her lucid thoughts on the matter. In 2014, in her song '***Flawless', Beyoncé recited Ngozi Adichie's definition of feminism as a person who believes in the socio-economic equality of the sexes. Two years later came this T-shirt, and then a whole wave of 'feminist' products. Hardly any company that speaks to women – even just a bit – can now afford not to position itself as 'feminist' or fail to engage in a bit of 'femvertising' (feminist advertising): creams, shampoos, shoes, clothes, but also celebrities, films, series and books all surf the feminist wave. Because feminism is no longer disgusting; it's fashionable. Though to what extent this fashion really serves the cause is questionable. On the one hand, it has freshened up feminism's dusty image and re-established women's rights as a topic in the public discourse. On the other hand, it gives the impression that emancipation is easily achieved. That it's enough to fork over a few banknotes and buy yourself 'empowerment'. Perhaps, to dispel this illusion, the next T-shirt ought to be printed with the words of American journalist and women's rights activist Gloria Steinem: 'This is a revolution, not a public relations movement.'

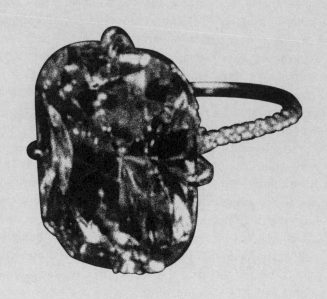

KIM KARDASHIAN'S RING

2016

From a pop culture and women's history perspective, Sunday, 23 October 2016 was an eventful day. It began with bestselling author Elena Ferrante, who had been writing for years under this pseudonym with the explanation that she preferred to remain anonymous, being unmasked against her will (though, it has to be said, this purported identity has been consistently refuted by her publisher ever since). And it ended at around 3 a.m. with an assault on reality-TV and social-media star Kim Kardashian. She was in Paris for Fashion Week and alone in her hotel room near the Place de La Concorde when masked men suddenly burst in, threatened her with a weapon and shouted repeatedly in poor English, 'The ring! The ring!' What they meant was this ring, a fifteen-carat diamond, which Kim's then-husband, Kanye West, had given her as a second engagement ring, and which she had shown in close-up in an Instagram selfie taken just a couple of hours before.

Both events caused a great stir. The first chiefly attracted criticism: if someone wants to remain anonymous, let them. The second drew mainly schadenfreude: anyone who shows off their ostentatious wealth deserves what they get. But more than any of this, both cases posed two questions, each in their own way. First, how much success is a woman ever permitted to enjoy before she has to 'pay' in some way? And secondly, what degree of exhibition or privacy is a woman actually permitted in the twenty-first century – and, more precisely, how far is she allowed to determine this for herself? Both women were, and still are, hugely successful; both had chosen a radical – and radically different – way of being a public figure: all or nothing. The topic has long been controversial: until not that long ago – well into the nineteenth century – women were considered to have exhibitionist tendencies if they were seen at the windows of their own homes (clothed, mind you).

Nowadays, those who want to be seen are still accused of pathological narcissism, yet those who would prefer to live hidden are dragged out from behind the curtain: in Ferrante's case, the journalist who 'unmasked' her claimed that it wasn't for a successful author to insist on anonymity; her readers had a right to know who was writing the books they loved so much. Her unmasking was 'inevitable', according to the magazine that published it. In Kim Kardashian's case, on the other hand, the assault was seen as a kind of punishment for her female pride: if a woman puts her life and wealth on display like that, and shows off on Instagram with a ring worth millions, she shouldn't be surprised if someone tries to steal it, the gleeful critics said. The more malevolent voices among them even suggested she'd staged the entire thing so as to catapult herself into the headlines. In general, both women were accused of choosing to hide or show themselves not out of personal preference – in the same way that some people are extroverts and some introverts – but as part of a PR strategy intended to manipulate the market and earn them even more money.

In the case of Ferrante, it's hard to say to what extent her anonymity inspires admiration, to what extent her fame and fortune have been generated not just by her writing but also by the mystery in which she is shrouded. But even if that were the case: why not? When it comes to Kim Kardashian, however, we can spare ourselves the trouble. After all, it's true. It's her job to exhibit herself and her private life – or, at least, something that looks satisfyingly like it to other people – this is how she earns her money. You can find this a stupid or rather thin career concept, but it's worked: by now, Kardashian and her various businesses are said to be worth almost one billion dollars. Not for nothing was she wearing a ring like this that October evening. She understood that exhibiting yourself isn't without its risks, but does also bestow power. Ever since the seventeenth century and the first paintings of women engaged in their morning toilette (today's 'beauty routine'), we've known that people crave insights into women's intimate lives. It was precisely because women were kept apart for so long and no one knew what actually went on in 'ladies' areas' that people were so desperate to peep through the keyhole. Kardashian merely turned the tables on this age-old curiosity: whereas celebrities, especially women, spent decades hiding behind bushes, under caps or behind big sunglasses, and fleeing restaurants through the fire exit to escape the press and its intrusive stalking, she took the wind out of voyeurism's sails by showing us absolutely everything, even before we knew we wanted to see it. When Kim Kardashian's sex tape was leaked in 2006, she didn't hide remorsefully behind the couch like we might have done, but instead went on the offensive and turned an embarrassing moment to her advantage: her family made a show out of it, *Keeping Up with the Kardashians*, became a brand in their own right, and used the then-new emergence of social media as an extension of reality TV to create a permanent advertising platform for their own products.

It might be pure exhibitionism, but perhaps it's also just a different, modern-day form of storytelling. At least, this space of self-presentation is the first one in which women have had the power to decide when and how they are seen, to shape their image in the way they want and to earn money with it. When Kim Kardashian appeared on the cover of *Forbes* magazine a couple of months before the attack, in summer 2016, because turning her privacy into a profitable venture had made her a successful businesswoman, she wrote a tweet for all the haters who voiced the accusation that putting yourself on display wasn't really a talent: 'Not bad for a girl with no talent.' In the photo series that accompanied the article, she was wearing: the ring. The ring.

THE MOBILE PHONE

21ST CENTURY

Confident, independent women and telephones – no, confident, independent women and mobile phones – go hand in hand. This isn't something we only started thinking when celebrities like Kim Kardashian began earning unprecedented sums with the help of their phones. You may also remember the poster for the 1990s cult teen film *Clueless*, a modern remake of Jane Austen's *Emma*: it shows Alicia Silverstone, alias 'Cher', flanked by her two friends, making their majestic way down the staircase of her luxurious home, all three of them with enormous phones – brand new back then, very old-school now – pressed to their ears. It didn't matter that they only chattered inconsequentially into these devices; we all understood that a young woman with a mobile was cool, important and successful, or at least on her way to being it.

And you could say it had always been like that. Ever since the 1870s, when mobiles didn't even exist, and their predecessor, the telephone, had only just been invented, it was women who enthusiastically embraced this new technology. As with many other technological novelties, the men who had invented it initially had their difficulties. Perhaps they just had no desire to battle with the switchboard, which of course you had to go through; perhaps they found the static annoying or the handset unwieldy. Whatever it was, they didn't warm to the newfangled machine quite as quickly as their wives did. One of the reasons will have been that, unlike the ladies, they didn't actually need it. Men went out and met people, 'in real life'. Women were stuck at home more; back then, the telephone was what the mobile phone is to some these days: a window to the world. But also, a means to independence. Thanks to the telephone, women could take action themselves if they needed something. They could ring the plumber, order things, and also get help: alert the doctor if their child was sick, call the police if their husband was violent. Today, in the fight against femicide – the murder of women by their partners – mobile phones are one of the most important weapons, and it all began with the telephone. It helped a little to break the *huis clos* (no exit) of the home and make women feel less alone and vulnerable. It gave them strength and courage.

In less dramatic situations, it simply presented an opportunity to talk to people who had nothing to do with their partner or parents. They could discuss confidences ear to ear, without another ear listening in as well (at least, that was the idea). Just as some people apparently believe that mobile phones tempt women to betray their husbands and therefore ought to be forbidden to them, a couple of men back then will have worried that this new apparatus would give their spouse a whole new kind of freedom. And they probably weren't wrong. A phone call with your lover was more discreet than a letter; a message on a mobile even more so, of course. Long before phones and dating apps, the telephone gave love lives in general a wonderful shake-up and lent women's voices a whole new significance. Instead of writing long letters or casting shy glances from behind an ice cream sundae, you just got on the phone. It was more innocuous, more relaxed; people had fewer inhibitions. Above all, however, this was the first time it wasn't all about a woman's appearance. In 1911, *Life* magazine impressed upon its male readers that they shouldn't meet their potential future wife in person, but instead should speak to her on the phone: 'Selfishness, sympathy, shallowness, cultivation, reserve strength, control, and the capacity to bore – all these things and many more are revealed in a woman's voice.' In England, young women were even given special elocution lessons, because a 'good voice' was suddenly an important aspect of female attractiveness. Sounding light and gentle but still clear was ideal, though at some stage this changed – or perhaps women simply started setting less store by having a pleasing voice. At any rate, according to one study, women's voices became consistently deeper over the course of the twentieth century.

Nonetheless, the slowly vanishing obsession with the female voice probably has its roots in those early days and what was then a completely new interest in the way such voices sounded. Until then, to put it bluntly, it had been preferable for women not to speak at all, but now they too were able to seduce with words. The first switchboard operators, for example, were deluged with offers from men who wanted to chat, flirt, banter with them. We recognise this in 1970s films like François Truffaut's *The Man Who Loved Women*: the protagonist has flings with several women, but one of his most important relationships is with a telephonist. Speaking of telephonists: just as smartphones have enabled many women today to become self-employed and start a business from their bedroom, so too did the telephone present new job opportunities back then. After young men had failed to make themselves terribly popular on the switchboards, brusque and impatient as they were, they were replaced with young women who would thenceforth spend many decades breathing 'Number, please' into the receiver several hundred times a day. Fulfilling, it certainly wasn't; they earned very little and worked a lot, but it was still a new route to independence and, at worst, better than a factory. Today, the power-women and girl-bosses of our cities have at least two or three constantly blinking, ringing and vibrating phones to hand. In other parts of the world, the mobile phone is a male affair. Various organisations have been working for years to close this 'mobile gender gap'. Because, then as now, having access to a smartphone enables women to be more independent, confident, successful – and, in turn, free.

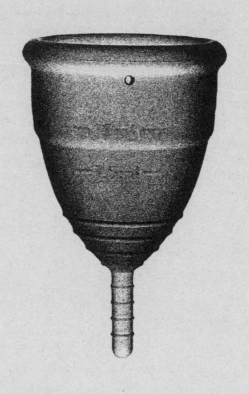

MENSTRUATION CUP

2010s

In the 1979 adaptation of Stephen King's first bestseller, the gruesomely brilliant *Carrie*, the pivotal scene – the one that sets off the entire chain of events – has to do with menstruation. In the communal showers after a school sports lesson, Carrie gets her first period and clearly has no idea what's happening to her. Apparently, no one has ever told her she'll start bleeding one day, so instead she believes she's dying and appeals to her classmates for help. Alas, they merely laugh at her and pelt her with tampons and sanitary towels. And when her fanatically religious mother later boxes her ears and locks her in the broom cupboard (because, of course, there would be no female menstruation without female sin), Carrie's tragic tale – one of newly awakening powers, of shame and of female fury – begins to take its course.

If Stephen King had written his story a couple of decades later, Carrie might not have been laughed at, and all that horror would simply have fizzled out. The other girls might not have given her the feeling that she needed to be ashamed of what was happening to her, that it was something dirty and disgusting; instead, they might have told her it was normal. Not always pleasant, true, but definitely not embarrassing or bad or something she needed to hide. They might not have thrown things at her, but, if anything, have handed her a tampon, or advised her to steer clear of those outmoded things altogether and instead get herself one of these contemporary, environmentally friendly menstruation accessories: the menstruation cup. Over the past couple of years, such cups have become wildly popular among women, at least in the West. Recent years have seen them advertised widely as though they were brand new, but in fact they've been around since the 1930s, when an American actress, one Leona W. Chalmers, patented a rubber cap that could be pushed into the vagina to collect menstrual

403

blood. At the time, women didn't have many options: they could simply let the blood flow, cobble together something to soak it up, or use sanitary towels that were kept in place by unattractive constructions known as 'sanitary belts'. Now, Ms Chalmers apparently set great store by being able to wear white silk dresses even during her period – but a sanitary belt wasn't a good look underneath such a garment, and nor did she want to go about with red stains on her backside. And so she launched the cup – which had actually been invented by someone else a couple of decades before – but never really found many takers. Probably because the tampon followed shortly after and was somehow easier to use. But maybe also because the menstruation cup forced women to look at something they still found frightening, disgusting and shameful: the blood that flowed out of their bodies each month.

When a girl gets her period for the first time, she's overcome by a terrible feeling of disgust, according to Simone de Beauvoir. Disgust at the blood, at the smell of decaying violets (aha!), disgust at the colour and her changing body: 'This is when she feels most acutely that her body is an alienated opaque thing,' she wrote in *The Second Sex*, referring to the centuries-old – no, millennia-old – taboo around menstruation, which, good will and menstruation cups notwithstanding, is still proving difficult to shake.[1] Even now, in our Western society, it apparently isn't all that unusual for a young woman to go to her mother with news of her first period only to get a slap, as though to say: *Welcome to womanhood! It'll be great!* In the Middle Ages, women who had their period were kept away from church, kitchen, pretty much all aspects of life, because menstrual blood was regarded as unclean and frightening – yet, at the same time, the blood of Christ was venerated fanatically. During the notorious witch-hunts of the early Renaissance, both menstrual blood and its absence – the menopause – were dangerous, signs of a woman's connection to Satan, the devil who glowed permanently red. And even if, in the centuries that followed, blood was thought to turn to milk in pregnant women and so constituted a form of nourishment, the shame didn't lessen. At the end of the nineteenth century, some people even claimed that menstruating women were more aggressive and more likely to commit crimes.

---

1 de Beauvoir, Simone, *The Second Sex*, Vol. II, Part I, tr. Constance Borde and Shelia Malovany-Chevallier (London: Vintage, 2011), p. 42

Still, it wasn't just in the twenty-first century that periods became feminist terrain. I've already mentioned Germaine Greer, who in the 1970s wrote in *The Female Eunuch*: 'If you think you are emancipated, you might consider the idea of tasting your menstrual blood – if it makes you sick, you've a long way to go, baby.'[1] Nowadays, few women want or need to go that far; current debates centre less on its taste and more on normalising the sight of menstrual blood. Through pictures, for example; through sanitary-towel adverts that use red instead of blue liquid; and also through cups like these, which don't spare you the sight of blood. Incidentally, if we look at the history of colours, red doesn't stand for shame, but for strength, joy, love – quite simply, for life.

1   Greer, Germaine, *The Female Eunuch* (London: Harper Perennial, 2006), p. 57

THE PUSSYHAT

2017

If at some point in the distant future someone looks back on the beginning of the twenty-first century and considers the situation of women, the year 2017 will stand out as particularly trailblazing, or at least especially loud. It was the year which – social media and a few magazines claimed – rang in the 'female revolution', maybe even the 'end of the patriarchy', because a couple of patriarchs were toppled and the power of several others challenged. And the most politically overt accessory of this eventful year and its feminist revolution was this hat, the so-called 'pussyhat'.

Discovered as a symbol right at the beginning of the year, it was already gracing the cover of American *Time* magazine by February 2017: it was pictured on its own in front of a pale-grey background, a cat-shaped shadow looming into view behind it, almost as if Catwoman herself was about to come round the corner and avenge anguished women everywhere. Above it, pink lettering proclaimed: 'The Resistance Rises. How a March Becomes a Movement.' Yes, the talk was of marches and movements, but what we saw was nothing but a little pink woolly hat, a hand-knitted nothing, not exactly beautiful, maybe even a little big ugly. Why? Because the pussyhat had become such a strong symbol of resistance that this object stood – better than any photo of a demonstration could – for a protest movement that was growing by the day. By this time, it could even be found fulfilling its role of 'contemporary witness' in museums – the Smithsonian, the British Museum, London's V&A. If we wanted to exaggerate just a little bit, we could compare it to the headwear sported during the French Revolution: the Phrygian cap. Both were worn by people who wanted to smash existing power structures and fight for greater equality, but while women were forbidden from wearing a Phrygian cap, the pussyhat was designed by women, for women – though it can and should also be worn by everyone else.

Let's quickly remind ourselves of the context in which it was created. It was October 2016 when, in the course of what was already a ridiculous election campaign, we encountered a snippet of conversation on a leaked tape in which Donald Trump, then presidential candidate for the Republican party, was heard proudly telling his interlocutor that the best thing about being famous was that you could do whatever you liked with women: 'You can do anything [. . .] Grab 'em by the pussy. You can do anything.' It had seemed clear for quite some time that this luminous-orange real estate mogul was neither an upstanding chap nor a gentleman, yet despite his many embarrassing appearances and dubious intentions he still enjoyed a following. After this episode, however, the so-called 'locker room talk', it was widely (and naïvely) believed that no one would want to elevate such a clearly misogynistic monster of a man to a position as important as president of the USA. Sadly, this was a gross error. When he was eventually elected fifty-third president of the United States in December 2016, many considered it a brutal wake-up call, a clip round the ear for a society which seemed to be announcing that it didn't give a damn about the rights of women and a few other minorities besides. Nor was it even ashamed of that.

This, more or less, is where the story of the hat begins. When Krista Suh and Jayna Zweiman, two young women from California, heard about the Women's March on Washington, a protest against Trump's election that was to take place on 21 January 2017, the day after his inauguration, they started to wonder: how could they create an eye-catching symbol of community and solidarity? Even the suffragettes had recognised the importance of images; in the era of social media, Instagram and co., this was doubly true. Because both women knew that protest marches are usually filmed from above, they hit upon the idea of a hat: the pussyhat was (and is) easy to make – you don't even really need to be able to knit – it cost pretty much nothing, was pink (ostensibly a female colour) and had the rough shape of cat's ears, as in 'pussycat'. It was a direct reference to Donald Trump's comment, 'grab 'em by the pussy', and in turn said: the president sees the pussy, the vagina, as a symbol of vulnerability, something any idiot can assault, but we're going to turn this symbolism on its head. We're going to turn it into a symbol of power, community and rebellion.

The pussyhat was, if you like, an unexpected revival of the power of Baubo (see the fifth object in this history), and simultaneously rooted in a tradition that tied together knitting and rebellion: as far back as the French Revolution, women – the so-called *tricoteuses* – sat knitting in their revolutionary women's clubs and National Convent and, apparently, even stood in front of the guillotine with their needles clacking while heads rolled at their feet. In the First World War, it's said, spies knitted secret messages into their scarves; knitters even played a role during the American War of Independence – as a diversionary tactic. A knitting woman always came across as matronly and unthreatening, but the pussyhat of 2017 proved otherwise. In photos of the demonstrations that took place on 21 January 2017, the biggest in the history of the USA, uniting several million people – no matter their sex, sexuality, race or age – in over six hundred locations around the country, we don't see any individual points, but a sea of pink. A sea of pussies.

This hat, as one of its creators once explained, was intended as an object that wordlessly proclaimed: 'You are not alone. When you speak up, you're not alone.'[1] As such, the pussyhat and what it symbolises can be seen as a forerunner of the #MeToo movement that would explode just a few months after that first Women's March, in October 2017. It, too, said exactly the same: violence and abuse of power don't just exist in Hollywood, not just at the very top and the very bottom, but everywhere. You are not alone. There are lots of us. And, from now on, we will speak up. As the year drew to a close, the cover of *Time* magazine tellingly published not a picture of a little hat crouching beneath a giant shadow, but a group photo of the women whose statements had contributed to the fall of Hollywood producer Harvey Weinstein and incited the global wave of #MeToo. It was the beginning of a new revolution.

---

1   Krista Suh quoted in *Forbes* magazine, 26 June 2018, available at: <https://www.forbes.com/sites/macaelamackenzie/2018/06/26/co-creator-of-the-pussyhat-krista-suh-talks-craftivism-and-building-a-movement/>

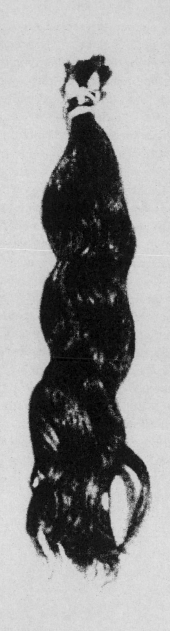

BUNCH OF HAIR

2022

This chapter needs to start with a confession, with an explanation for the omission of an object. An object which, since the beginning of antiquity, has been closely associated with the image of women and their place in society, which has often been taken as a symbol of a woman's virtue or vice, as a sign of belonging, which has stood for repression at many points in history, but in others also succeeded in representing a form of self-empowerment. An object, then, which evades clear categorisation, whose interpretation varies depending on who is looking at it, and in what period and part of the world, and which is thus a constant source of heated debate. The object in question is, of course: the headscarf, the veil.

The decision not to include it as an object, not to address it as one of these 101 things, was a decision that was made consciously and will be adhered to even in this last piece of the puzzle of women's history. The reason for this is not a desire to ignore a subject of great importance to so many women, but far more the deep-seated feeling that this theme is too complex and too charged to be discussed in a mere few pages. Particularly in view of the fact that I, the author of this book, consider myself neither qualified nor called upon to contribute anything new to this debate; nor do I think much of making judgements from the position of my cultural background on which feelings of freedom – or lack of freedom – women might associate with this particular garment. Instead, then, of entering the noisy room of contradictory interpretations, opinions and discussions, and singling out a piece of fabric that was, historically, first laden with significance by men, this chapter is about what's usually hidden underneath it – or, to be more precise, what's usually *supposed* to be hidden underneath it: women's heads. The very heads on which society still stages its internal and external battles, at whose expense it works through trauma or even affirms its virility (see *The Shaved Woman of Chartres*, object 78). The heads which are repeatedly made to serve as an indication of whether a nation is progressive or retrogressive (as though they would be able to bear such a weight!). The heads which some women are now reclaiming with an unbelievably courageous gesture, a gesture deserving of all the respect in the world. This chapter is about the Iranian women's rebellion and, by association, the part of the female body that has become a symbol of what might just be the most significant women's revolt of the early twenty-first century: hair. Or, to be more precise: a severed bunch of hair. A braid. A hank.

Since time immemorial, women's hair has attracted all manner of passions; throughout history, it has regularly become a battlefield in the fight against women's liberation, but sometimes also territory for their own self-assertion. None of this is new. But the way in which the women of Iran have occupied and subverted this battlefield, and above all the vigour they have unleashed far beyond the headscarf debate, most certainly is. Let's quickly recap the events that led up to this point, to January 2023. It all began on 13 September 2022, when a twenty-two-year-old Kurdish woman, Jina Mahsa Amini, was arrested by the so-called morality police during a visit to Tehran because her headscarf was sitting too loosely and too much of her hair was visible. The very same day, a few hours after her arrest, Amini was delivered to hospital unconscious. Three days later, she was dead. According to official statements, she had suffered heart failure. Her sudden, brutal death triggered a wave of anger and disgust never before seen in her country. By the time of her funeral on 17 September, thousands of people had assembled to protest against the Ayatollah's regime and the brutal repression of women; many of those women took off their headscarves and chorused, 'Jin, Jiyan, Azadi' – 'Women, Life, Freedom'. And the rebellion hasn't abated. Women and men have been taking to the streets together to demand the end of the regime and, in doing so, risking everything – in the worst cases, their lives. Several protestors have already been executed; others have disappeared without trace.

Now, one of the most distinctive gestures of this uprising – perhaps budding revolution – isn't just the demonstrative removal of headscarves, the calls for 'death to the dictator' and other similar protest cries, but the cutting of hair. On the street and on the internet, women (and men) have been demonstratively reaching for their scissors or razors and cutting off a braid or hank of hair, sometimes even shaving their heads bare. In Iran, cutting off your hair is a gesture of mourning, so this marks a collective mourning for the injustice to which Mahsa Amini was subjected and which many other women continue to encounter every day. But perhaps it's also an act of self-empowerment, as though to say: this hair, which is supposed to be kept hidden, these few strands for which a girl was killed – they belong to us. These heads that you want to oppress are free and willing to fight for that freedom, no matter the cost. And this time, it seems, their cry has been heard far beyond the borders of Iran. In the autumn, European actresses like Juliette Binoche, Isabelle Huppert and others copied the gesture with their own scissors; in October, the Swedish MEP Abir Al-Sahlani cut off her braid at the speaker's podium in the European Parliament and held it aloft, saying, 'Women, Life, Freedom'.

This isn't the first time that uprisings or even revolutions have begun with women. In eighteenth-century France, it was the market women who led the march on Versailles and forced the king to go with them; in Russia, it was women who took to the streets to demand bread, peace and the abdication of the tsar. In both cases, it was women who fired the starting gun of revolution, yet in neither was the issue at stake their existence as women, their rights as women. The likelihood that the masses would have followed them in such a cause was not terribly high. And this is exactly why the revolt in Iran seems so unique: women are rebelling against the violent oppression of women, reacting to the injustice to which women are subjected, holding thoroughly feminine attributes like bunches of hair aloft, chanting 'Women, Life, Freedom' and thereby succeeding in uniting what had been a fractured opposition and even the international public behind them. Not in a debate for or against the headscarf, but in a fight for freedom, to do and be allowed to do as they please. As women, as humans. With their heads, their hair, their bodies, their lives. It's as though these women, with their bunches of hair in their hands, have managed, perhaps for the first time ever, to make everyone understand that women's rights aren't special rights, aren't a luxury, aren't an extra that can be negotiated or put off until later, but fundamental human rights. And that a society which tramples all over them will never be in a position to guarantee and protect other fundamental rights. And so, in this spirit: Women. Life. Freedom.

SELECT BIBLIOGRAPHY

Lisa Appignanesi, *Mad, Bad and Sad: A History of Women and the Mind Doctors from 1880 to the Present*, Virago, 2008

Hannah Arendt, *Mary McCarthy*, ed. Carol Brightman, *Between Friends: The Correspondence of Hannah Arendt and Mary McCarthy*, Harcourt, Brace, 1995

Séverine Auffret, *Une histoire du Féminisme de l'Antiquité grecque à nos jours*, L'Observatoire, 2018

Jane Austen, *Emma*, Penguin Books, 1973

Elisabeth Badinter, *The Myth of Motherhood: An Historical View of the Maternal Instinct*, Souvenir Press, 1982

Anna Banti, *Artemisia*, tr. Shirley D'Ardia Caracciolo, Hope Road, 2020

Marie Bashkirtseff, *The Journal of a Young Artist, 1860–1884*, Hard Press, 2012

Simone de Beauvoir, *A Transatlantic Love Affair: Letters to Nelson Algren*, The New Press, 1998; *The Autobiography of Simone de Beauvoir: After the War: Force of Circumstance, I: 1944-1952*, tr. Richard Howard, Paragon House, 1992; *The Second Sex*, tr. Constance Borde and Shelia Malovany-Chevallier, Vintage, 2011

Quentin Bell, *Bloomsbury Recalled*, Columbia University Press, 1997

Rebecca Benamou, *Sur la bouche: Une histoire insolente du rouge à lèvres*, 1er Parallele, 2021

Arthur Christopher Bensons, *Viscount Esher (eds), The Letters of Queen Victoria, Vol. III, 1854–1861*, John Murray, 1908

Shari Benstock, *Women of the Left Bank: Paris 1900-1940*, Virago, 1987

Cécile Berly, *Lettres de Madame de Pompadour: Portrait d'une favorite royale*, Éditions Perrin, 2014

Dorlis Blume, Monika Boll, Raphael Gross, *Hannah Arendt und das 20. Jahrhundert*, Piper, 2020

Nellie Bly, *Ten Days in a Mad-House: A Story of the Intrepid Reporter*, Dover Publications, 2019; *Around the World in Seventy-Two Days and Other Writings*, Penguin Classics, 2014

Gisela Bock, *Frauen in der europäischen Geschichte: Vom Mittelalter bis zur Gegenwart*, C.H. Beck, 2005

Daniel J. Boorstin, *The Americans: The Democratic Experience*, Knopf Doubleday, 2010

Jorge Luis Borges, *Victoria Ocampo: Dialogue*, Bartillat, 2014

Silvia Bovenschen, *Die imaginierte Weiblichkeit*, Suhrkamp, 2003

Ann Braude, *Radical Spirits: Spiritualism and Women's Rights in Nineteenth-Century America*, Indiana University Press, 2001

Charlotte Brontë, *Jane Eyre*, Penguin Classics, 2006

Emily Brontë, *Wuthering Heights*, Penguin Classics, 2003

Barbara Burman, Ariane Fennetaux, *The Pocket: A Hidden History of Women's Lives 1600-1900*, Yale University Press, 2020

Andreas Capellanus, *The Art of Courtly Love*, tr. John Jay Parry, W.W. Norton, 1969

Hélène Carrère d'Encausse, *Alexandra Kollontai: La Walkyrie de la Révolution*, Fayard, 2021

Leonora Carrington, *The Debutante and Other Stories*, Silver Press, 2017

Mona Chollet, *In Defence of Witches: Why Women Are Still on Trial*, tr. Sophie R. Lewis, Pan Macmillan, 2023

Claudine Cohen, *Les femmes de la préhistoire*, Éditions Tallandier, 2021

Colette, *The Complete Claudine: Claudine at School, Claudine in Paris, Claudine Married, Claudine and Annie*, tr. Antonia White, Farrar, Straus and Giroux, 2001; *The Pure and the Impure*, tr. Herma Briffault, New York Review Books Classics, 2000; *Chéri*, tr. Antonia White, Vintage, 2001

Kara Cooney, *When Women Ruled the World: Six Queens of Egypt*, National Geographic, 2020

Christine Desroches Noblecourt, *La reine mystérieuse: Hatshepsut*, Éditions Pygmalion, 2002

George Duby, *Dames du XIIe siècle*, Folio Histoire, 2020

George Duby, Michelle Perrot, *Histoire des Femmes en Occident 1: L'Antiquité*, Éditions Perrin, 2002; *Histoire des Femmes en Occident 2: Le Moyen Âge*, Éditions Perrin, 2002; *Histoire des Femmes en Occident 3: XIVe-XVIIIe siècle*, Éditions Perrin, 2002; *Histoire des Femmes en Occident 4: Le XIXe siècle*, Éditions Perrin, 2002; *Histoire des Femmes en Occident 5: Le XXe siècle*, Éditions Perrin, 2002

Marguerite Duras, *Hiroshima Mon Amour*, Gallimard, 1960

George Eliot, *Adam Bede*, J.M. Dent & Sons Ltd, 1911
Lauren Elkin, *Flâneuse: Women Walk the City in Paris, New York, Tokyo, Venice and London*, Vintage, 2017
Annie Ernaux, *Happening*, tr. Tanya Leslie, Fitzcarraldo Editions, 2022
Charles Fourier, *Le nouveau monde amoureux*, Presses du réel, 2013
Betty Friedan, *The Feminine Mystique*, Penguin Classics, 2010
Artemisia Gentileschi, *Actes d'un procès pour viol en 1612. Suivi des lettres de Artemisia Gentileschi*, Éditions Des Femmes, 1984
Virginie Girod, *Les femmes et le sexe dans la Rome antique*, Éditions Tallandier, 2013
Edmond & Jules Goncourt, *La femme au 18ème siècle*, Flammarion, 1993
Germaine Greer, *The Female Eunuch*, Harper Perennial, 2006
Susan Griffin, *The Book of the Courtesans: A Catalogue of Their Virtues*, Broadway Books, 2002
John Harrison, *A Manual of the Typewriter*, I. Pitman & Sons, 1888
Elke Hartmann, *Frauen in der Antike*, C.H. Beck Verlag, 2021
Marjorie Hillis, *Live Alone and Like It: The Art of Solitary Refinement*, Virago, 2005
Margaret R. Hunt, *Women in Eighteenth-Century Europe*, Routledge, 2009
Asti Hustvedt, *Medical Muses: Hysteria in Nineteenth-Century Paris*, Bloomsbury, 2011
Margaret L. King, *Women of the Renaissance*, University of Chicago Press, 1991
Francine Klagsbrun, *Lioness: Golda Meir and the Nation of Israel*, Schocken, 2021
Thomas Laqueur, *Making Sex: Body and Gender from the Greeks to Freud*, Harvard University Press, 1992
Madeleine Lazard, *Les Avenues de Fémynie: Les femmes et la Renaissance*, Fayard, 2001
Titou Lecoq, *Les grandes oubliées de l'histoire*, L'Iconoclaste, 2021
Hallie Lieberman, *Buzz: A Stimulating History of Sex Toys*, Pegasus Books, 2017
Uwe Lindemann, *Das Warenhaus: Schauplatz der Moderne*, Böhlau Verlag, 2015
Deborah Lutz, *The Brontë Cabinet: Three Lives in Nine Objects*, W.W. Norton & Company, 2015
Janet Malcolm, *Forty-One False Starts: Essays on Artists and Writers*, Farrar, Straus & Giroux, 2014
Guy de Maupassant, 'Une femme', *Gil Blas*, 16 August 1882
Adrienne Mayor, *The Amazons: Lives and Legends of Warrior Women Across the Ancient World*, Princeton University Press, 2016
Victor Margueritte, *La garçonne*, Payot, 2013
Mary McCarthy, *The Group*, Virago, 2009
Rebecca Messbarger, *The Lady Anatomist: The Life and Work of Anna Morandi Manzolini*, University of Chicago Press, 2010
Tiya Miles, *All That She Carried: The Journey of Ashley's Sack, a Black Family Keepsake*, Random House, 2022
Nancy Mitford, *Madame de Pompadour*, Vintage, 2011
Lothar Müller, *Freuds Dinge*, Die Andere Bibliothek, 2021
Victoria Ocampo, *Victoria Ocampo: Writer, Feminist, Woman of the World*, tr. Patricia Owen Steiner, University of New Mexico Press, 1999
Marylène Patou Mathis, *L'homme préhistorique est aussi une femme*, Allary Éditions, 2020
Leslie P. Peirce, *The Imperial Harem: Women and Sovereignty in the Ottoman Empire*, Oxford University Press, 1993
Charlotte Perkins Gilman, *The Yellow Wallpaper & Herland*, Macmillan Collector's Library, 2021
Régine Pernoud, *La femme au temps des cathédrales*, Le Livre de Poche, 1997
Michelle Perrot, *Mon histoire des femmes*, Seuil, 2006, *Les femmes ou les silences de l'histoire*, Flammarion, 2020
Sarah Pomeroy, *Goddesses, Whores, Wives & Slaves: Women in Classical Antiquity*, The Bodley Head, 2015
Virginia Postrel, *The Fabric of Civilization*, Basic Books, 2021
Eileen Power, ed. M.M. Postan, *Medieval Women*, Cambridge University Press, 1995
Janina Ramirez, *Femina: A New History of the Middle Ages Through the Women Written Out of It*, W.H. Allen, 2022
Maura Reilly, *Women Artists: The Linda Nochlin Reader*, Thames & Hudson, 2015
Nicolas-Edme Rétif, *L'Anti Justine: The Delights of Love*, tr. Charles Carrington, Locus Elm Press, 2014
Monika Richarz, *Jewish Life in Germany: Memoirs from Three Centuries*, Indiana University Press, 1991
Jutta Rosenkranz, *Mascha Kaléko*, dtv, 2012
Evke Rulffes, *Die Erfindung der Hausfrau: Geschichte einer Entwertung*, HarperCollins, 2021
George Sand, *Story of My Life*, tr. Thelma Jurgrau, State University of New York Press, 1991; *Gabriel*, tr. Kathleen Robin Hart and Paul Fenouillet, MLA Texts & Translations, 2010; *Little Fadette*, tr. J.M. Lancaster, Hawthorne Classics, 2020; *Rustic Legends: Twelve Ghostly Tales*, tr. Hannah Hoyt, Dragonet Classics, 2017
Sappho, *If Not, Winter: Fragments of Sappho*, tr. Anne Carson, Virago Press, 2003
Joanna Scutts, *The Extra Woman: How Marjorie Hillis Led a Generation of Women to Live Alone and Like It*, Liveright, 2017

Elizabeth Cady Stanton, Susan B. Anthony and Matilda Josyln Gage (eds), *History of Woman Suffrage*, Vol. III, Susan B. Anthony, 1886

Valerie Steele, *Corset: A Cultural History*, Yale University Press, 2003

Susie Steinbach, *Women in England, 1760–1914: A Social History*, Phoenix Paperback, 2004

Guy Thuillier, *Pour une histoire du quotidien au XIXème siècle en Nivernais*, Mouton, 1977

Judith Thurman, *Secrets of the Flesh: A Life of Colette*, Ballantine Books, 2011

Alice B. Toklas, *The Alice B. Toklas Cookbook*, Harper Perennial, 2021

Joyce Tyldesley, *Daughter of Isis: Women of Ancient Egypt*, Penguin, 1995

Simone Veil, *A Life*, The Armchair Traveller at the Bookhaus, 2017

Élisabeth Vigée Le Brun, *Souvenirs 1755–1842: 'Les femmes régnaient alors, la Révolution les a détrônées'*, Éditions Tallandier, 2015

Fabrice Virgili, *La France Virile*, Payot, 2019

Virginia Woolf, *A Room of One's Own*, Penguin Classics, 2020

Marguerite Yourcenar, *With Eyes Open: Conversations with Matthieu Galey*, tr. Arthur Goldhammer, Beacon Press, 1984

Vera Zingsem, *Lilith: Adams erste Frau*, Reclam, 2009

Émile Zola, *The Ladies' Paradise*, tr. Brian Nelson, Oxford World's Classics, 2008

ACKNOWLEDGEMENTS

I would like to thank my editor, Johanna von Rauch, for her ideas, her encouragement, all the conversations, walks and evenings, and for her sheer endless patience. My friend Carolin Würfel for accompanying me through every century of this history of women and commenting on the most bizarre stories with her clever thoughts. My friends Miriam Stein, Alexandra Link, Nadia Pantel, Jonathan Drews and Niklas Maak, for their important suggestions and encouragement. Tarun Kade, for our Dante Bad Sessions. My father, Uve, for his unexpected enthusiasm for women's history. My mother, Danièle, without whom this book would never have been finished.

My husband, Olivier, Olive, for everything.

ANNABELLE HIRSCH has German and French roots. She studied art history, dramatics and philosophy in Munich and Paris, and works for *Frankfurter Allgemeine Zeitung (FAZ)* and various magazines. She writes short stories and translates French literature. She lives between Rome and Berlin.

@annabellehirsch

ELEANOR UPDEGRAFF was born in London and studied English Literature, German and Russian at Durham University. She is a literary translator and author, ghostwriter and editor, and reviews books for various publications online and in print. She lives in Vienna.

Cover design adapted by Rafaela Romaya, adapted from original design by Maurice Ettlin
Author photo © Tanja Kernweiss